OGLALA RELIGION

OGLALA RELIGION

William K. Powers

UNIVERSITY OF
NEBRASKA PRESS
Lincoln/London

Manufactured in the United States of America

First Bison Book Printing: November 1982
Most recent printing indicated by the first digit below:
3   4   5   6   7   8   9   10

Library of Congress Cataloging in Publication Data

Powers, William K.
  Oglala religion.

  Bibliography: p. 215
  Includes index.
  1. Oglala Indians—Religion and mythology. 2. Oglala Indians—
Social life and customs. 3. Oglala Indians—Ethnic identity. 4. Indians
of North America—Great Plains—Religion and mythology. 5. Indians
of North America—Great Plains—Ethnic identity. I. Title.
E99.03P68   299.7   76-30614
ISBN 0–8032–8706–2 (pbk)

Title page photographs: Victory dance on the Pine Ridge Reservation, 1945. (*Courtesy of the Smithsonian Office of Anthropology.*)

To

FRANK AFRAID OF HORSES

Ate na kola

AND

THE OGLALAS OF PINE RIDGE, SOUTH DAKOTA

CONTENTS

Contents

LIST OF
TABLES AND FIGURES

INTRODUCTION

THE PERSISTENCE OF VALUES

The purpose of this book is to explicate how one society of Native Americans, the Oglalas, preserves its social and cultural identity over time. Despite formidable attempts by the United States government to eliminate indigenous tribal societies, through either military strategy or congressional legislation, values which are distinctly Oglala continue to persist within the macroenvironment of Anglo society. This book focuses on the nature of those values, their modes of cultural expression, and the processes by which they are replicated synchronically and diachronically. I am also interested in demonstrating how these synchronic and diachronic dimensions are related to each other conceptually and perceptually.

THE PROBLEM: CONTINUITY AND CHANGE

How is it possible that, despite overwhelming odds in favor of assimilation into the "mainstream" of American society, the Oglalas maintain a distinct social and cultural identity? I approach this problem by addressing myself to the phenomena of continuity and change: I regard both as aspects of the same phenomenon, a posture largely ignored in American anthropology.

Traditionally, the literature related to North American Indians in general, the Oglalas and their antecedents in particular, has been historically oriented. Most treatments of social structure focus on kinship and marriage, and kinship terminologies (Bowers, 1950; Eggan, 1937, 1950; Swanton, 1905). Monographs written by others such as Boas (1897, 1966); Lowie (1935); and Radin (1923) describe Indian tribes in terms of cultural institutions and traits, but do not generally explain the relationships between these institutions within the same tribe. Other works (Fletcher, 1904; Walker, 1917) investigate institutions out of cultural context.

In particular, the literature related to acculturation studies tends to be biased, by definition, in favor of showing change and adaptation, but not continuity (Colson, 1949; Linton, 1940; Redfield, Linton, and Herskovits, 1936; and Spindler and Spindler, 1971). Most anthropologists studying acculturation assume that all aspects of Native American culture have, or will become, "Americanized" without examining to what extent aspects of Euro-American culture have become "Indianized." The tenacity of Oglala cultural values, however, seems to negate that assumption and affirm the validity of the latter approach. Thus anthropologists may argue over the extent to which native religion, for example, has been influenced by Christianity, without recognizing that these intrusive elements may not be regarded as Christian at all by native adepts.

By treating continuity and change as two aspects of the same phenomenon, I hope to avoid the one-sidedness of acculturation studies. Interestingly, anthropologists have been led to describe and analyze societies by two sets of principles. One set applies to the investigation of a homogeneous society in which culture is stated to be transmitted over generations (in Tylor's sense [Tylor, 1871]). However, in dealing with cultures in contact, anthropologists employ another set of principles, which is intended to describe and analyze culture change collaterally, that is, between the same generations of two originally independent societies, one dominant, the other subordinate. The principles of the second approach are often taken to exclude the principles of the first. I believe that it would be profitable in terms of explaining culture contact to apply the principles of both generational and collateral transmission: as we investigate the extent to which one society influences another, we should concurrently explore the continuitive process of generational transmission in one (or both) of the societies under investigation.

The notion of continuity and change as two aspects of the same phenomenon may be stated more concretely. For the purpose of this study I regard the opposition continuity-change as analagous to the opposition Oglala-Euro-American. We may regard both sets of terms as opposite ends of a scale. Most people in contemporary Oglala society operate in the midrange of the scale (cf. Leach, 1954, for his treatment of myth and ritual in this same context). For purposes of satisfying one's felt needs (Goodenough, 1963:49-60), Oglalas in the midrange of the scale are mobile: they move back and forth from the Oglala to the Euro-American extreme on a day-to-day basis, or situationally. Sometimes this mobility is conscious (people use their Indianness or whiteness), and sometimes they do so spontaneously (they respond in a culturally conditioned way). This scale should not be regarded as exclusively geographic or locational, although there are some circumstances in which certain areas are more Oglala (a sacred butte) than Euro-American (a bar). Rather, the scale is ideational: people pass back and forth from one end of the scale to the other independently of locations (with exceptions like those mentioned above). Those who identify with that which is Oglala may not necessarily live on a reservation or in an Indian community. They may also not be active in Indian celebrations, secular or sacred. Their ethnicity transcends geographic or locational boundaries; Oglala personnel move through it (Barth, 1969: introduction), a point to which I shall return below.

In addition to its ideational qualities, the Euro-American end of the scale is also technological and materialistic. The Oglalas readily identify it: the federal government, education, public health, employment, military service, and material things derived from each. But most Oglalas do not participate in this extreme of the scale; most are in the midrange: school dropouts, underemployed or unemployed, the sick, welfare cases, the politically powerless. Their felt needs are satisfied at the Oglala extreme of the scale, along with those of the traditional Oglalas—the hereditary chiefs, the medicine men, and the common people whose primary allegiance is to kin and local communities.

It is in these Oglala extremes of the scale that we find persistence in Oglala values. Here, one's felt needs are satisfied through the medium of a religious system. It is here in the local communities that we find social relationships reminiscent of those of bygone days, relationships that now manifest themselves in novel ways, but ways which are nevertheless more Oglala than they are Euro-American. It is here in the local communities that we find the persistence of Oglala society, not in the form in which it appeared at contact time, but in one which differentiates itself from Euro-American society on the basis of religious values. What contributes to this persistence is a transformation: extended family hunting groups, whose survival once depended on the leadership ability of a hunter-warrior, have been transformed into local communities whose social and cultural survival now depend on the acumen of a ritual specialist. In the process of this transformation, developing out of social conflict, the structures underlying the patterns of behavior between groups and leaders have remained relatively constant, but the Oglalas' mode of expressing these relationships have changed.

RELIGION AND ETHNIC BOUNDARIES

In addition to explicating how the Oglalas have preserved their social and cultural identity over time, I am interested in defining "the framework within which things can change without shattering the society that strives to perpetuate its identity despite the repeated blows of history" (Maranda, 1972:331). In this regard, the work of Fredrik Barth is instructive, and I consider the Oglalas as an ethnic group which, inter alia, "has a membership which identifies itself, and is identified by others, as constituting a category distinguishable from other categories of the same order" (Barth, 1969:11). I agree that "the organization of ethnic identities does not depend on cultural diversity *per se*, as generally assumed in anthropology, but rather on the assignment of particular social meanings to a limited set of acts" (Blom, 1969:74).

The limited set of acts which delineate the boundaries of Oglala ethnicity is inhered in a belief system which has persisted for more than 250 years, that is, from the historical period in which the Oglalas evolved as a politically discrete unit to the present. This belief system is also shared with other Tetons, as well as with other constituents of the Oceti Šakowin (Santees and Yanktons), and other Siouan-speakers. What I seek to demonstrate is that the boundaries of Oglala ethnicity are synonymous with the boundaries of religious belief. In the transformation from the extended family under hunter-warrior leadership to local communities dependent on religious leadership, religion has become institutionalized.

By convention in the English language, I use the term *religion* to refer to this belief system which has become institutionalized. I recognize that the Oglalas express the concept differently, and, in fact, have no cognate word, except in those invented by missionaries, and acceptable to some Oglalas as a convention in Lakota, their native language.

I am concerned not so much with what religion is but what religion does (cf. Spiro, 1966:122), that is, to what extent the concepts people have about religion can help us explain how a society functions and persists. I thus regard religion as an aspect of social organization (Middleton, 1970) distinguishable from other aspects on the basis of intervening supernatural beings and powers (Spiro, 1966). I regard religion as a cultural system which provides a model of and for reality, and subscribe to Geertz's paradigm that "sacred symbols function to synthesize a peoples' ethos—the tone, character, and quality of their life, its moral and aesthetic style and mood—and their world-view—the picture they have of the way things in sheer actuality are, their most comprehensive ideas of order" (Geertz, 1966:3).

Inasmuch as I will be analyzing myth and ritual, their relationship to each other, as well as their relationship to other aspects of social organization, I find Wallace's analytical definition of religion instructive: *religion is a set of rituals, rationalized by myth, which mobilizes supernatural powers for the purpose of achieving or preventing transformations of state in man and nature* (Wallace, 1966:107). Wallace's definition also obtains well for the Oglalas, who do not differentiate between supernatural beings and impersonal supernatural force in terms of their own concept of religion. I also acknowledge Wallace's debt to Van Gennep's categories of *rites de passage* (Van Gennep, 1908) and rites of intensification (Chapple and Coon, 1942; Wallace, 1966:107). In some instances,

Oglala rituals are not rationalized by myths, but rather complement them. Here I am inclined to follow Leach's suggestion that
"myth regarded as a statement in words 'says' the same thing as
ritual regarded as a statement in action." They are both to be
regarded as forms of symbolic statement about the social order
(Leach, 1954:13–14).

Although Oglala beliefs have changed over the past 250 years,
particularly in association with the transformation mentioned
above, they have done so as if they were molded by the same set of
templates which have been used to "express the persistence of
certain themes of belief, from which replication occurs only when
other elements in the social and physical environment combine to
permit this" (Ardener, 1970:156). The rituals, myths, songs, dances,
prayers—in essence, the contents of religious belief (Ardener's
realien, loc.cit.)—change circumstantially. But the ways in which
they change, and the relationships which are maintained, are determined in a conscious or unconscious manner both synchronically
and diachronically. This process, which calls for the rearrangement of culturally finite elements, can be explained in part by
methodological considerations first advanced by Lévi-Strauss.

Social Structure and Social Relations

My own analysis of Oglala religion calls for an understanding of
Lévi-Strauss's fundamental distinction between social structure
and social relations. According to Lévi-Strauss, "the term 'social
structure' has nothing to do with empirical reality but with models
which are built up after it" (Lévi-Strauss, 1962a:322). Social
relations consist of the raw materials out of which the models are
constructed (ibid). What I hope to demonstrate, in my own analysis of the transformation from a sociopolitical system into a religious institution, is that the social structure of both are similar, but
the social relations are manifested differently.

Lévi-Strauss further defines a structure as a model meeting
several requirements:

> First, the structure exhibits the characteristics of a system. It is
> made up of several elements none of which can undergo a change
> without effecting changes in all other elements.

In the second place, for any given model there should be a possibility of ordering a series of transformations resulting in a group of models of the same type.

In the third place, the above properties make it possible to predict how the model will react if one or more of its elements are submitted to certain modifications.

And, last, the model should be constituted so as to make immediately intelligible all the observed facts. [Ibid.:322]

Contrasting social structure and social relations in another way, we may also speak of conscious and unconscious models. For Lévi-Strauss, structural models may be either one or the other without affecting the nature of the model. However, conscious models, or norms, make poor models because "they are not intended to explain the phenomena but to perpetuate them" (ibid.: 324). Social structure is essentially a deep-level structure and is unconscious; social relations are at a conscious level and may be equated with social organization. This is the distinction to which Lévi-Strauss alludes when he cites Firth: "social structure...[is] outside the time dimension, and social organization [is] where time reenters" (ibid.: 327; Firth, 1951:40). Placing Firth's statement in its full context is relevant:

The concept of social organization is important also for the understanding of social change. There are structural elements running through the whole of social behaviour, and they provide what has been metaphorically termed the social anatomy, the form of a society. But what is this form? It consists really in the persistence or repetition of behaviors; it is the element of continuity in social life. The social anthropologist is faced by a constant problem, an apparent dilemma—to account for this continuity, and at the same time to account for social change. Continuity is expressed in the social structure, the sets of relations which make for firmness of expectation, for validation of past experience in terms of similar experience in the future. Members of a society look for a reliable guide to action, and the structure of the society gives this—through its family and kinship system, class relations, occupational distribution, and so on. At the same time there must be room for variance and for the explanation of variance. This is found in the social organization, the systematic ordering of social relations by acts of choice and decision. Here is room for variation from what has happened in apparently similar situations in the past.

Time enters here . . . . Structural forms set a precedent and provide a limitation to the range of alternatives possible. . . . In the aspect of social structure is to be found the continuity principles of society; in the aspect of (social) organization is to be found the variation of change principle. [Firth, 1951:39–40]

Consonant with Firth's contention that structural forms provide a limitation to the range of social and cultural alternatives possible, in this case, to the Oglalas, is Lévi-Strauss's analogy between the construction of mythical thought and *bricolage*. *Bricolage* is intended to explain the finite number of elements and their recombinable forms which a society employs to construct new assemblages of mythical thought (Lévi-Strauss, 1966). Lévi-Strauss analogizes the primitive myth maker with a *bricoleur*, someone "who works with his hands and uses devious means compared to those of a craftsman" (ibid.: 16–17). Furthermore, he states:

The "bricoleur" is adept in performing a large number of diverse tasks; but unlike the engineer, he does not subordinate each of them to the availability of raw materials and tools conceived and procured for the purpose of the project. His universe of instruments is closed and the rules of his game are always to make do with "whatever is at hand," that is to say with a set of tools and materials which is always finite and is also heterogeneous because what it contains bears no relation to the current project, but is the contingent result of all the occasions there have been to renew or enrich the stock or to maintain it with the remains of previous constructions or destructions. [Ibid.: 17]

Lévi-Strauss's concept of *bricolage* as it relates to the raw materials and combinations of elements out of which mythical thought is constructed can be extended to apply to Oglala ritual and other aspects of social organization. I will later demonstrate that the techniques employed to analyze relations in a mythical sense are also appropriate for analyzing other such aspects. The contents of all these aspects are constantly changing circumstantially and systematically, as Firth has stated above. But because social relations are constructed out of a limited or finite set of sociocultural tools and materials, the resultant changes bear similar structural relationships to previous ones. These "bundles of such relations" (Lévi-Strauss, 1963:207), as I shall demonstrate, appear synchronically and diachronically in Oglala society, serving as reliable guides to action and as markers of ethnic boundaries.

At the sociopolitical level, an etymological analysis of terms used by the Oglalas to identify politically discrete units (e.g., Tetons, Oglalas, Sicangus, Hunkpapas, etc.) reveals that these terms are related to each other structurally. Diachronically, as new politically discrete units evolve, new terms are created to identify them in such a way that these new terms are structural replications of previous ones.

At the level of ritual and myth, religious concepts and actions likewise bear similar structural relationships to each other synchronically and diachronically. The symbols employed to synthesize the Oglala ethos are manifested in the contemporary rituals and ceremonies: the sweat lodge, vision quest, sun dance, and curing rituals such as *Yuwipi*. These, as well as the ritual use of time and space, are structurally related not only to similar ceremonies and rituals of prior times, but also to the terms employed to identify politically discrete units.

In order to underscore these synchronic and diachronic relationships, I intend to reconstruct the social system of the Oglalas at contact time, roughly 1700, using documentary materials and field data; provide an ethnography of Oglala religion based on contemporary field data as well as relevant literature; and analyze the structural relationships implicit in both the reconstructed system and the contemporary system, and show that the structure of contemporary Oglala religion replicates the social structure of the reconstructed periods.

I shall demonstrate that these structural relationships have remained relatively stable over time and space, but that the social relations—the modes of cultural expression—have changed. Through this transformation, native religion has become the means by which the Oglalas express their social and cultural identity and delineate the boundaries of their ethnicity as distinguished from other American Indian and non-Indian societies.

Although at an earlier period religion was diffused throughout all aspects of social organization, the Oglalas increasingly focused on native religion as other cultural aspects related to power and authority, and technoeconomic traditions lost significance, predominantly through Euro-American contact. In the process of this transformation initiated by conflict between a traditional society and a bureaucratic one, religion has become institutionalized, and it is within this framework that Oglala society has striven to perpetuate its identity.

For expository purposes, this book is divided into four parts, each containing a number of chapters relevant to a single theme, all of which are integrated in the analysis. Part I, "The Seven Fire-places," treats the Oglalas in a larger sociopolitical context, i.e., their relationship to the Oceti Šakowin, and some problems in the nomenclature related to the political and linguistic classification of this larger category of people. It also deals with the migration of the Western Sioux onto the plains from their earlier home in Minnesota and the affects of the acquisition of the horse on tribal society. During this historical period, the Oglalas can be identified as a discrete sociopolitical unit, and I attempt to reconstruct their history and social organization from 1700 to the reservation period, about 1868.

Part II, "Sacred Things," deals with Oglala concepts and percepts of supernatural beings and powers, with particular focus on sacred numbers, concepts of time and space, as well as other sacred categories. I investigate the role and responsibility of the intermediaries—the shamans, medicine men and women, and other ritual specialists. I introduce abstracts of the myths related to the cosmology, the origin of people, and the acquisition of the sacred pipe. I then discuss the seven rituals of the mid-nineteenth century Oglalas: the sun dance, vision quest, sweat lodge, spirit keeping, *Hunkayapi*, a women's puberty ceremony, and the sacred ball game.

Part III, "All My Relations," deals with contemporary Oglala social organization: the setting, the conflict between the traditional Oglalas and those who identify with the federal power structure, and the notion of symbolic illness as a primary integrative factor, particularly among traditional members of the tribe. I also review the remaining sacred ceremonies, the influence of Christianity on native religion, and the introduction of the Native American Church as an alternative to native religion and Christianity. In dealing with religion as an institution, I focus on the nature and structure of Yuwipi, a phenomenon which has been described as a modern-day healing ritual (Kemnitzer, 1968); it is in this phenomenon that the transformation to religious institutionalization is realized.

Part IV, "Continuity and Change," investigates and analyzes the formal properties of sociopolitical organization and compares them with the formal properties identified in myth and ritual, revealing the similarity in the underlying structures common to all aspects of Oglala society, synchronically and diachronically. A transformation model, based on the contrast between sacred and profane, and mediated through the dialectic of social conflict, serves to explicate mythical and ritual transformations, as well as the transformation which accounts for the present social organization of the Oglalas.

Since my analysis requires the use of native terms, Appendix A contains a phonological key and Appendix B a note on the sources.

PART I

THE SEVEN
FIREPLACES

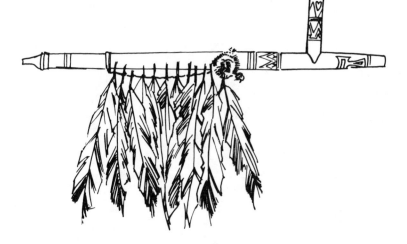

Chapter 1

PROBLEMS IN NOMENCLATURE

THE SEVEN FIREPLACES

Inasmuch as I am concerned with explaining religion first as an aspect of social organization, and second as an institution synonymous with ethnic or tribal identity, perhaps it is appropriate to begin with a clarification of the nomenclature traditionally employed to classify the Oglalas and their antecedents. Historically, the term *Oglala* has appeared in anthropological literature in combinatory forms—Oglala Sioux, Oglala Dakota, Oglala Division of the Teton, Oglala Lakota, etc. In this chapter I propose to explain how the Oglalas differentiate themselves from those cognate tribes which have been classified under the Siouan linguistic family and the pseudo-political and linguistic designation Dakota. I will begin by tracing the historical development of these terms and explain how and why they have been treated ambiguously in anthropological, historical, and linguistic literature.

The basic problem in nomenclature stems from failure by investigators to differentiate between dialectal, political, and geographic designations as they relate to that native American population which prior to white contact called itself Oceti Šakowin, usually translated as The Seven Council Fires (Robinson, 1904; Hyde, 1937, 1956, 1961) (from *oceti* 'stove, fireplace' and *šakowin* 'seven'). *Fireplace* is a term widely used by a number of American Indian tribes as a metaphor for various levels of social and political organization. "Father, mother, and children [are] ...what the Iroquois called the 'fireside family'" (Hertzberg, 1966:55). The Iroquois "likened their confederacy to a long house, having partitions and separate fires" (Morgan, 1851:51). The tribal name Potawatomi signifies "people of the place of the fire" (Wright, 1951); and together with the Chippewas and Ottawas they were known as the Three Fires. The Prairie Band of Potawatomis was also known as the Fire Nation (Les Gens de Feu). The Osages divided themselves into three constituent units, each of which had seven fireplaces (*u-dse-the pe-thonba*, LaFlesche, 1921). Radin also asserts that the Osage term for the clan was *peda* ('fire') and that the dual organization of the Winnebagos was reflected in the arrangement of fireplaces when they were on the warpath (Radin, 1923).

I have elsewhere indicated a preference for "fireplace" as a gloss for *oceti* (Powers, 1972); "stove" is the modern gloss, but the concept of fireplace predates the introduction of the modern cooking stove. "Seven Fires" is the gloss used by DeMallie (1971:104 and passim), but this disregards the wider semantic range of the native term, i.e., a specific place in the tipi, "tipi-bottom; fireplace at center, inside the tipi" (Walker, 1914:99); or possibly a named or otherwise delineated space. (Compare *oce*ti and mak*oce*, the former term being derived from *oce + ti* 'to live, dwell', and *maka* 'earth, land' + *oce*, which signifies a specific area of land, territory, as in *Lakota makoce* 'Indian land'. *Oce* may be an attenuated form of *caje* 'name' or *(w)ocaje* 'class, kind'.)

The numbers four and seven are regarded as sacred numbers among most North American Indians. Heptadic structures are found among a number of Siouan-speakers. In addition to the Seven Fireplaces comprising the antecedents of the Oglalas, and the seven fireplaces of the Osages mentioned above, Fletcher and LaFlesche report seven "gentes" for the Poncas (Fletcher and LaFlesche, 1911); and Howard's principal informant states that the Poncas were divided into seven "bands" (Howard, 1965). The Omahas were governed by a council of seven chiefs (Fletcher and LaFlesche, 1911). Dorsey reports on the belief in seven *wakandas* by the Omahas, Poncas, and Kansas. He also describes what appears to be fire or hearth worship among the Osages and Kansas in which a certain number of fireplaces were consecrated before ordinary fires could be made by the common people. The consecrated fireplaces were arranged in two parallel rows, seven on one side and six on the other among the Kansas, and seven on each side among the Osages (Dorsey, 1894).

Since 1640, the Seven Fireplaces have been more popularly known as the Sioux. The term itself was recorded by Jean Nicolet during his visit to the Winnebagos of Green Bay in the Jesuit *Relation* for 1640 (Thwaites, 1959). The earliest spelling of the term was *Naduesiu*, a French corruption of the Algonquian *nadowe-is-iw-ug* 'lesser, or small, adder' (*Nadowe* 'adder, enemy'; *is*, diminutive; *iw-ug* 'they are'), which was used by the Ojibwas to distinguish the Seven Fireplaces from the Iroquois, whom they called *nadowewok* 'real adder' (Densmore, 1918:1). It is from the pejorative *Sioux* that the linguistic designation *Siouan* is derived.

Over the years, the term *Oceti Šakowin* was eventually supplanted by the term *Sioux*, and today, when speaking English, the Oglalas and others refer to themselves as Sioux to indicate the relationship between all members who once identified themselves collectively as Oceti Šakowin. *Sioux* as a substitute for *Oceti Šakowin* seems acceptable inasmuch as the latter term became dysfunctional after the original constituents of the federation were dispersed. However, in addition to the political designation *Sioux,* the people themselves, when speaking their native language, employed other cognate terms which in a general sense may today be glossed as "Indian." Since the Seven Fireplaces did not speak a common language, but rather three mutally intelligible dialects of the same language, there was in fact no single term in their native language which could be employed to classify all members of the Seven Fireplaces other than *Sioux*. The designations of these dialects—Dakota, Nakota, and Lakota—eventually became terms which various investigators employed to define and classify political units, rather than dialectal ones; and in the process, *Dakota* became the favorite term under which the collective membership of the old Seven Fireplaces was subsumed. Furthermore, as the constituents of the original Seven Fireplaces were dispersed and migrated from their original homes in Minnesota to the prairies and plains, additional terms suggesting geographic relationships were combined with dialectal terms in order to provide more specific labels for various divisions of social and political units. The in-

discreet application of combined political, dialectal, and geographic designations gave rise to nearly all possible permutations
of the three variables. Thus the literature abounds with such
designations as Western Sioux, Teton Dakota, Oglala Sioux, Oglala
Dakota, Middle Sioux, Eastern Sioux, etc., ad infinitum. In an
attempt by authors to be specific as to precisely what group of
Sioux they were discussing, the terminology related to the discreet
groups became, in fact, even more ambiguous. Dakota finally
became the "official" designation of the Seven Fireplaces by
anthropologists after Powell's monumental classification of Indian
languages (Powell, 1891).

The ambiguities were accepted in anthropology, but references to the Seven Fireplaces were always self-conscious. Robinson's classical history is entitled *A History of the Dakota or Sioux
Indians* (Robinson, 1904). Boas and Swanton called their contribu-
tion to the *Handbook of American Indian Languages* Siouan
Dakota (Boas and Swanton, 1911). Boas also collaborated with Ella
C. Deloria on "Notes on the Dakota, Teton Dialect" (Boas and
Deloria, 1932). Wissler's monograph on sodalities was entitled "Societies and Ceremonial Associations in the Oglala Division of Teton Dakota" (Wissler, 1912). Lowie wrote on "Dance Associations
of the Eastern Dakota" (Lowie, 1913). Walker has a similarly ex-
haustive title for the monograph "The Sun dance and Other
Ceremonies in the Oglala Division of Teton Dakota" (Walker,
1917).

The above titles serve to illustrate the apparent bias of the
writers toward using the term *Dakota* even though, as I will demonstrate, there were other choices which agreed more closely with
how the Seven Fireplaces and their constituents perceived themselves in relation to other members. The "Dakota" bias and other
considerations led to technical deficiences in the classification of
Siouan-speakers and obfuscated references to political organization as employed by the Sioux themselves.

WILL THE REAL DAKOTA PLEASE STAND UP!
THE PROBLEM OF DIALECTS

The rules of linguistic classification of native North America,
which also contributed to the classification of political units, were

standardized in John Wesley Powell's *Indian Linguistic Families of America North of Mexico* (Powell, 1891). In this historic work, Powell paid homage to Albert S. Gallatin's *Synopsis of the Indian Tribes within the United States East of the Rocky Mountains, and in the British and Russian Possessions in North America* (Gallatin, 1836) by stating as the first rule: "The law of priority relating to the nomenclature of the systematic philology of the North American tribes shall not extend to authors whose works are of date anterior to the year 1836" (Powell, 1966:86 [1891]). Rule II stated that the name given to a linguistic family by the person first identifying it should be retained to the exclusion of all others. In Rule III, family names were restricted to one word. In Rule IV, a family name, once established, could not be canceled in any subsequent divisions of the group. Rule V stated that family names should terminate in *an* or *ian*. Rule VI applied to the interchangeability of the terms *family* and *stock*. Rules VII and VIII related, respectively, to identifying the habitat of the family and retaining the orthography of the original classifier (ibid: 86-87).

Gallatin had called *Siouan* a family divided into the Winnebagos, the "Dahcotah proper" and Assiniboins, the Minitaris, and the Osages and southern kindred tribes (i.e., Degiha-speakers). He identified the "Dahcotah proper" as the Mdewakantons, Wahpetons, Wahpekutes, and Sissetons to the east, and the Yanktons, Yanktonais, and Tetons to the west. According to his rules, Powell adopted Gallatin's designation *Siouan,* stating that although the term was derived from the Algonquian *nadowe-ssi-wag*, 'the snakelike ones, the enemies', its variations, Nadowesig, Nadowessies, and final corruption, Sioux, had been used by early missionaries, as if this in itself were a sanction for its adoption. In Powell's classification, *Dakota* was used for a major subclass because "owing to the fact that 'Sioux' is a word of reproach and means snake or enemy, the term has been discarded by many later writers as a family designation, and 'Dakota', which signifies friend or ally, has been employed in its stead" (ibid: 188).

Powell states that Gallatin used the term *Siouan* to indicate all of the kindred speakers of the family and that "the term 'Dahcotah' (Dakota) was correctly applied by Gallatin to the Dakota tribes proper as distinguished from the other members of the linguistic family who are not Dakotas *in a tribal sense.* The use of

the term with this signification should be perpetuated" (*ibid.;*
italics added). He does not make clear why the inimical *Siouan* was
retained as the family designation, while the amicable *Dakota* was
applied to some of its constituents "in a tribal sense." There was
never a Dakota tribe, only a Dakota dialect. And the Dakota
dialect was spoken only by four politically discrete divisions of the
Oceti Šakowin, that is, by the group known collectively as the
Santees, comprised of the Mdewakantons, Wahpetons, Wahpekutes, and Sissetons. Another division, comprised of the Yanktons
and Yanktonais (and their relatives, the Assiniboins), spoke a
dialect called Nakota (Nakoda in Assinboin), while the Tetons, by
far the largest of all the divisions of the Oceti Šakowin, spoke a
dialect called Lakota. Most of the constituent members of Powell's
"Dakota" subclass theoretically could not even say Dakota, much
less be one.

Under the subclass "Dakota" Powell listed the political divisions of the Oceti Šakowin: Santees, Yanktons, Yanktonais, and
Tetons. He further divided these political groups into smaller entities, such as the Oglalas, Sicangus, Hunkpapas, etc., members of
the Teton division. But he did not indicate that these divisions
spoke separate dialects; *Dakota* was only, for Powell, a tribal
designation.

Similarly, in his introduction to "Siouan Dakota" Boas writes:
"The following sketch of Siouan grammar is based mainly on the
Santee and Teton dialects of the *Dakota language,* which em-
braces four dialects—Santee, Yankton, Teton, and Assiniboine.
Santee and Yankton are spoken by the eastern *Dakota bands,*
Teton by the western bands" (Boas and Swanton, 1911:879; italics
added). In this brief passage, Boas makes a number of remarkable
assumptions. First, he establishes a Dakota language (it is a dialect). Second, he claims both Santee and Teton to be dialects of
Dakota (the former is Dakota; the latter is not). He then calls
Yankton and Assiniboin dialects of the Dakota language (the perti-
nent dialects are, respectively, Nakota and Nakoda). And finally,
he adds the modifiers *eastern* and *western* to *Dakota bands,* im-
plying that the Tetons are western Dakotas (they are Lakota-
speakers).

In 1891, Powell only stated that the Dakotas were principal speakers of "Siouan." It would follow then that Santee (which is synonymous with Dakota) would be a dialect of Siouan, not Dakota. Similarly, Teton, Yankton, and Assiniboin would also be dialects of Siouan (but not Dakota). Boas is correct (by Powell's standards) in calling these Siouan-speakers eastern and western bands, but no living "western Teton" would call himself Dakota.

Recognizing that the dialects spoken by the Santees, Yanktons, and Tetons were mutually intelligible, one can understand the intuitive need for a single term to include the three dialects. Yet Siouan, the most tempting, was irrevocably linked to the family classification according to Powell's rules. A second choice, despite its pejorative connotation, Sioux, might have been a likely candidate, except for Powell's mentioning it as a term of reproach (plus the fact that it could not meet the requirements for Rule V without duplicating the family name, Siouan). The original *Oceti Šakowin* might have been reduced to *Shakowinian,* but then this term was a political designation, not a linguistic one. The only recourse to being specific about what tribal or linguistic group was being referred to was by juxtaposing a number of modifiers—dialectal, political, and geographic—to *Dakota.* In trying to be specific, however, ambiguities arose.

THE CASE OF THE IMPROPER DAKOTA

Although the anthropologists, historians, and linguists mutually agreed upon the notion of a "Dakota language," there were some inherent problems in trying to adhere to the Powell classification and at the same time report on other aspects of the Dakotas proper. Dakotas simply did not all call themselves Dakota. Moreover, at the same time Powell was cautioning against the use of *Sioux* because it was a pejorative label, this was precisely the term that was used by the Santees, Yanktons, and Tetons to designate themselves when speaking English. It may have been scientifically improper to call these Indians Sioux, but it was what they were calling themselves, collectively.

Wissler and Lowie adhered to the Powell and Boasian dicta. In describing the Tetons, Wissler used *Teton Dakota* (Wissler, 1912). In describing the Santees, Lowie preferred *Eastern Dakota* (a redundancy) rather than simply *Santee* (Lowie, 1913). Walker used *Teton Dakota* in the title of a monograph on the sun dance, but throughout the text he changed to *Lakota*, recognizing that his dialect group did not respond to *Dakota*. (He later changed to *Oglala*, the name of the principal Teton division [Walker, 1917]).

As more and more was published on the Sioux, there seemed to be no manner in which investigators could be consistent with tribal designations. Wissler in *Indians of the United States* classifies the "Dakota tribes" of the Siouan family as "Eastern Dakota," "Santee-Dakota," "Teton-Dakota," and "Yankton" (Wissler, 1945:154). He offers no explanation why Eastern and Santee are differentiated and why the Yanktons are not "Yankton-Dakota." Under the subtitle "The Dakota," Wissler states: "In the popular mind, Sioux symbolizes war, horses and buffalo as exemplified in the Dakota, the *true name* for the most powerful member of the family. In the literature of the last century and even now the word (Sioux, Dakota) seems dynamic" (ibid:156; italics added).

This need to clarify the terms *Sioux* and *Dakota* was shown earlier in Robinson's book, *A History of the Dakota or Sioux Indians*. Even in 1963, Feraca and Howard were to title a paper "The Identity and Demography of the Dakota or Sioux Tribe," as if neither one term nor the other was sufficient. They also added a footnote that "some Dakota also resent the pejorative connotations of 'Sioux,' though most are unaware of its original meaning" (Feraca and Howard, 1963: n.p.).

Hassrick wrote on "Teton Dakota Kinship Systems" in the *American Anthropologist* (1944) but called a later book *The Sioux: Life and Customs of a Warrior Society* (Hassrick, 1964), stating in the introduction that "the Sioux Indians with whom this book deals call themselves Lakotas, as distinguished from their relatives the Nakotas, or Yankton Sioux, and the Dakotas, or Santee Sioux. All of these groups speak closely related dialects of the Siouan language. However, because the word Sioux has been identified with the Lakotas in the American mind...the term is used throughout this book" (ibid:ix).

Apparently the "popular" (Wissler) and the "American" (Hass-rick) minds are just as undecided as are the anthropologists as to what to call the people with whom they associate *Sioux* so strongly. Of the two authors, however, Wissler is the more inconsistent. In four publications he discusses "Decorative Art of the Sioux" (1902), the previously mentioned "Societies...in the Oglala Division of Teton Dakota" (1912), "Some Oglala Dakota Myths" (1907a), and "Some Protective Designs of the Dakota" (1907b). All the divisions he discusses are politically Teton, dialectally Lakota, and geo-graphically Western.

LANGUAGE, POLITICS, AND GEOGRAPHY: THE EMIC MODEL

As mentioned before, the need to be specific about a seemingly vague entity known to themselves first as the Oceti Šakowin, and later as Sioux, created a classification system largely based on the juxtaposition of linguistic, political, and geographic designations. None of these designations are incorrect when used properly; however, they are redundant. Table 1 shows the proper relation-ship between these three classificatory criteria.

TABLE 1
POLITICAL, DIALECTAL, AND GEOGRAPHIC DESIGNATIONS APPLIED TO THE SEVEN FIREPLACES.

Political Designation	Dialect	Geographic Relationship
Teton	Lakota	Western
Yankton	Nakota	Middle
Santee	Dakota	Eastern

At one time, Table 1 might have been labeled "Oceti Šakowin," but that term has fallen into disuse. Today, the Indians call them-selves Sioux when speaking English, and Lakota, Nakota, or Da-kota when speaking their native language. These dialectal terms may be glossed either as "Indian" or "Indian language." The cor-rect classificatory label for Table 1 can only be "Sioux." However, the "Dakota" bias still persists. For example, DeMallie states that

the Seven Fires are divided into three dialectal groups: Santee, consisting of the Mdewakanton, Sisseton, Wahpeton, and Wahpekute;
Yankton, consisting of the Yankton and Yanktonai; and Teton. Their
common self-designation is *Dakota* (and dialectal variations *Nakota*
and *Lakota*) signifying 'ally.' Walker analyzed the term as *da-* 'to
esteem,' and *koda*, 'friend' (MS. 1:30A,1). *Dakota* is a verbal concept,
nominal forms being created by infixing pronouns. [DeMallie,
1971:106-7].

The problem here is that the "common self-designation" for the
"Seven Fires" is not Dakota, and Nakota and Lakota are not
variations of Dakota: the three dialects are "equal." Walker's
analysis is purely fictional. *Da* as a prefix does not mean "to esteem," although as a suffix it might mean "to consider." On the
other hand, *da* might also indicate a diminutive or a superlative.
Furthermore, *Dakota* is not a verbal concept as such; it is a nominal
one. It is precisely verbal forms that are created out of nominal
(and other) forms by infixing (actually, affixing, inasmuch as verbal forms may take prefixes or infixes).

To illustrate infixing, DeMallie goes on to provide the following example "in the Teton dialect" (i.e., Lakota):

> *lamakota,* 'I am a Dakota'
> *unlakotapi,* 'we are Dakotas'
> *lakotapi,* 'they are Dakotas'
> *lakota,* 'he is a Dakota'
> [Ibid.]

This paradigm is erroneous for two reasons. First, there is an
error of fact. The first person is not infixed in the verbalization of
the nominal form, *Lakota*: it is prefixed, *maLakota*. Secondly,
maLakota, unLakotapi, etc., could never be glossed as "I am a
Dakota," "we are Dakotas," etc. The significance can only be "I am
a Lakota," "we are Lakotas," etc. "I am a Dakota" is expressed by
maDakota; "we are Dakotas" by *unDakotapi*, etc. Here we see the
persistence of the "Dakota" bias carried to extremes.

In Table 2, I provide a model of the Seven Fireplaces which is
an elaboration of the political designations indicated in Table 1.
The political constituents of the Tetons are also shown. In the two
columns I employ rather conventional anglicized forms of the
Lakota terms and conventional glosses of the terms.

TABLE 2

POLITICAL ORGANIZATION OF THE SEVEN FIREPLACES, INCLUDING SUBDIVISIONS OF THE TETONS

DIVISION	GLOSS
	(TETON)
1. Teton	prairie dwellers
a. Oglala	they scatter their own
b. Sicangu	burned thighs (also known by the French term, Brulé)
c. Hunkpapa	end of the circle
d. Mnikowoju	planters beside the stream
e. Sihasapa	black foot (not to be confused with the Algonquian tribe of the same name)
f. Oohenunpa	two boilings, or two kettle
g. Itazipco	without bows (also known by the French term, Sans Arcs)
	(YANKTON)
2. Yankton	end dwellers
3. Yanktonais	little end dwellers
	(SANTEE)
4. Mdewakanton	spirit, or mystery lake dwellers
5. Wahpeton	leaf dwellers
6. Sisseton	fish scale dwellers
7. Wahpekute	leaf shooters

By way of emphasis, I should point out that *Teton* is a collective term which identifies its constituents, but there is no Teton tribe as such. The same obtains for *Santee.* However, *Yankton* refers to a collectivity of two fireplaces, and at the same time is a political designation for one of the two. In employing binary terms to identify any of the Seven Fireplaces, it only makes sense to combine geographic terms with *Sioux,* e.g., Western Sioux. All other combinations are ambiguous or redundant.

Other complications have arisen as the result of using the combination *Teton Sioux.* Frances Densmore's *Teton Sioux Music* (1918) is a good example. While the songs she collected were unmistakably Teton, all were from the Standing Rock Reservation in North Dakota (a few were collected at Sisseton, South Dakota) and thus came from the Hunkpapas, one of the seven constituents of the Tetons. Since there is some dissimilarity between the songs of the Hunkpapas, and those of, say, the Oglalas, particularly in style of presentation, that which is typically Hunkpapa may not necessarily be Oglala or representative of all Tetons. The same problem exists for the Yanktons and Santees, inasmuch as the former represent two political divisions, and the latter, four.

This rather lengthy discussion of problems in the nomenclature related to the Seven Fireplaces is important because it helps to provide a rationale for my use of the term *Oglala* as a marker for an ethnic boundary. At the same time, it demonstrates that the ambiguous or arbitrary usage of nomenclature can obfuscate the real identity of American Indian people. Deloria has briefly touched upon this point (Deloria, 1974).

It is somewhat ironic that the majority of anthropologists and linguists have selected *Dakota* over any other choice for a classificatory label. The majority of descendants of the Seven Fireplaces speak Lakota. Most dictionaries and grammars published in the native language have rightfully been labeled Dakota where they deal with the language of the Santees. Buechel, however, disregarded Powell's regulations and published *A Grammar of Lakota* (1939) and, posthumously, *A Lakota-English Dictionary* (1970) since both deal with Lakota.

Chapter 2

THE SEVEN
FIREPLACES

CULTURAL-HISTORICAL BACKGROUND

The conventional model of Sioux social organization (Chap. 1, table 2) must be regarded as a typology restricted to a specific time period, probably no earlier than about 1700. Prior to that time, one must postulate that the Tetons, as well as other Siouan-speakers, were redistributing their populations because of migrations, economic pressures, and warfare with the Central Algonquians. Thus, the Oglalas did not exist as a discrete political entity before about 1700. However, it is probable that the term *Oglala*, possibly in some variant form, served to identify a segment of the Tetons. As I shall demonstrate, a number of political designations found among contemporary Sioux existed at a prior time, but in another context.

My purpose here is to present a historical summary of the Seven Fireplaces which will place the Oglalas in their proper diachronic perspective. For a more comprehensive treatment of Sioux history, see DeMallie (1971), Hyde (1937, 1956, 1961), and Robinson (1904). In addition to describing the historical and cultural context out of which the Oglalas emerged, this summary will also provide a basis for understanding contemporary Oglala myth and ritual. The myths which I will later analyze, for example, refer to this earlier period of time. Contemporary rituals also emerge out of this cultural and historical milieu, and the social organization of the Oglalas is a replication of the Seven Fireplaces.

Although some investigators have speculated that a time existed when the three dialectal groups of Sioux formed a proto-Siouan entity along with their linguistic cognates, the Assiniboins, Missouri River peoples (Crows, Mandans, Hidatsas), the Degiha

(Kansas, Omahas, Osages, Poncas, Quapaws), Chiwere (Otos, Missouris, Iowas), and other tribes located in the southeastern United States, there is no archeological or glottochronological evidence to indicate just what this protoculture might have resembled. Sioux prehistory is at best conjectural, despite the fact that some outlandish claims have been made linking the Sioux with Adena-Hopewellian populations (see particularly Hyde, 1962; Terrell, 1974).

On the other hand, the amount of literature devoted to Sioux history is staggering, and much has been documented about the early history of the Seven Fireplaces, beginning with the mid-seventeenth century.

EUROPEAN CONTACT

The first positive mention of the Sioux appears in the *Jesuit Relation* for 1640 (Thwaites, 1869–1901), in which appear tribal names collected by Jean Nicolet a few years earlier. Nicolet first learned of the people called Naduesiu from the Winnebagos at present Green Bay, Wisconsin. However, it was not until 1660 that two French explorers, Pierre Esprit Radisson, and Médard Chouart, sieur des Groseilliers, encountered the Sioux in what is now northwestern Wisconsin or eastern Minnesota at an annual Feast of the Dead. Here, the Sioux regarding the French as demigods "wept copiously and smoked the calumet with the strangers" (Meyer, 1967:1-2). Subsequent encounters by the missionaries Claude Jean Allouez, Jacques Marquette, and Louis Hennepin, and the military men and traders Daniel Greysolon, sieur Duluth; Nicolas Perrot; and Pierre Charles Le Sueur, provide the first ethnographic accounts.

By the beginning of the sixteenth century, the people known as the Oceti Šakowin had established themselves on the headwaters of the Mississippi. The French who first encountered them regarded them as formidable warriors. Historians state that when the Seven Fireplaces were not fighting their enemies, mainly the Central Algonquians, they were fighting each other, despite the fact that their dialectal names (Dakota, Nakota, Lakota) signify "friendly" or "allied" (compare *kola* 'friend'; *wolakota* 'peace'; *okolakiciye* 'association, sodality'). Hennepin classified the Sioux into the Sioux of the East (east of the Mississippi), comprising the Mdewakantons, Wahpetons, Wahpekutes, and Sissetons, and the Sioux of the West, comprising the Yanktons, Yanktonais, and Tetons. The four divisions of the Sioux of the East were also known collectively as Santee (from *isan* 'knife' and *ti* 'to dwell'), the name—also spelled Izatys—of the principal village of the Mdewakantons near present Mille Lacs, Minnesota.

Le Sueur in 1700, estimated the population of the Seven Fireplaces at 4,000 families. In 1736, a census reflecting the opinions of voyageurs estimated the population at from eight thousand to ten thousand. Wars between the Sioux and the Chippewas and Crees were in part responsible for an out-migration of the Eastern division from their homes around Mille Lacs, since the Chippewas were armed by the French traders. Missionaries state that the attraction of traders operating around the junction of the Mississippi and Missouri Rivers also contributed to the abandonment of the original homeland. DeMallie suggests that the desirability of homes farther west also contributed to the early migrations (DeMallie, 1971). Around 1750, the Santee village was attacked by Chippewas, an event which one investigator calls "the most readily identifiable...in the process by which [the Sioux] were transformed from a typical tribe of the Eastern Woodlands culture to a people at least on the margin of the Plains Indian culture" (Meyer, 1967:14).

After the French and Indian Wars, in 1766, the Sioux were visited by Captain Jonathan Carver, who made observations on their customs and began compiling a dictionary of their language. He divided the Seven Fireplaces into River Bands and Prairie Bands, and estimated their total population at two thousand. Carver was followed by Peter Pond, a trader who embarked upon an expedition into Sioux country in 1773–75 and built a fort on the lower Minnesota River. His journal describes the Sioux living in tipis and owning a great number of horses and dogs (DeMallie, 1971).

The first official representative of the United States to reach the Sioux was Lt. Zebulon M. Pike, who attempted to establish American sovereignty on the upper Mississippi in 1805–06. He signed a

treaty with the Mdewakantons in which they ceded 100,000 acres
of land to the United States and for which they received about $200
worth of gifts and liquor on the spot and the promise of an unspecified sum of money (Meyer, 1967). Pike estimated the total
population of the Sioux at 21,675. He identified all the major components of the Seven Fireplaces, stating that the Wahpekutes
"were the most stupid and inactive of all the Sioux" (cited in
Meyer, 1967:27). I shall return to this point below.

Pike was followed in 1817 by the expedition of Major Stephen
H. Long, the purpose of which was to identify sites for the con-
struction of forts. The territory of the Eastern Sioux at the time of
Long's expedition was reported as

> bounded by a curved line E. of N. from Prairie du Chien on the
> Mississippi, so as to include all the E. tributaries of the Mississippi, to
> the first branch of Chippewa r.; thence westwardly to Crow Wing r.,
> Minn.; and up that stream to its head; thence westwardly to Red r. and
> down that stream to Pembina; thence southwestwardly to the E. bank
> of the Missouri near the Mandan villages; thence down the Missouri to
> a point probably not far from Soldiers r.; thence E. of N. to Prairie du
> Chien, Wis. [Hodge, 1907–10:376]

The territory of the Sioux of the West was a vast region west of
the Missouri from the Yellowstone River southward to the Platte.

Social Organization

As Howard has pointed out (Howard, 1960; Feraca and Howard, 1963), the Santees, Yanktons, and Tetons can best be understood by regarding them as not only dialectally but culturally
separate entities, each uniquely adapting to a particular environment. At the time of French contact, the Seven Fireplaces exhibited the cultural traits of the Woodland Indians, ones they shared
with the Central Algonquians. Their economy was based on hunting, fishing, and gathering, all of which was supplemented by slash
and burn horticulture.

DeMallie has recently challenged Howard's theory, calling it
oversimplified (DeMallie, 1971). This is partly due to Howard's

claim that the Santees represent an "older Dakota culture," while the Yanktons and Tetons, in their westward migrations, adapted to new locales and cultural influences (Howard, 1960:250; DeMallie, 1971:15-16). DeMallie asserts that there is no reason to assume that the earlier culture is necessarily represented by nineteenth-century Santees, and that "it is untenable to assert without evidence that Santee culture remained stable for two or three centuries while that of their western neighbors developed in new directions" (DeMallie, 1971:16).

However, within the passage cited by DeMallie, Howard states that the Santees did in fact undergo some changes, "presumably minor...subsequent to the separation" (Howard, in DeMallie, 1971:16). I believe that both arguments can be reconciled if we regard the focus of subsistence patterns and other cultural traits, changing spatially from east to west, and temporally. Thus at some historic period we would find traits of "true" Woodland and "true" Plains types in all three divisions of the Sioux. In terms of focus, however, we would find a primary focus on horticulture, canoe travel, and semisedentary village life among the Santees, and on horse nomadism and buffalo hunting among the Tetons. The Yanktons would, in theory, occupy an intermediary position.

The change of focus in time and space also helps explain another problem in Sioux social organization, one which centers on principles of descent. I believe it is fair to say that again Howard and DeMallie represent the contemporary opposing points of view. Howard, in keeping with the original investigations of Morgan (1871), regards the Sioux as originally living in patrilineal clans. He believes that because of migrations and the breakdown of the village, the clans were ultimately transformed into cognatic groups which helped them better adapt to a nomadic, buffalo-hunting subsistence pattern. DeMallie, on the other hand, follows the reasoning of Lesser (1928, 1958), who holds that the "bilateral" family was the "underlying structure of all Siouan later social organization (Lesser, 1928, cited in DeMallie, 1971:6). Again, I believe the argument is reconciled by suggesting a change of focus over time and space between lineal and cognatic principles of descent, the latter being more strongly associated with the Tetons.

VILLAGE ORGANIZATION AND LEADERSHIP

French, British, and American travelers to Sioux country all reported the presence of villages along waterways which bisected prairie and marsh lands. Each village was under the leadership of one or more chief and subchiefs. Hickerson states that among the Santees and Yanktons, their several villages were autonomous:

> Each was represented by one or more chiefs in matters related to treaties, war and peace, and trade. War was carried on independently by several villages, and it was not unusual for one village to be fighting while its nearest neighbor was in a state of truce. In treaties with the government, the separate villages usually acted separately. Their territories were demarcated one from the other, and presumably each village acted as a separate economic unit. [Hickerson, 1970:77]

Hickerson further emphasizes the emergence of the village as the discrete political and territorial unit. Despite the autonomy of these villages, alliances were often formed for the purpose of waging war. One must assume that because of the combined pressures of warfare and encroachment by Europeans, the villages of the Seven Fireplaces were in a constant state of flux. Meyer states that when the Mdewakanton chief Wabasha moved a segment of his band, a portion of the village remained, forming the nucleus of a new band: "This was the pattern followed earlier and later; a subchief might take a few of his followers and establish a new village, or the principal chief might leave without taking all of the members of his band along. In this way the historic villages of the Mdewakanton Sioux were formed" (Meyer, 1967:21).

I would hastily add that in this way the subsequent camps of Yanktons and Tetons were also formed after their migration onto the prairie. The same pattern in which chiefs and subchiefs formed and re-formed new villages and bands among the Mdewakantons was to be replicated by the westernmost groups of Sioux. Presumably the reasons for the reformulation and redistribution of populations were numerous: war, economic pressures, hostility between chiefs and subchiefs, and petty arguments. However, the manner in which these populations were redistributed remained relatively constant over time and space: the mental template which

The Seven Fireplaces

21

gave rise to new local populations was indelibly etched in the social structure of the Seven Fireplaces.

Etymolgical Considerations

The conventional terminology for the Seven Fireplaces (Santees, Yanktons, Tetons), particularly in its anglicized form, and the conventional glosses which anthropologists and linguists have perpetuated over time tend, I think, to support the idea that the Seven Fireplaces represented a social and cultural system which was ideally unified. This unification, I believe, is largely illusory. Rather, I see the Seven Fireplaces as being in a state of constant flux, forming temporary alliances, constantly shifting leadership and nuclei of villages and bands. This notion of flux and movement is suggested in the etymology of the native terms for autonomous political entities, and also becomes a major theme of the myths that rationalize the origins of the Oglalas. A perusal of the native terms for autonomous units over time presents an insight to the dialectic of change in Sioux social organization. But at the same time it elucidates some principals of continuity; certain native terms are reused again and again.

A reconsideration of the social organization of the Seven Fireplaces, based on etymologies of the native terms, reveals the following model:

1. *Mdewakanton* is derived from *mdewakantunwan* (*mde* 'water, lake' [compare *mni* 'water' and *ble* 'lake']; *wakan* 'sacred'; *tunwan* 'village'). The conventional gloss is "Spirit Lake People" (Howard, 1966); DeMallie translates it "Sacred Lake" (for Mille Lacs), a better gloss (DeMallie, 1971:104), but *tunwan* signifies "village" (compare the modern Lakota term for town, city, *otunwahe*) and should be part of the translation.

William H. Keating, chronicler of the Long expedition, identifies four Mdewakanton villages: Oanoska, the village under Big Eagle; Tetankatane; Taoapa; and Weakaote (Keating, 1825). There is some problem in deciphering the orthography. The second is probably "old buffalo" (*tatanka tanni*); the third possibly is "strikes the wound" (*tao* 'wound' and *apa* 'to strike');

the fourth may be "strikes many women" or "crowded with women" (*winyan* 'woman' and *kaota* 'to strike many' or *kaotins* 'crowded in'). Keating also cites the names of Mdewakanton bands by their leaders: Wabasha's band is called Keoxa (*kiyuksa* 'to break in half'); Red Wing's is noted as Eanbosandata (?); and Little Crow's is called Kapoja (*Kapoja* 'light [weight]'). The first and last names are important insofar as they appear again as subdivisions of the Oglalas.

2. *Wahpeton* is derived from *wahpetunwan* (*wahpe* 'leaf' and *tunwan* 'village'). Howard translates it as "Dwellers among the Leaves" (Howard, 1966), and DeMallie as "Leaf Village." Both suggest that the Wahpetons wandered away from the Mdewakantons to the deciduous forests of the south, hence the name (DeMallie, 1971).

3. *Wahpekute* is from *wahpekute* (*wahpe* 'leaf' and *kute* 'to shoot'). Howard calls them "Shooters among the Leaves," and DeMallie "shoot in the leaves [village]." Interestingly, this is the only Fireplace that does not identify itself as a village (*tunwan*); above it was quoted that these Sioux were regarded as the most "stupid and inactive" among the tribe. They are also identified as being a group of renegades who deserted the Wabasha band and who were also known as Gens de la Feuille Tire, or Fire-Leaf band (Meyer, 1967:29).

4. *Sisseton* comes from *sinsintunwan* (*sinsin* or *sisin* 'to smell of fish' [Riggs, 1890:435] or 'besmeared, slimed, as with fish'; also 'dried on, glued, or glazed over' [Buechel, 1970:454]). Howard calls this band "People of the Boggy Ground," and DeMallie, "slimy village." Riggs and DeMallie attribute the name to the fact that the Sisseton village stank like fish. Hickerson states that fish were not regarded highly by the Dakotas, and that any allusion to fish is one suggesting poverty (Hickerson, 1970).

5. *Yankton* is derived from *ihanktunwan* (*ihanke* 'end, termination, border, boundary' [Buechel, 1970:216] and *tunwan* 'village'). Conventionally glossed as "End Village" or "End Dwellers," this term refers to a relative position in a camp circle rather than to a topographical area as do the preceding four.

6. *Yanktonais* is derived from *inhanktunwanna* (*ihanke* 'end'; *tunwan* 'village'; and *na*, diminuitive suffix), conventionally glossed as "Little End Village" or "Little End Dwellers."

Both the Yanktons and Yanktonais are also referred to by other Sioux as Wiciyela or Wiciyena, glossed as "Those Who Speak like Men" by Howard (1966) and "our people, those who are ours" by DeMallie (1971) (probably from *wica*, third person plural [objective]; *iye* 'to speak'; and *la*, suffix which connotes either diminution or proper name, hence 'speakers').

According to Howard, the Yanktons were divided into seven subdivisions, to which an eighth, the "Half-Breed," was added. The Yanktonais were divided into the Upper Yanktonais and Lower Yanktonais (also called Hunkpatina). Of these two divisions, the former was divided into six subdivisions, the latter into seven. I shall return to these subdivisions at a later point insofar as we again find terms used by the Santees and Tetons employed by the Yankton groups. As a matter of historical note, it is from the Yanktonais that the Nakoda-speaking Assiniboins emerged allying themselves with the Crees.

7. *Teton*, according to all sources, is derived from *tintatunwan* (*tinta* 'prairie' [in Dakota dialect]; and *tunwan* 'village'), and the conventional gloss is "prairie dwellers." *Tinta* does not appear in Lakota; it is replaced by *tiiȟeyab* (*ti* 'to dwell'; and *iȟeyab* [from *iȟeyapa* 'away from, beyond']). Thus I believe that both *tinta* in Dakota and *tiiȟeyab* in Lakota are metaphors signifying "prairie," but in the sense of "village beyond the other dwellings." Furthermore, *iȟeyab* is composed of *i*, preposition 'at' or 'toward'; *ȟe* 'mountain'; and *yab* (from *yapa* 'moving toward'). Thus *iȟeyab* as it is used in the proper name may be regarded as a double metaphor, i.e., away from or beyond is actually "toward the mountains from." Another form, *ȟeyata*, is used with *wicasa* 'man' to indicate one of two divisions of the Sicangus, a constituent of the Tetons, hence *ȟeyata wicaša* 'upper men' distinguished one group of Sicangus from the *kul wicaša* (*kuta* 'low, below') 'lower men'. As we have just seen, the upper-lower dichotomy also appears among the Yanktonais.

What I believe is important here is that although *Teton* has been conventionally glossed as "Prairie Dweller," the important distinction between this division and other members of the Seven Fireplaces is that its name bears no relationship to the others. That is to say that while the Dakota-speakers favor names that refer to their original homes in the Woodlands, i.e., lakes and forests, and the Nakota-speakers are named after relative positions in a metaphorical camp circle, i.e., the ends, the Lakota-speakers emerge with a generic name which refers to neither toponymic nor village-related concepts. The Tetons are, in fact, unique.

In the next chapter, I shall follow this etymological analysis with one of native terms which designate the constituents of the Tetons, the primary one being the Oglalas.

Chapter 3

THE OGLALAS

The Tetons

The Tetons are perhaps the best known of all the Sioux. They may be regarded as the "typical" Plains Indian: they lived in tipis, hunted buffalo on horseback, and were involved in numerous battles with other tribes and with Euro-Americans, including the Red Cloud wars of the 1860s, the Custer battle of 1876, and the Wounded Knee massacre of 1890.

After migrating from their original homelands in Minnesota, this constituent of the Seven Fireplaces adapted to a Plains environment, an adaptation which lasted for 150 years and ended with their political subjugation at Wounded Knee and their final retirement to reservations in North and South Dakota, Montana, and Saskatchewan. For an excellent summary of their migrations onto the Plains, see Hyde (1937, 1956, 1961).

As the Tetons migrated onto the Plains, groups of extended families fused with others to form what have conventionally been called bands or subbands. Other, larger groups splintered, some members joining other extant bands or forming new ones. This pattern of fusion and fission was not unlike that described for the Eastern villages. Just as the Santees followed prominent chiefs and subchiefs in their semisedentary haunts, the Tetons similarly based group affiliation on the prowess of one or more men who were adept at hunting and warfare.

Teton, of course, is a collective term. The straggling groups of Westerners who entered upon the Plains aligned themselves in such a way as to replicate the original structure of the Seven

Fireplaces. These seven subdivisions, with an etymological analysis of their native names, are as follows:

1. *Oglala* is conventionally glossed "they scatter their own" (from the reflexive form of *okala* [*o* 'in or on'; *kala* 'to scatter as grain'; Buechel, 1970:281]. *Okala* means 'to scatter in or on, e.g. to sow grain; pour out into; sow; plant' [ibid.:383]). Properly, *oglala* means "to scatter one's own."

2. *Sicangu* is derived from *sican* 'thigh' and *gu* 'burned, scorched, branded' and is conventionally glossed as "Burned Thighs." This group is also known in the literature by the French term, Brulé.

   The Oglalas and Sicangus were the first of the Tetons to enter upon the Plains, and for some time remained together as a unit (Hyde, 1937).

3. *Hunkpapa* is usually translated as "Campers at the Horn, or End of the Camp Circle," and is derived from a reduplicated form of *hunkpa* 'entrance to a camp'. Compare this with *Hunkpatina* (the term for the Lower Yanktonais) and *Ihanktunwan*. Both *hank* and *hunk* are variants of *ihanke* 'end'. *Pa* means "head," hence the entrance to a camp circle is metaphorically both the end and head of a camp.

4. *Mnikowoju*, also spelled Minneconjou in the literature, is usually glossed "Planters beside the Stream." It is derived from *mni* 'water'; *ki*, a prefix indicating that an action takes place in the middle, or between something (compare *kiyuksa* 'to break in half'); and *oju* 'to plant'.

5. *Itazipco* signifies "No Bows," or "Without Bows," and is derived from *itazipa* 'bow' and *cola* 'without'. This group is also known in the literature by the French term, Sans Arcs.

6. *Oohenunpa* is usually translated as "Two Kettle" or "Two Boilings," and is derived from (*w*)*o*, noun prefix; *ohan* 'to cook, boil, specifically something that can be cooked at once in one pot'; and *nunpa* 'two'.

7. *Sihasapa* is glossed "Blackfoot," always with the caveat that it should not be confused with the Algonquian Blackfeet. It is derived from *si* 'foot'; *ha* 'hide, skin'; and *sapa* 'black'.

   The latter five divisions of the Tetons followed the Oglalas and Sicangus onto the Plains and remained together for some time, occupying areas north of the Oglalas. They are sometimes referred to collectively as the Saones, a word which Hyde discusses at length and unconvincingly glosses as "Shooters among the Trees." He mentions that older Sioux state that the term "came from *Sanyoni wichasha* ('Saone Men') and was a nickname formerly applied by the Oglalas and Brules to the Miniconjous, Sans Arcs, and Two Kettles, while others insisted that the name came from *Sanyona*" (ibid.: 13). Howard lists Sanona as a division of the Lower Yanktonais, but provides no gloss. I suggest that the term is probably an orthographic corruption of *canoti* 'wood'; *o* 'in'; *ti* 'to dwell'), or 'forest dwellers'.

THE OGLALAS

Although the native terms related to the Santees are obviously toponymic names which describe or identify the original villages, the origins of Teton names are obscure. Hyde presumes that the stories which account for the provenience of the Oglalas are apocryphal. The most common story, one still told, is that two chiefs quarreled, one insulting the other by throwing dirt in his face. This caused the followers of the two to go separate ways.

Yet historically, the Oglalas did not emerge until 1700, when they were encountered by Le Sueur at a trading fair at the mouth of the Minnesota River. Le Sueur called these people Ojalespoitan, Village Divided into Many Small Bands. Again we are faced with a corrupted orthography, one rationalized by Hyde in the following manner:

> There is no "j" in the Sioux tongue, this sound being represented in the Teton dialect by "gl." This name was therefore *Oglales-poit-ton:* from *Oglala* (scattered or divided) and *ton* (village). The *poit* is puzzling, but seems to be an Algonquian word (*poituc,* "men" or "people") which the early French often employed in writing Sioux tribal names. [Ibid.:8]

Le Sueur was probably attempting to spell the Santee version of *Oglala* (*Ohdada*) or the Yankton (*Okdada*). Fortunately, his translation of "Village Divided into Many Small Bands" is more useful than his attempt to orthographize the Siouan. Of course, we do not

know what Hyde means when he states that there is no *j* in Sioux
(nor do we know what he means by *Sioux* in this context), but he is
correct in assuming that this is the first mention of the people under
discussion.

Hyde also mentions that Le Sueur did not make any reference
to the Sicangus at that time, and accounts for this by stating that
they simply did not exist under that name until after 1750. It is
reasonable to speculate, I think, that possibly the "apocryphal
myth" which accounts for the establishment of the Oglalas might
indeed have been an altercation between the Oglalas and Sicangus,
since they migrated together.

Although there is some disagreement over when the Oglalas
first obtained horses (about 1750), it is evident that when the
scattered groups of people first reached the Great Bend of the
Missouri River, they were on foot, carrying their meager belongings on their backs and on dog travois. They first came into contact
with the powerful Arikaras, who numbered some twenty thousand, and who had already adapted to an equestrian life. According to the Sioux traditions of this period, they were alternately
friendly and hostile to the Arikaras, and it was from those riverine
Caddoan-speakers that the Sioux first obtained horses.

The strength of the Arikaras prevented the Oglalas from making any westward advances until an epidemic of smallpox struck
the former, reducing their numbers drastically. The Oglalas
crossed the Missouri about 1775, and by that year, according to
their own traditions documented by means of winter counts
(*waniyetu iyawapi* [*waniyetu* 'winter'; *i* 'with, by means of';
yawapi 'they count'; i.e., pictographic calendars]) reached the
Black Hills, there engaging in battle with the Kiowas and Crows
and, finally extirpating the two tribes from the region. The following account of their social organization at that time is largely ex-
tracted from Hyde (1937).

Lewis and Clark met the Oglalas in 1804 and identified two
"bands," the True Oglalas and the Siyos ("prairie chicken"). The
latter band, however, later joined the Sicangus. Wissler cites the
report of the Commissioner of Indian Affairs for 1875, which gives
four Oglala divisions: the "Ogallallas, Kiocsies, Onkapas, and
Wazazies" (Wissler, 1912:3). Wissler's own investigations led him

to believe that the Oglala "tribal government was composed of the Oglala, Kiaksai, Oyuhpe, and Wazazies, (the latter of which) according to Two-crow...were but a subdivision of the Kiaksai while the fourth division was the Pahabyapi" (ibid.: 7).

Schoolcraft lists six Oglala bands for 1850, but he neglects to include the Kiyaksas (Wissler's Kiaksai, Kiocsies), who are known to have been established at this time. His six are the True Oglala; Minisha, or Red Water Band; Old Skin Necklace Band; Peshla, or Short Hair Band; Night Cloud Band; and Red Lodge Band (Schoolcraft, 1851). Hyde himself records seven subdivisions of the Oglalas for 1879, the year in which the Sioux were placed on reservations. He lists the following: Payabsa (Wissler's Pahabyapi); Tapishlecea; Kiyuksa (Wissler's Kiaksai, Kiocsie); Wazhazha (Wissler's Wazazies); Iteshicha; Oyukhpe (Wissler's Oyuhpe); and Waklukhe (Hyde, 1937:313–14). Hyde comments, interestingly, "Thus by 1850 the Oglalas had a camp circle *of the ideal Sioux type, consisting of seven bands*" (ibid.:312; italics added).

Before providing an etymological analysis of the seven subdivisions of the Oglalas, it is perhaps appropriate to make some mention of the fissiparous nature of the Oglalas at that time. Rivalry between leaders was not uncommon, as I have suggested above. When faced with survival, it is likely that the people chose leaders who exhibited strength in hunting and warfare. But as the lives of the Oglalas and others were increasingly manipulated by traders and military men, it appears that petty jealousies based on popularity became more common. Hyde relates an interesting story about hostility between two rival chiefs, one also recorded by Francis Parkman during his stay among the Oglalas and by Dr. Charles A. Eastman (Parkman, 1846; Eastman, 1920). The story concerns Bull Bear and Smoke, two leaders with extensive followings around 1840.

Apparently, Bull Bear was a tyrannical chief who had an on-going feud with Smoke. The feud reached a crisis when local traders encouraged the latter to challenge the former. One day, Bull Bear stationed himself in front of his newly acclaimed rival and demanded that Smoke come out and fight. When Smoke did not appear, Bull Bear in a fury stabbed the chief's horse and left for his own camp. Smoke made no immediate response, but later he and his friends, including Red Cloud, devised a plan to retaliate, and waited. In the autumn of 1841 Bull Bear happened upon Smoke's camp on the Chugwater, a few miles from Fort John. An abundance of liquor had been provided by the traders, and the warriors from each band began arguing. Bull Bear attempted to stop the fight, but was instantly shot down as he emerged from his lodge. A wild fight ensued in which Red Cloud's brother, Yellow Lodge, and six other warriors were killed, and many more were wounded (Hyde, 1937:53–54). According to winter counts, this event created a division in the tribe, and forty years later on the reservation, the two divisions were still known as the Bear People, after Chief Bull Bear, and the Smoke People.

It is worthwhile to note here that in addition to reaching the ideal Sioux type of social organization based on seven subdivisions (like the Yanktons and Yanktonais), the Oglalas also divided into two major sections, later to be known as the Northern and Southern Oglalas.

ETYMOLOGICAL CONSIDERATIONS OF OGLALA DIVISIONS

Placing the native terminology of Oglala divisions into a standard orthography allows the following etymological analysis:

1. *Payabya* is derived from *pa* 'head' and *yabya* 'to cause to go toward'. It is glossed as "pushed aside" by Hyde, who states that they were almost destroyed by Red Cloud and his band of Itešica in 1864–74. According to Feraca, the Payabyas were originally called Hunkpatilas and were under the leadership of Old Man and Young Man Afraid of His Horses. He attributes the change of name to the Itešicas (Feraca, 1966:5). My own informant, John Colhoff, translated the name of the division as "head of the circle," which is closer to the original Lakota (Powers, 1963).

2. *Tapisleca* is derived from *tapi* 'liver' and *šleca* 'split'. Hyde glosses it as "Split Liver" and acknowledges that it was also known as Shkopa (*škopa* 'bent, curved'). Colhoff translates it as "Spleen" (the term for spleen is in fact "split liver"), and identifies its leaders as Yellow Bear and White Bird (ibid.).

3. *Kiyaksa* is from *ki*, prefix that indicates action takes place in the middle, between; *ya*, instrumental prefix indicating that action takes place by means of the mouth; biting, chewing, speaking, singing; *ksa* 'to sever, cut'. Hyde spells it Kiyuksa and glosses it as "breaks his own," "Cut-off," and "Bit-the Snake-in-Two," and states that it refers to the breaking of a marriage custom. "Bite-the-Snake," he suggests, comes from a woman's test of virginity. Feraca also spells it Kiyuksa and glosses it as "Breakers of the Rule" (Feraca, 1966). Colhoff spells it Kiyaksa and glosses it as "Cut Band." *Kiyaksa* is best glossed as "to divide by speaking," which is in keeping with Feraca's "breakers of the rule." Buechel states that the name Kiyaksa came from the custom of relatives intermarrying in this division. Both forms, Kiyaksa and Kiyuksa, are in current usage.

According to Hyde, these three bands constituted the half of the tribe under Bull Bear. They settled on Medicine Root Creek on the Pine Ridge Reservation.

4. *Wajaje* is an interesting appellation for an Oglala division. It is a Siouan word but not Lakota, and is the term used by the Osages to identify themselves. It has often been translated as "snake," but is probably a cognate to the Lakota *wocaje* 'class, kind' (from *wo*, noun prefix, and *caje* 'name'). They are regarded as a people who settled between the Bear and Smoke People.

5. *Itesica* is from *ite* 'face' and *šica* 'bad'. This is Red Cloud's original band. The name is said to be derived from their manner of painting their face for war. "Bad Faces" is the accepted gloss.

6. *Oyuhpe* is the verb *oyuȟpe* 'to throw down, away'. Hyde translates "throw down or where they lay down their packs." Feraca and Colhoff gloss it as "Untidy," which is acceptable. This band was under the leadership of Red Dog and Big Road.

7. *Wagluhe* is derived from *wa*, noun prefix, and *gluge* 'to pick or gather up scraps from the floor' (Buechel, 1970:156). Buechel also identifies this division as the Loafer band of the Oglalas and glosses the name as "to live with one's wife's relatives, to be a hanger-on" (ibid.:516). Most authorities agree that the proper gloss is "Loafers." The term seems to refer to the Oglalas who hung about Fort Laramie looking for handouts. A number of mixed-blood Oglalas (*ieska*) belonged to this division.

The last three bands constituted the second half of the Oglalas, those under Chief Smoke.

Hyde states:

These seven bands of 1879 were made up of little camps, each with its own name. Among these obscure bands were the formerly proud true Oglala, now not considered important enough to have a place of its own in the tribal circle. Some of these little bands had formerly been strong and prominent, like the True Oglala. Leadership either made or ruined an Oglala band. An unimportant little camp with a strong leader would surge suddenly to the front, draw strength from the other bands and for a time lead the tribe, only to sink back into obscurity when a younger warrior from some other camp pushed the older leader aside and took his place. [Hyde, 1937:315]

Chapter 4

SOCIAL ORGANIZATION

In the preceding chapters I have attempted to describe the sociocultural and historical milieu out of which the Oglalas emerged as an autonomous political entity. My analysis of the Seven Fireplaces in their original Minnesota homeland and of the divisions which emerged during and after their migration onto the prairie has been confined largely to etic considerations. Through this analysis we have seen that there has been a preeminence of the number seven in determining the ideal structure of Sioux divisions. In addition, there has been a tendency for Sioux groups to form two major subdivisions in the process of their autonomous development.

In this chapter I am more concerned with emic considerations, and offer a model (about 1700) of how the Oglalas classified their own social organization. I am here interested in native concepts of the social universe, the means by which order was maintained among the Oglalas through tribal government. I am also interested in the manner in which relationships were established between the Oglalas and various divisions and subdivisions of other Siouan and non-Siouan peoples.

Levels of Social Organization

At one level of social organization we find seven villages in Minnesota which call themselves Oceti Šakowin, the Seven Fireplaces. Each of the villages (with the exception of Wahpekute) is distinguished by the suffix *tunwan* 'village' to its proper name. *Oceti* 'fireplace' may be regarded as a synonymn of *village*. The

Seven Fireplaces stands in contradistinction to all nonmember Siouan-speakers, and, of course, this would include non-Indians. The native term for nonmembers is *toka*, usually glossed "enemy" but perhaps better translated as "outsider" inasmuch as even friendly outsiders such as the Cheyennes and Arapahos are today regarded as *toka*.

At the second level, we find the Teton village giving rise to seven divisions, the largest of which is the Oglala. At this historical period, however, the *tunwan* suffix is missing. The constituents of the Tetons are not village-based. Instead, we find the Oglalas and other members of the Tetons referring to themselves as *oyate* 'people'. Today, *oyate* is not only the generic term for *people*, but is also used ritually to refer to animals (e.g., *Mato Oyate* 'Bear People') and birds (*Wanbli Oyate* 'Eagle People'). In its ritual context, anthropologists have tended to translate *oyate* as "nation." This is somewhat misleading because it gives the impression that the Oglalas differentiate between *Oglala oyate* and *Wanbli Oyate* (i.e., Oglala people, but Eagle Nation). There is no reason to assume that the Oglalas in fact do differentiate, at least in ritual contexts.

At a third level we find the Oglalas giving rise to seven divisions which in terms of emic categorization are neither *tunwan* nor *oyate*. The Lakota term for this third level of social organization is *tiyošpaye* (from *ti* 'to dwell' and *ošpaye* 'a drove, a herd consisting of different kinds of animals, a company separated from the main body' [Buechel, 1970:406]; *ošpaye* is derived from *ošpe* 'a piece, a part'). *Tiyošpaye* has previously been glossed in a number of ways: "a band, a division of a tribe, a community" (ibid.:491); "lodge group, or group that lives together" (DeMallie, 1971:110); "they live together" (Feraca, 1966:1); "family hunting group" (Hassrick, 1964:11); "camp" (Howard, 1966:3); and "ti-ospayepi" (tipi-divisions-bands) (Walker, 1914:98). The *tiyošpaye* has been regarded by most authors as the smallest sociopolitical unit which operated under one or more chiefs throughout most of the year.

With respect to these three levels of social organization, an Oglala would theoretically identify himself in the following way:
1. At the first level he would regard himself as a member of the Titunwan.

2. At the second level he would regard himself as a member of the Oglala *oyate*.
3. At the third level he would regard himself as a member of the Kiyaksa (or other) *tiyospaye*.

His membership in the above would be determined by his birth.

RESIDENTIAL GROUPS

At still another level of social organization, an Oglala would be a member of *wicoti* (from *wica*, third person plural [objective]; *o* 'in'; and *ti* 'to dwell'), the generic term for camp, encampment. A *wicoti* may be comprised of several families from the same *tiyospaye*, or several families representing a number of different *tiyospayes*. An Oglala belonged to the same *tiyospaye* from birth to death but could change his residence from one *wicoti* to the next as he desired. He regarded everyone in his *tiyospaye* and *wicoti* as kin, and was required to seek a spouse outside these bounded units. According to one Oglala, old men would gather their grandchildren around them and admonish them by saying, "Grandchildren, do not choose a wife from the corner of your household!" (*Takoja, tiokahmi etan tawicutun šni po!*) The grandchildren were carefully taught their kinship terms so that they might know who among them were eligible for marriage. They were cautioned to climb to the top of a hill and look for a wife on the other side.

The *wicoti* was comprised minimally of two or more *tiwahe*. *Tiwahe* is the generic term for family. It is derived from *ti* 'to dwell' and *wahe* which is related to *wohan* 'cooking' (compare with Oohenunpa 'Two Kettle' or 'Two Boilings'; *han* in final position becomes *he*). Each *tiwahe* was comprised of one or more tipis which accommodated a man, his wife or wives, unmarried children, and possibly elderly parents.

To summarize, the rank order in which an Oglala claimed membership in what has been arbitrarily identified as nation, tribe, band, etc., may be expressed in the following taxonomy:

tunwan	nation
oyate	tribe
tiyoŝpaye	band
wicoti	camp
tiwahe	family

KINSHIP AND MARRIAGE

I have already alluded to the lack in the literature of adequate explanations of kinship, marriage, and descent (cf. Buechel, 1939, 1970; DeMallie, 1971; Hassrick, 1944; Lesser, 1928, 1958; Mirsky, 1937; Morgan, 1871, Murdock, 1949, Walker, 1914). The Oglalas, as well as other Tetons, are regarded as having Iroquoian cousin terms and a tendency toward patrilocal residence (Murdock, 1949). Membership in a *tiyoŝpaye* was predicated on cognatic principles, that is to say, there were some choices as to which *tiyoŝpaye* an Oglala could claim allegiance to. According to some investigators (Hassrick, 1944), boys chose the *tiyoŝpaye* of their father, and girls, of their mother. This is reflected in the kinship terminologies collected by Buechel (1939, 1970) but not in others. Since all members of the *wicoti* and *tiyoŝpaye* regarded themselves as kin, men were required to obtain spouses from another *tiyoŝpaye*. The distinction between one's own *tiyoŝpaye* and another's is reflected in some kinship terminology still employed by the Oglalas.

The generic term for relations, relatives, kinsmen is *otakuye* (*o*, noun prefix, and *takuye* 'to have, regard, consider related' [*takukiciyapi* 'relatives' is derived from this, from *takuya* 'to have as a relative'; *kici* reflexive infix "each other"; *pi* third person plural, subjective, glossed as "they call each other kin"]). With sororal polygyny, the sororate, and levirate excepted, no one could marry another in the class of *otakuye*. Another term which also applies to relative, relations, kinsmen is *titakuye*. *Titakuye* is currently glossed as "his (her) side of the family" and signifies the relatives in one's own *tiyoŝpaye* as opposed to relatives in one's spouse's.

The alliance of members of two *tiyoŝpayes* gives rise to another term which cannot be precisely glossed in English, *omawahetun*.

Buechel calls it a term of address between parents, aunts, uncles, and grandparents of a married couple. Etymologically, the term may be derived from *unma* 'other'; *wahe* 'cooking, boiling' (?) (cf. *tiwahe*, Oohenunpa, above); and *tun* 'to bear, given birth to'. I think it is worthwhile to note here that *tun*, which signifies "birth, creation, giving rise to," is the radical element of *tunwan* 'village.' The term also appears significantly in my later discussion of Sioux religious concepts, particularly those related to life and death. Finally, related to *omawahetun* is the term *owahecun*, the generic term for kinship terminology. It is probably derived from *o*, noun prefix; *wahe* and *ecun* 'to do'. Walker glosses it as "do-marker," but this is suspect.

It is unlikely that marriage prohibitions were intended to encompass the *omawahetun* relationship, for this would in fact militate against the exogamous principle of marrying someone from another *tiyošpaye*. Today the term is conventionally employed to indicate a relationship created by marriage, but for which there is no kinship term. When I revealed to a man that I was adopted by the grandfather of his daughter-in-law, he immediately remarked, "*Wan! Omawahetunciye!*" (My god! We're related!).

The notion of finding a spouse in another *tiyošpaye* is still highly valued today. Oglalas have told me that most of the arguments in their communities revolve around accusations that persons are inbred. The term for incest, *wogluze* (also "taboo") is derived from *winyuze* 'to marry', but literally, 'to catch a woman'. *Wogluze* signifies "one who marries one's own (kin)." The products of incestuous relationships are called *wicogluzewin* (girl) and *wicogluze hokšila* (boy). A social dance song which is still sung on the Pine Ridge Reservation underscores the dictum to look for a spouse from another *tiyošpaye*:

> *Dearie, wanciyanka wau na waun welo.*
> *Leciya otakuye wanice lo.*
> *Unkokihi kin he unkotanin kte lo.*

> Dearie, I'm here and I want to see you.
> There's no relationship over here.
> We can tell the whole world what we're doing.

FAMILY ORGANIZATION: BIRTH-ORDER NAMES

Up to the reservation period the Oglalas maintained a peculiar system of classifying children based on birth-order names. This system has been reported for the Oglalas by Walker (1914), for the Canadian Dakotas (Wallis, 1947), for the Winnebagos by Radin (1923), and for other societies by Lévi-Strauss (1962b). Riggs (1890) and Buechel (1970) also list birth-order names in their dictionaries.

Unfortunately, orthographic corruptions make it almost impossible to translate some of the names. The Oglalas, like the Winnebagos of Radin's time, neither employ the terms any more, nor do they agree that the terms had any meanings. However, the speculations made for the Winnebagos are applicable to the Santees, and implicitly to the Oglalas. Table 3 provides a comparison of birth-order names for the Santees (Riggs), the Canadian Dakotas (Wallis), and the Oglalas (Walker). Despite the lack of glosses for some terms, other relationships are implicit. I offer an analysis in Chapter 15.

TABLE 3

COMPARISON OF BIRTH-ORDER NAMES

ORDER	SANTEES		CANADIAN DAKOTAS		OGLALAS	
	Male	Female	Male	Female	Male	Female
First-born	Caske	Winona	Tcaské	Winóne	Caske	Wi-tokape
Second-born	Hepan	Hapan	Hepó	Hápe	Hepan	Hapan
Third-born	Hepi	Hapistinna	Hepí	Hápsti	Hepi	Hepistanna
Fourth-born	Catan	Wauske	Watcáto	Wiháki	Catan	Wanska
Fifth-born	Hake	Wihake	Haké	Hapóna	Hake	Wi-hake
Sixth-born	——	——	Tatcó	Hapstina	Hakata	Hakata
Seventh-born	——	——	——	Wihakéda	Cekpa	Cekpa

SOURCE: Riggs, 1890; Wallis, 1947; Walker, 1914.

According to all authorities, the birth-order names were maintained until the child received another name during a life-crisis ritual. The new name usually bestowed by a kinsman or berdache, the latter of whom were considered to have auspicious powers related to childbirth and child rearing. In some cases, however, a birth-order name might be retained as an endearing nickname analagous to "bro" or "sis" in American usage.

Despite the inconsistencies in the orthographies in table 3, some speculation is in order. First, most of the terms are in some abbreviated form, and others appear in a diminutive form. *Caske,* which appears consistently as the name for the first-born male, is probably related to *kaška* 'to bind' (*icicaške* 'to bind together'). *Winona* (*Wino'ne*) is a diminutive form of *winu,* glossed by Riggs as "female captive." Interestingly Buechel glosses *witoka* as the Lakota form of "female captive," the term used by Walker for first-born female. It would appear, if the first to be born are the first to be married and customarily among the Oglalas, a man might steal a wife (Walker, 1914:98), that the two terms are reciprocal and express the marriage relationship in the metaphor of capture. The term *winu* still survives in Lakota as the radical element in *winuȟcala* 'old woman', a word also used as a synonym for "mother-in-law."

The other terms are not so easy to decipher. *Hapan* and its variations may be an attenuated form of, if not baby talk for *scepan* 'sister-in-law' (female speaking); and *Hepistanna* may be the shortened form of *scepanši* 'female cross-cousin' (female speaking). The phonemic changes in the male series for these same terms may be sex indicators. Although this does not hold for these terms in modern Lakota, there are still some surviving terms which employ phonemic changes to indicate sex differentiation (e.g., *cinkši* 'son'; *cunkši* 'daughter'; *tunjan* 'niece'; *tunska* 'nephew').

The terms for fourth-born male and female, with the exception *Wiha'ki,* almost defy translation (but I return to them in the analysis). The others refer to last-born (*hakakta* 'last-born child'; *wihakta* 'last-born female child'; *hoihakakta* is the term for the youngest of a man's wives). The last entry in Wallis's list of males is a term for an offspring of a mixed-blood marriage, while Walker's last two terms refer to twins.

Faulty orthography notwithstanding, I believe the most interesting point about birth-order names is found in Wallis's list for females. Here we see more or less the ideal Sioux type of organization, not only in terms of the number seven, but in the manner in which the seven are differentiated, a manner reminiscent of the structure of the original Seven Fireplaces, particularly the manner in which the dialects cluster (see Chapter 1, table 2).

AUTHORITY AND CONTROL: THE CAMP CIRCLE

Throughout most of the year the Oglalas operated in small groups enabling them to exploit the environment with maximum efficiency. Each of the *wicotis* and *tiyošpayes* was under the leadership of one or more men commonly designated as *itancan* 'chief, leader, boss'. A man was elected leader and maintained that status with the consent of the people who followed him. If he was unable to find game or lead warriors against their enemies, he could be replaced with another, more capable warrior-hunter. On the basis of what we know about social organization from documented sources, it is unlikely that the organization of the *wicoti* and *tiyošpaye* was stable. Yet the Oglalas maintained a complex political organization, at least as an ideal.

Wissler may be credited with making the first systematic attempt to analyze Oglala sociopolitical organization, one in which he focused on the organization of *okolakiciye*, or "societies." The following description of Oglala leadership and the maintenance of authority and control is abstracted from his seminal work (Wissler, 1912). It focuses mainly on the Red Cloud *tiyošpaye*.

The Chief Society (locally known even today as *Tezi Tanka* 'Big Bellies', from the fact that the men were forty or older) served as a governing council which in turn elected seven chiefs for lifetime service. The seven chiefs were known as *wicaša itancan* 'leader of men' (today the preferred form is *wicašitancan* from *wicaša* 'man' and *itancan* 'chief'). Wissler states that this position could be handed down from father to son, but that the governing council had the right to approve. The modern Oglalas still assert that chieftainship was hereditary, and most of the contemporary *itancan* bear the names of famous leaders of another generation.

The seven chiefs, or *wicašitancan,* delegated authority to four younger men, who were known as *wicašayatanpi* (from *wicaša* 'man and *yatanpi* 'they praise', or praiseworthy men). The *wicašayatanpi* were also called "shirt wearers" from their particular badge of office, the so-called scalp shirt, or hair shirt. These men essentially controlled the camp.

Together, the Chief Society—the seven *wicašitancan*—and the four *wicašayatanpi* appointed four men to serve as *wakicunze* (from *wakunza* 'to determine, influence' [compare *wokunze* 'influence']; *wakicunze* may be glossed as "to determine for"). It was the *wakicunze* who determined where camps would be set up and when hunting would be permitted. They controlled the general social, political, and economic aspects of Oglala life.

The decisions of the *wakicunze* were carried out by men known as *akicita* 'marshal, soldier', among whom was appointed an *akicita itancan* 'marshal, soldier chief'. The *akicita* were members of an *akicita okolakicye* 'soldier society'. Whether real or ideal, an organization such as this was required only when *tiyošpayes* or segments of them came together for communal buffalo hunts and the annual sun dance. Smaller divisions of Oglalas operated throughout the year under only one *itancan*.

When an annual gathering of the *tiyošpayes* occurred, they formed a camp circle whose opening, or *tiyopa* 'door', was to the east. The entrance to the camp was also called *hunkpa* 'camp entrance', or *hoihanke*, referring to the two ends of the camp entrance. The circle was often concentric, with younger married couples camping in front of their parents' lodges. In the center of the camp circle was the *tiyotipi* or soldiers' lodge, and/or the *tiyokihe* 'lengthened tipi', made by attaching two tipi coverings together to form a large area for dancing and councils. The *tiyotipi* and *tiyokihe* faced east. The space inside the perimeter of outer tipis was referred to as *hocoka* (from *ho* [which as a radical can be translated a number of ways but here refers to camp] and *coka* 'center, middle').

Symbolically, the camp circle was representative of unity and social solidarity. Everything inside the camp circle, that is, everyone and everything within the parameters of the *hocoka*, was irrefutably Oglala, despite the fact that during most of the year the constituents of the camp circle were in a state of flux. Outside the *hocoka* were the enemies, the inconsistencies of everyday life, the evil spirits, and later the white man. Everything within the circle was safe, knowable, auspicious. The sacred circle was represented in a number of symbolic ways; in design elements, artifacts, songs, and dances. Metaphorically, the camp circle was called *cangleška wakan*, 'the sacred hoop'.

It was during the formation of the camp circle by several *tiyošpayes* that young men and women could look for spouses. It was a time when there was general feasting and visiting. Dances were held, and members of the warrior societies recounted their deeds of valor. Buffalo were pursued under the jurisdiction of the *akicita* lest some young man stampede the herd in his personal quest for food and fame.

It was also during the formation of the camp circle that the great religious ceremonies were performed. These religious performances were under the jurisdiction of another class of leaders, the *wicaša wakan*, the holy men. Many of these men banded together in *okolakiciye* consisting of members who had all shared in the same kinds of visions. They were not the chiefs, the warriors, or the feast makers. Their responsibilities revolved around another kind of authority and control. They were the intermediaries between common man and the supernatural spirits and powers, who, by proper propitiation, could be coaxed to enter the *hocoka*.

Part II

SACRED THINGS

Chapter 5

THE SUPERNATURAL

THE MEANING OF *Wakan*

If we mean by religion a "binding back together" (the literal sense of the root elements of the English word), then we are hard pressed to accept the conventional gloss provided by Christian missionaries in their attempt to translate scripture into Lakota. The term *wocekiye* (*wo*, noun prefix and *cekiya* 'to cry for, to pray') corresponds to their translation for "religion, prayer." The Oglalas, however, regard the totality of superhuman beings and powers that control their universe quite differently from Christian theologians.

To the Oglalas, the totality of natural and cultural phenomena are capable of undergoing transformations which require that behavior toward these phenomena be altered, or somewhat modified. The causes of these transformations and the Oglala explanation for concomitant changes in behavior are subsumed under the concept of *taku wakan* 'sacred thing(s)'. The phenomena which are regarded as *taku wakan* may be temporarily or permanently transformed. Those which are permanently transformed are regarded collectively as *Wakantanka*, traditionally glossed as "Great Spirit" or "Great Mystery" (*wakan* 'sacred' and *tanka* 'great, large, big'). This term has become the conventional gloss for "God." Although singular in form, *Wakantanka* is collective in meaning. *Wakantanka* is not personified, but aspects of it are. These aspects are often personified or manifested in the sun, moon, sky, earth, winds, lightning, thunder, and other natural phenomena.

Man exists as an integral part of nature, not as one wishing to
control its vicissitudes, but as one wanting to live in harmony with
it. Man is innately powerless and cries out to be pitied when con-
fronted with danger, famine, and the unexplainable. When an
Oglala is in need of supernatural help, he asserts his powerlessness
by intoning "Wakantanka unšimala ye" (Wakantanka, pity me).
Man's relation to nature is always unšike 'pitiable'. By crying out to
Wakantanka he at once addresses the sum total of supernatural
help at his disposal.

Wakantanka may also be addressed in the metaphor of kinship.
Thus an Oglala says "Ho Tunkašila Wakantanka..." (Ho, Grandfather Wakantanka...). Or he may say "Ate Wakantanka" (Father
Wakantanka). Here Grandfather is used to appeal to Wakantanka
independent of any manisfestation; Father is used to appeal to an
aspect of Wakantanka which is capable of being manifested, such
as the sun (Brown, 1953:5–6). The same metaphor of kinship is
used to differentiate between the potentiality of the earth to grow
things (unci 'grandmother') and the actual manifest produce of the
earth (maka ina 'mother earth') (ibid.).

The ways in which Wakantanka manifests itself are limited.
According to Sword:

> When Wakan Tanka wishes one of mankind to do something he
> makes his wishes known either in a vision or through a shaman....
> The shaman addresses Wakan Tanka as Tobtob Kin.... This is part
> of the secret language of the shamans.... Tobtob Kin are four times
> four gods while Tob Kin is only the four winds. The four winds is a
> god and is the akicita or messenger of all the other gods. The four
> times four are: Wikan and Hanwikan; Taku Skanskan and Tatekan
> and Tob Kin and Yumnikan; Makakan and Wohpe; Inyankan and
> Wakinyan; Tatankakan; Hunonpakan; Wanagi; Waniya; Nagila; and
> Wasicunpi. These are the names of the good Gods as they are known
> to the people.
>
> Wakan Tanka is like sixteen different persons; but each person is
> kan. Therefore, they are all only the same as one. [Walker, 1917:153]

The recognition that one's behavior differs with respect to
phenomena which have undergone transformations is embodied
in the concept of wakan (here as a matter of convention glossed as
"sacred"). Wakan has been regarded as analagous to orenda of the

Iroquois, the Shoshone *pokunt*, Algonquian *manitu*, Kwakiutl *nauala*, Tlingit *yek*, and Haida *sgana* in North America, as well as the Melanesian *mana* (Durkheim, 1912:221–23). About the meaning of *wakan* Sword states:

> *Wakan* means very many things. The Lakota understands what it means from the things that are considered *wakan*; yet sometimes its meaning must be explained to him. It is something that is hard to understand. . . . Every object in the world has a spirit and that spirit is *wakan*. Thus, the spirit of the tree or things of that kind, while not like the spirit of man, are also *wakan*. . . . *Wakan* comes from the *wakan* beings. These *wakan* beings are greater than mankind in the same way that mankind is greater than animals. They are never born and never die. They can do many things that mankind cannot do. Mankind can pray to the *wakan* beings for help. [Ibid.:152]

That *wakan* refers to things that are hard to understand is implicit in the words which were applied to items newly obtained from other Indians and the white man: horses (*šunkawakan* 'sacred dog'), guns (*mazawakan* 'sacred iron'), and whiskey (*mniwakan* 'sacred water'). An etymology of *wakan* leads to further interesting speculations. For example, the radical element *kan* signifies 'aged, worn out with age'; *kanheca* 'ragged, tattered'; *kanhi* 'to live to be old, reach old age'; *kanit'a* 'to die of old age' (Buechel, 1970:283). *Kan* also appears in *tunkan* and *tunkaši* 'father-in-law' and *tunkan*, "in the sacred language, a sacred stone supposed to have great power and used in the *oinikage tipi* [sweat lodge]. This stone is also called the *yuwipi wašicun*" (ibid.:502). *Kan* provides the basis for *tunkašila* 'grandfather' and *tunkaši* (the *n* is dropped before *ši*), and also *wakanka* 'old woman' (presumably in sacred language) (Buechel, ibid:526). In summary, it would appear that *wakan* carries the connotation of ancient, old, and enduring.

THE SACRED NUMBERS

The Oglalas classify all natural and cultural phenomena by fours and sevens, and to some extent by the products of four, and four and seven (but not by products of seven). To illustrate, I draw from examples in the literature and my own field work. According to Sword:

In former times the Lakota grouped all their activities by four's. This was because they recognized four directions: the west, the north, the east, and the south; four divisions of time: the day, the night, the moon, and the year; four parts to everything that grows from the ground: the roots, the stem, the leaves, and the fruit; four kinds of things that breathe: those that crawl, those that fly, those that walk on four legs, and those that walk on two legs; four things above the world: the sun, the moon, the sky, and the stars; four kinds of gods: the great, the associates of the great, the gods below them, and the spirit kind; four periods of human life: babyhood, childhood, adulthood and old age; and finally, mankind had four fingers on each hand, four toes on each foot, and the thumbs and the great toes of each taken together are four. Since the Great Spirit caused everything to be in four's, mankind should do everything possible in four's. [Walker, 1917:159–60]

Sword also states that the four great virtues of all Lakotas should practice were bravery, generosity, truthfulness, and begetting children (ibid.).

Standing Bear reiterates much of Sword's account and adds that the Oglala camp was often divided into four circles, the center of which formed the *hocoka*. He recalls two songs:

> *Wankatanhan heyau welo*
> *Wankatanhan heyau welo*
> *"Mitahocoka topa wanlaka nunwe"*
> *Heyau welo*
> *Hanhewi kin heyau welo*
> E ya ye yo.

> That is what she is saying coming from above
> That is what she is saying coming from above
> "May you see my four camp circles"
> That is what she comes saying
> That is what the moon comes saying
> E ya ye yo.

> *Wankatanhan heyau welo*
> *Wankatanhan heyau welo*
> *"Mitawicoȟan topa wanlaka nunwe"*
> *Heyau welo*
> *Anpewi kin heyau welo*
> *Heyau welo*
> E ye ye yo.

That is what he is saying coming from above
That is what he is saying coming from above
"May you see my four deeds"
That is what he comes saying
That is what the sun comes saying
That is what he comes saying
E ye ye yo.

According to Standing Bear, these songs were received by sacred men and sung over the sick. The four deeds in the second song refer to the creation of the four winds and signify that the power of the sun reaches to the four corners of the earth (Standing Bear, 1933:216; my orthography, phrasing, and translation).

Ideally, ceremonies took place over a four-day period or over a period of time divided into four-day segments (Walker, 1917). According to Sword, the White Buffalo Calf Woman (to whom I will return later) stayed with the people for four days, during which time she gave them the seven great ceremonies. In handling ritual objects, she feigned at them three times before picking up on the fourth, a practice still observed among the Oglalas, particularly in handling a sacred pipe (Sword, n.d.).

As noted above, *Wakantanka* has sixteen aspects (four times four). My own informants stated that the ideal number of willow saplings needed to construct a sweat lodge was sixteen (four for each direction). The four divisions of time may be further divided into four segments:

LAKOTA	FREE TRANSLATION	LITERAL TRANSLATION
1. *omaka*	year, season	form of "land"
waniyetu	winter	breath
wetu	spring	blood, sap
bloketu	summer	potato
ptanyetu	autumn	turn over
2. *wi*	month	moon
witanin	new moon, crescent	visible moon
wiyašpa	half-moon	bitten-off moon
wimimela	full moon	round moon
wit'e	waning moon	dead moon

3. *anpetu*	day	day, light
wihinapa or *anpo*	sunrise or dawn	sun comes into the lodge, light
hihanna *wicokanhiya*	morning	arrives (?)
sam iyaye	noon	sun comes to the middle and goes past
wimaheya	sunset	sun goes into
4. *hanhepi*	night	night, covering shade, shadow
ȟtayetu	dusk	dim
hanyetu	evening	night, covering, etc.
hancokan	midnight	night, middle, center
hanwakan	aurora	night, sacred

As noted above, a camp circle of seven constituents is an ideal Sioux type. According to Black Elk, the White Buffalo Calf Woman brought seven sacred ceremonies to the Sioux (Brown, 1953). As I describe later, invoking all the supernaturals of the universe requires praying, singing, and/or smoking to seven directions: west, north, east, south, zenith, nadir, and the messenger. Prayer offerings, consisting of seven small bundles of tobacco, are often left in trees and on hillsides.

The product of four and seven is also regarded as sacred. There are seven sun dance songs, each of which is sung four times. As to the importance of four times seven, Black Elk states:

In setting up the sun dance lodge, we are really making the universe in a likeness; for, you see, each of the posts around the lodge represents some particular object of creation, so that the whole circle is the entire creation, and the one tree at the center, upon which the twenty-eight poles rest, is *Wakan-Tanka*, who is the center of everything...And I should tell you why it is that we use twenty-eight poles. I have already explained why the numbers four and seven are sacred; then if you add four sevens you get twenty-eight. Also the moon lives twenty-eight days, and this is our month; each of these days of the month represents something sacred to us: two of the days represent the Great Spirit; two are for Mother Earth; four are for the four winds; one is for the Spotted Eagle; one for the sun; and one for the moon; one is for the Morning Star; and four for the four ages; seven are for our seven great rites; one is for the buffalo; one for the fire; one for the water; one for the rock; and finally one is for the two-legged people. If you add all these days up you will see that they come to twenty-eight. You should also know that the buffalo has twenty-eight ribs, and that in our war bonnets we usually use twenty-eight feathers. [Ibid.: 80]

CONCEPTS OF LIFE AND DEATH

The philosophical interpretation of the meaning of life and death, the concept of the hereafter, and the transmigration of the soul are in the purview of the ritual specialists who have received the power of interpretation through communion with the super-natural. Although I deal with the sacred people, the cosmology, and rituals in following chapters, I believe it is instructive first to summarize the salient features of Oglala religion. I should offer some caveats. First, there is no general agreement either in the literature or among informants as to the true nature of religious ideas. Beliefs concerning a hereafter, for example, range from a belief in an unspecified place in which the spirits of humans and animals live in a world reflective of the "real" world, to the idea that there is no hereafter, but that all spirits reside visibly and invisibly near the place of their kinsmen.

Second, I recognize the danger in attempting to explain basic Oglala religious concepts either directly or by analogy through the eyes of a Western observer. Thus in treating certain concepts basic to understanding Oglala religion, I will provide the widest seman-tic range possible for each concept rather than translation labels. Finally, the tenets of Oglala belief, as I present them, should be regarded as analytical, and as such they reflect the consensus of sacred men's thinking; but the language and order of ranking of these tenets are my own. These are the tenets:

The universe is composed of a finite amount of energy; good and evil are thus two aspects of the same energy.

The good aspects of energy are controlled by *Wakantanka*; evil aspects are controlled by *wakan šica* (evil sacred).

Man may harness good energy toward his own ends by propitiating *Wakantanka*; he may harness evil energy by propitiating *wakan šica*.

Wakan šica is subordinate to *Wakantanka*, and man is subordinate to both.

Energy has two aspects: visible and invisible. The potential to transform visible energy into invisible energy, and the reverse, is called *tun*. The *tun* of every invisible aspect is its visible aspect.

The transformation from visible to invisible, and the reverse is called *wakan*, as is the resultant state.

Invisible aspects are to be feared.

Life and death are both *wakan* because in the former an invisible aspect is transformed into a visible one and in the latter the reverse takes place. The Lakota term for birth, creation is *tunpi* (e.g., *"Tohan nitunpi he?"* 'When were you born?').

Life is manifested in *ni* 'breath, life, steam'. If a person becomes weak, he must strengthen himself by participating in a sweat lodge, *inikagapi* 'to make live, breath, steam'.

When a person dies, his *ni* leaves him.

All supernatural beings and powers and all animate and inanimate objects have innate power manifested in the concept of *šicun*. Every animate object is born or created with his own personal *šicun*, which is immortal. At the time of birth, a man is given a *šicun* by the supernaturals; it is his guardian spirit and it will help him ward off evil. When he dies, the *šicun* is returned to the supernaturals. The *šicun* accounts for vacillation between good and evil, for a man may borrow another's *šicun*, or be permanently invested with it by means of a special ceremony. He may accumulate many *šicun*, which he turns for help when in need; but one's gain is another's loss. Because the *šicun* of things is immortal, reincarnation is possible. Sacred men are usually invested with the *šicun* of a deceased sacred man.

A sacred man becomes powerful through visions with the supernaturals. To increase power, he must accumulate the *šicun* of as many animate and inanimate objects as possible.

To help other people ward off sickness and evil, he must invest them with some of his own accumulated *šicun*. Thus he is faced with a paradox: the more people he helps, the more *šicun* he gives away; the more *šicun* he gives away, the more power he loses.

Every animate and inanimate object has a counterpart which is eternal but not vital. It is called *nagi*. *Wanagi* is the common word for "ghost, apparition." The *nagi* of someone or something is often regarded as its shadow or shade.

When a person loses *ni* 'life or breath', his body eventually decomposes, but his *nagi* lingers on. The *wanagi*, particularly right after death, is dangerous because it grieves for its loved ones and will try to entice its family to join it. In order to appease the *wanagi*, the parents or loved ones will "keep" it for one year. Ghost keeping is accomplished by feeding the *wanagi*. Sacred men can learn things from it, particularly how to cure the sick.

The *wanagi* of humans and animals dwell on buttes in the west. After one year, they are fed for the last time and they depart to the south along the *wanagi tacanku* 'ghost road', i.e., Milky Way. The aura of the Milky Way is caused by their campfires.

Somewhere at the end of the Milky Way they are met by an old woman who assesses their deeds on earth. Those who were good are passed along the way to a place which is reflective of their life with *ni*; those who were bad are pushed over a cliff, and their evil spirits are left to roam the earth, where they endanger the living.

Some believe that the *wanagi* live forever near the place where they died.

Wanagi are particularly *wakan* because although they are invisible to common people, they are visible to sacred men.

SUPERNATURAL BEINGS AND POWERS

The Oglala universe is controlled by supernatural beings and powers. They have no beginning and no end. They created or helped create the universe, and they are responsible for the appearance of man on earth. Some of these beings are benevolent, others are malevolent. Intermediate between the two is the culture hero, Inktomi 'the Spider'. Here I propose to provide a dramatis personae of the supernatural beings and powers (after Walker, 1917) critical to understanding the religion of the Oglalas. Their relationship to each other and to mankind will be treated further in the chapters on myth and ritual.

Wakantanka represents the embodiment of all supernatural beings and powers in the Oglala universe. As we have seen, it has sixteen aspects in the sacred language and is referred to as *Tobtob* 'four-four'. The sixteen aspects are hierarchically ranked in groups of fours, the major classes being (1) *Wakan akanta* 'superior *wakan*'; (2) *Wakan kolaya* 'those whom the *wakan* call friends or associates'; (3) *Wakan kuya* 'lower, or lesser, *wakan*'; and (4) *Wakanlapi* 'those similar to *wakan*'.

The superior are comprised of the Wi, the Sun; Škan, the Sky; Maka, the Earth; and Inyan, the Rock. The associates of the superior are Hanwi, the Moon; Tate, the Wind; Woȟpe, the Falling Star; and Wakinyan, the Winged, or Thunder-being. The superior and their associates are thus linked in the following way: the Sun and Moon; Sky and Wind; Earth and Falling Star; and Rock and the Winged. Together, these two classes are called *Wakan kin* 'the sacred'. In the cosmology, they had no beginning, and they were responsible for creating the universe and man in it.

The lower, or lesser, *wakan* are comprised of Tatanka, the Buffalo; Hununpa, the Two-legged (both the bear and man); Tatetob, the Four Winds; and Yumni, the Whirlwind. Those similar to *wakan* are *Nagi*, the Shade, or Apparition; Niya, Life or Breath; Nagila, the Shadelike; and Šicun, the Potency. Together these two classes are called *Taku wakan* 'sacred things'. They were created by the *Wakan kin* and are at the same time part of them.

In addition to the sixteen aspects of *Wakantanka*, there are other supernatural beings and powers which figure prominently in Oglala belief, some benevolent, some malevolent. There is Wazi, the Old Man, and later in cosmological time, the Wizard; and Wakanka, the Old Woman, his wife, who later is transformed into the Witch. Their daughter, Ite, Face, is the most beautiful of super- natural women, and in the first period of time she is married to Tate, the Wind, and they have four sons, the Four Winds. Later, she is transformed into Anukite, Double-Face, and given a horrid countenance to complement her beautiful one as punishment for adultery.

There are also spirits which inhabit their respective parts of the universe: the Unkteȟi, Water Spirits; the Unkcegila, Spirits of the Land; the Canoti, Forest-Dwelling Spirits; and the Hoȟogica, the Spirits of the Lodge. These are all dangerous spirits that threaten mankind, but they may be warded off by the proper rituals, and especially by the aroma of sweetgrass and sage, and the smoke of a pipe.

Iya, sometimes called the Giant, or the Glutton, is the youngest son of the Rock and the Winged. He is associated with the cold of the north. During the winter he consumes people, and in the myths he is finally overcome by fire, which causes to regurgitate the people he has consumed. His older brother is Inktomi, the Spider, who is the culture hero of the Oglalas. It is the Spider that gives culture to man and entices him out of his subterranean world, only to trick him once man cannot find his way back. Inktomi himself is both human and non human, and just as man emerged from the earth, he too, as a trap-door spider, occasionally comes out of the earth carrying his scampering children on his back.

To conclude, the Oglalas recognize themselves as part of nature, yet somehow distinct from it, just as the lesser *wakan* are part *Wakan kin*, but distinct from them. Together, the supernaturals abide in the universe, and specialists may call upon them so that the common people may live in harmony with that which is otherwise inexplicable.

Chapter 6

THE INTERMEDIARIES

CATEGORIES OF RITUAL SPECIALISTS

Insofar as *taku wakan* 'sacred things' and the poteniality for transforming natural and cultural phenomena into *wakan* status were reflected in the entire Oglala universe, it is understandable that religion was widely diffused throughout all aspects of Oglala social organization. But as has been stated by Oglala informants, if common man was to accomplish things, it was necessary for *Wakantanka* to appear in a vision. Visions manifested themselves as uninduced revelations, or they might be sought in the vision quest (*hanbleceya* 'to cry for a vision, dream'). *Wakan* things were difficult to understand for the common man, and so certain persons were invested with the power of interpreting the multitudinous wonders of *Wakantanka*.

Those capable of mediating between the supernatural beings and powers and the common people were called *wakan* (*wicaśa wakan* 'man sacred'; and *winyan wakan* 'woman sacred'). Sacred persons were distinguished from *pejuta wicaśa* 'medicine men' and *pejuta winyan* 'medicine women', who administered *pejuta* (from *peji* 'grass' and *huta* 'roots', i.e., 'herbal medicine'). Although sacred persons might on occasion be instructed to administer *pejuta* by *Wakantanka*, they cured people mainly by supernatural means; whereas the *pejuta wicaśa* was primarily a medical doctor, and aside from prescribing internal and external medicines was capable of setting fractures and providing forms of physical therapy. The term *medicine man* is derived from this latter form of doctor, and while it is inappropriate to refer to *wakan* person by the same label, it nevertheless has become a convention among Oglalas when speaking English.

The *wakan* people attended to the everyday needs of the common people: they interceded with the sacred to ensure a fair day for hunting and ceremonies; they sought out the buffalo by mystical means, and predicted the outcome of war journeys by divination. They were capable of creating potions and powders which could make a horse strong-winded or aid a young man in wooing a woman. They found lost objects by employing the aid of sacred stones; they interpreted the natural and sacred signs of the universe; they bestowed names upon the newborn and upon those who earned new names through prowess in hunting and warfare.

The *wakan* people were also instructors, interpreters of the sacred myths, and directors of the great ceremonies. Some were generalists; other were specialists. Among the latter were those who cured illnesses which were induced by *wakan šica* 'evil wakan' or by other *wakan* persons who derived the power from the evil *wakan*, the *wicaȟmunga* 'wizard' and *wiȟmunga* 'witch'. The specialists in curing were known as *wapiye wicaša* or *wapiyapi* (from *wa*, prefix, 'a person who'; *piya* 'to renew, do over, repeat'; and *wicaša* 'man'; *wapiyapi* 'they who renew'). Even among the specialists, the techniques employed in curing varied, depending on the nature of the vision in which the *wakan* person received his power.

Wissler, in his systematic survey of Oglala sodalities, discusses a variety of so-called dream cults, associations comprised of people who had experienced similar visions. Among them he lists:

The *Heyoka*. A cult comprised of persons who had dreamed of the thunder-beings (*Wakinyan*). Upon receiving such a vision of lightning or thunder, it was required that members act in an antinatural manner. They dressed warmly in summer, wore no clothes in winter. They sometimes spoke backwards. In one of their major ceremonies, *Heyoka Kaga* 'clown making, ceremony', they plunged their hands into boiling-hot water in an effort to retrieve choice bits of dog meat, and complained of the coldness of the water.

The Elks (*Heȟaka ihanblapi* 'they dream of elks'). The members of this cult dressed up to represent elks in their ceremonies. The elk was imbued with special powers over women, and members of the cult were supposed to be privileged to steal women, and made a special concoction from the white of the eye, the heart, and fetlocks, which they mixed with other *pejuta* and ate. This special medicine was called *wincuwa* 'to chase women with'.

The Bears (*Mato ihanblapi* 'they dream of bears'). The members, during their ceremonies, paraded around the camp dressed in bearskins, growling like a bear and chasing people. Bear dreamers were particularly astute curers.

The Black-Tailed Deer (probably *Sinte sapela* 'black tails'). This cult was similar in dress and ceremony to the Elks. Like the Elks, the members were capable of killing people with their glance, or by capturing the reflection of another through a mirror, or by sighting them through a sacred hoop.

The Wolf Cult (possibly *Šunkmahetu ihanblapi* 'they dream of wolves', but Wissler provides no native term). The members wore wolf skins and were particularly adept at removing arrows from wounded warriors. They also prepared war medicines (*wotawe*) for protection against enemies.

The Buffalo Cult (*Tatang ihanblapi* 'they dream of buffalo bulls'). The members dressed as buffalos and stamped about the camp bellowing like buffalos. One member stalked another, shooting him and causing him to vomit blood. Still another healed the wound with a special medicine.

The Berdache Cult. Men who dreamed of a *wakan* woman or a hermaphroditic buffalo cow (*pte winkte*) were forever required to behave as a woman, sometimes marrying men, and doing the household chores of women. The *winkte* (*win* 'woman' and *kte,* enclitic, future tense, i.e., 'would-be woman') were regarded as sacred people, but it is unlikely that they formed an association. One of their primary responsibilities was naming children.

The Double-Woman Cult (*Anukite ihanblapi* 'they dream of face-on-both-sides' [my gloss]). As we shall see, Double-Woman is a supernatural who, being once beautiful, was punished for infidelity by acquiring a second, horrid face. (Note that Deloria identifies Anukite as a man capable of transforming himself into a woman [Deloria, 1932:46 et passim].) Those who dreamed of Anukite became proficient in the handwork of women, particularly quillwork and tanning. The Double-

Woman appears in a number of conventional forms: as a person with two faces, one beautiful, the other ugly; a single beautiful woman, most often a temptress; or two women who represent alternative answers to a single question, often of a divinatory nature. The two women often change into black-tailed deer at the conclusion of dreams. Thus a synonym for Double-Woman is *Sinte sapela win* ('black-tailed woman').

Women who dreamed of Double-Woman inherited powers to seduce men. Such women were not regarded as normal. Men who encountered Double-Woman in a vision were often required to choose between male and female utensils. The latter choice indicated that the man should live as a berdache.

Men were instructed to avoid lone women whom they might encounter on the prairie or in the woods, for they might be deer women. Deer women usually appeared as beautiful women who, upon seducing a man, turned into a deer and ran away. Sexual contact with a deer woman was fatal.

The Dreaming-Pair Cult (*wakan ićihanbla* 'to dream of each other sacredly') was one on which two people who had dreamed of each other made feasts for those who had similar experiences. Not much is reported about this cult.

Mountain Sheep Cult (*hecinškayapi ihanblapi* 'they dream of mountain sheep [*hecinškayapi* 'to make horn ladles, spoons']). There is some debate over the existence of this cult; some members were credited with having the ability to make strong war medicine.

A Rabbit Cult, Horse Cult, Women's Medicine Cult, Mescal Cult, and Dog Cult are also reported by Wissler, but it is questionable whether or not these cults had the same status as the others. The Horse Cult is probably the *Šunkwakan wacipi* 'horse dance', a reenactment of a vision related to dreaming of thunder. The Mescal Cult is the same as the Peyote Cult, now called the Native American Church. *Mescal* is a misnomer.

BECOMING A *Wakan* PERSON

Although Wissler focused on dream cults and the relationships between sacred persons who shared similar visions, many sacred persons derived their powers from unique experiences. Here it is important to distinguish between the concept of *ihanbla* 'to dream of' and *piyapi* 'to renew, cure'. The first term identifies the source of the power and the means by which a sacred person received instructions. The second refers to the process of curing, and is used as a marker to identify sacred persons and their specific means of curing. Thus one who received instructions to cure from the bear was said to have *mato ihanbla* 'dreamed of a bear'. As long as this sacred person cured by means of the aforesaid instructions, he was known as a *mato wapiye* 'bear curer'. Presumably Wissler did not idenfity some dream cults, or was unable to gather information on others because they did not exist as cults. For example, he does not mention *wanbli wapiye* 'eagle curer', nor does he mention *Yuwipi wicaša* because they both were apparently not of cult status. *Yuwipi*, a contemporary form of curing, existed during Wissler's time, but no mention is made of it, probably because it suggests a method of curing rather than a source of power. Although I will deal with *Yuwipi* in full in a later chapter, it should be noted here that *Yuwipi* centers on a sacred person who usually (but not always) conducts his ceremonies in a darkened room, and is often bound with rawhide thongs, which are later loosened by his spirit-helpers. This form of curing has been noted by Densmore (1910, 1918, 1932), Fletcher (1884), and Ravous (1883–84, cited in Wallis, 1947) among others.

Autobiographical sketches of sacred persons have appeared only recently in anthropological literature (Brown, 1953; Densmore, 1918; Lame Deer and Erdoes, 1972; Neihardt, 1932; Sandoz, 1942; Vestal, 1932; Walker, 1917; and Wallis, 1947). Additional insights are provided in the works of Dorsey (1894), Fletcher (1884), Lowie (1913), and Wissler (1912). The following developmental stages in the life of a sacred person are synthesized largely from these works and my own field work.

Mystical experience. Although statistically most sacred men and women assumed their duties upon reaching middle age (35–45, but actually "fortyish" is regarded as old age among Oglalas), many relate that they had experiences as a child which left them perplexed. Black Elk had his first vision when he was nine (Neihardt,

1932). As a child, Crazy Horse behaved unusually, preferring isolation to sociability (Sandoz, 1942). The initial experience might take the form of an uninterpretable vision or a feat of accomplishment in hunting or warfare which was far beyond the person's age or ability. Sitting Bull killed his first buffalo when he was ten, and his first enemy when he was fourteen. He soon after was able to communicate with birds, particularly the meadowlark, which the Sioux believe speaks Lakota. (Actually, a number of birds "speak" Lakota, and their responses to questions are used as divinatory devices.) The initial mystical experience was normally not acted upon immediately, but often obsessed the person throughout his early life.

Misfortune. In middle age, the potentially sacred person usually experienced a misfortune which took the form of a riding or hunting mishap or misadventure in war. He was often injured bodily, or his sensory modalities were temporarily impaired. Frequently, the person was haunted by a recurring vision which eventually demanded interpretation. He might also be bothered by strange voices, communications from animals and birds, or revelations from deceased members of his family. At some stage in his life, these misfortunes and perplexities led him to seek interpretation from an established sacred person.

Consultation. When it became apparent that interpretation was required, the person sought out an established practitioner. The vision or other mysterious experience was described to the sacred person, and after a few days an interpretation was offered. It required that the person go through an ordeal which would be both instructive and revealing to himself about the nature of the problem, and would allow the sacred person to provide an additional interpretation. The ordeal was the vision quest.

Crying for a vision. Under the direction of the sacred person, the novitiate, as he may now be called, underwent instructions related to *hanbleceya* 'to cry for a vision'. A sacred place, usually a hill or isolated place, was chosen, and the novice was required to stay there alone, usually for four days, until he received a vision. He

must show humility; he drank no water and ate no food; and his
only possessions were perhaps a blanket and, most important, a
pipe.

After a vision had been received, the novice returned to the
camp for further consultation with the sacred person. On the basis
of the vision, the sacred person decided whether or not the novice
should become an apprentice and begin to learn the sacred
knowledge of the Oglalas. Not all persons became sacred; some
were simply instructed to perform their visions for the people or to
take part in a ceremony such as the sun dance. But if the vision
signified potential power in the novice, he would be instructed to
learn the practices of the sacred person, under the tutelage of his
mentor (Walker, 1917).

Apprenticeship. During his apprenticeship, the novice learned the
sacred knowledge, the significance of the myths, the sacred language, and the techniques required to perform ceremonies or cure
the common people. Most important, he learned that he must be
unšike 'pitiable' because the power that he had gained could be
used for either good or evil. Sacred knowledge and the performance of rituals could be used for the welfare of all the people, but at
the same time, the power could be dangerous to the practitioner. It
could also be misused if the supernatural beings and powers were
not properly propitiated. The novice learned the meanings of
prayers and songs, and often served as an assistant to his mentor in
the great ceremonies such as the sun dance.

Ordination. After the conclusion of his apprenticeship, the novice
became established as a sacred person in his own right. It is not
always clear how long an apprenticeship was served. Frequently,
however, the novice slowly drifted away from the tutelage of his
mentor; and upon occasion, the newly established practitioner
might find himself in competition with his mentor. As a sacred
person, he now conducted his own rituals and assisted other sacred
persons with the duties of larger ceremonies. He was also active as
a counselor to the secular administration of the Oglala camp, and
his influence figured prominently in the selection of civil magis-
trates (Walker, 1917).

Renewal. In order to retain his powers and propitiate the supernaturals, the sacred person periodically visited sacred places and underwent the vision quest. The more frequently he sought visions, the more power he maintained. If he cured people and invested in them some of his own powers (*šicun*), he would have to compensate for the loss of these powers by continual renewal. Should he not participate in the vision quest, he would eventually lose all power or he would be susceptible to evil powers.

Abdication. Growing old was synonymous with losing power and finally abdicating the role and responsibilities of the sacred person. Power was lost because one's personal *sicun* were given away, or because one's memory failed and with it the ability to properly propitiate the supernaturals. The loss of this power was recognized by the common people, and they turned to a more powerful intermediary. In old age the *wakan* person was often subjected to ridicule and distrust by the same common people he had guided and cured. When he died, his ritual paraphernalia were burned because of its residual power. In some cases, an elderly sacred person, in anticipation of abdicating his position, might train his son in the duties of a ritual specialist and bequeath to him part of his remaining power and his ritual paraphernalia.

The Role of Women

By far more Oglala men than women became sacred persons. However, the woman's role in ritual affairs was prominent, particularly prior to first menstruation and after menopause. During these times there were no menstrual avoidance rules in effect, and women were not capable of ritually contaminating men's paraphernalia related to hunting, warfare, and the supernatural. Before the onset of menstruation, girls in fact played a more prominent role in ritual matters than boys. The *witanšna* 'virgins' were selected by men's warrior societies to perform rituals and sing certain songs (Wissler, 1912). The virgins also handled ritual objects and figured prominently in the sun dance (Walker, 1917).

After puberty, certain women received visions in which they were taught how to find herbs and roots which they later applied as medicine. Some women mediated between the common people and the supernaturals. During menstruation women were required to leave the camp and live temporarily in an *išnatipi*. *Išnati* 'to live alone' is a metaphor for menstruation as well as the name of the menstrual dwelling. During this period, women could not handle or be in the same dwelling with ritual paraphernalia lest it be contaminated. The menstrual bundle was carefully placed in trees in order to prevent animals, such as coyotes, from stealing it and ultimately holding power over the woman from whom it was stolen.

A woman past menopause could enjoy more ritual obligations inasmuch as menstrual restrictions were no longer applicable. An old woman might assist her husband in sacred rituals to the extent that the death of the wife might be regarded as a partial loss of power by the husband. The potency of women was underscored in the sacred myths. All of the sacred ceremonies of the Oglalas were given to them by a woman in her sexual prime, the White Buffalo Calf Woman.

RITUAL LANGUAGE

The sacred persons were distinguishable from the common people not only by their ability to interpret sacred knowledge and perform ceremonies, but by their ability to communicate with the supernaturals and each other in a special language unintelligible to the uninitiated. According to Densmore, "a language of this kind was said to be necessary in order that persons intimate with supernatural things could communicate without being understood by the common people" (Densmore, 1918:120). Densmore gives no evidence why a secret language was necessary, and there is no evidence that there was a conscious attempt by sacred persons to exclude common people from sacred discourse. Common people heard the ritual language during the ceremonies, and the ritual vocabulary was familiar to them. They did not understand the ritual language because they did not comprehend the sacred knowledge which gave rise to it.

Ritual language was not entirely standardized, but it contained some lexical items which were mutually intelligible between sacred persons. The vocabulary was constructed from archaisms, metaphors, metonymns, abbreviated words, grammatical inversions, and common words and phrases to which uncommon meanings were applied. Mankind was referred to as *wahununpa* or *hununpa* 'two-leggeds' and the animal kingdom as *wahutopa* or *hutopa* 'four-leggeds' rather than the common Lakota, *ikce wicaša* 'common, ordinary man' or *wamakaškan* 'animal'. The sick were called *wakangle* or *wowakangle* 'to be in a sacred state' instead of the more common *wicakuje* 'sick'.

The Oglalas likened the white man to a supernatural power, calling him *Wašicun* (from *šicun*). It is likely that this term was initially part of the ritual language, inasmuch as Parkman records the common Lakota word for white man as *Meneaska* (*Mniaškan* 'moves on water') during his stay with the Oglalas in 1846 (Parkman, 1846). The white man was also referred to as *Ska wicaša* 'white man' (but properly, *wicaša ska*) and the generic term for Indians was *Ša wicaša* 'red man' (again an inversion). The latter term remains today as the generic term for Indian in common Lakota. Items of trade, as well as ideas, manners, and customs introduced by the white man, were called *wašicun witunšni* 'white man's lies, falsehoods'. Today the products of white man's technology are called *wakasotešni* 'permanent things' (literally, "things that can't be destroyed").

The common stone or rock was called *inyan*, but in ritual language the sacred stone employed to help the sacred persons find lost objects or cure people were referred to as *tunkan,* a term recognized by the Oglalas as having a relationship with *tunkašila* 'grandfather'. These stones had their own *šicun* and could be invested with others by the sacred person. A common person often carried his "guardian spirit" in the form of a small stone called *wašicun tunkan,* and the stone was named after the deceased or a supernatural being or power that originally owned the *šicun.*

Common language was often rendered sacred by means of its context. The best example of lengthy discourses in ritual language are found in songs learned in vision quests. Nonhuman species are regarded as human (*Wanbli oyate* 'Eagle nation', *Tatanka oyate* 'Buffalo nation', *Heȟaka oyate* 'Elk nation, etc.'). Sacred persons are often referred to in songs by common metaphors such as *Hocoka wanji iyotake cin* 'the one who sits in the middle of the camp circle' (i.e., the universe). The spirits that give instructions to the sacred persons are described in some activity reminiscent of olden times, e.g., *Šunka wakan yutapelo* 'They are eating dog sacredly', i.e., the spirits are participating in a dog feast. Most of these songs required interpretation inasmuch as they represented personal experiences shared by the sacred persons and the supernaturals.

The sacred persons often called each other *ieska*, a term intelligible to the common man. *Ieska* means "interpreter, translator," and in a ritual sense, "medium." Literally, *ieska* means "to talk white" and is the common term used for offspring of Indian and white marriages, mixed-bloods. But the term also carries another connotation. At one time the Lakota-speakers differentiated those who spoke a mutually intelligible language from those who did not. The former were called *skaiela* 'white speakers', and the latter *šaiyela* 'red speakers'. *Šaiyela (Sahiyela)* is the Lakota name for the Cheyennes. *Ieska* is an inverted form meaning "to make clear."

Ritual language was the means of expressing cosmological concepts and we find it used extensively in Oglala mythology. In Walker's collection of myths, some of which I investigate in the next chapter, we find an abundance of abbreviated terms. These terms were, according to Walker, part of the ritual language of his informants. The validity of these abbreviations (more than the content of the myths) was regarded by some of Deloria's later informants as untenable. However, Walker is considered by other Sioux specialists (DeMallie, 1971; Hassrick, 1964) as a good ethnographer who used capable informants. Although Walker's texts appear only in translation, one of his informants, Sword, provided another series of myths in the native language (Sword, n.d.). A comparison of the two series demonstrates that the concepts treated by Walker are consonant with those provided by Sword and other Oglalas.

In summary, the sacred persons were predominantly men, but women sometimes also assumed the sacred role. They provided the medium of communication between the common people and the supernaturals. They were the instructors and depositories of sacred knowledge, recounted in the myths and enacted in the rituals. Their authority was founded in the visionary experience, usually after personal misfortune had befallen them. They spoke in a sacred language unintelligible to common people, and those who had similar visions banded together in dream cults, sometimes depicting their visions in music and dance for the benefit of the uninitiated. Others remained isolated, and at times there was conflict between sacred persons, the eventual powerlessness of an old man succumbing to the auspiciousness of a younger one. Sacred persons were unique in their ritual performance, and just as there was individualism in other aspects of Oglala society, so there was in the realm of religion.

Chapter 7

COSMOLOGY

Reconstruction

In this chapter and the next I will reconstruct the concepts related to cosmology, cosmogony, and ritual for the period of time during which the Oglalas lived as a politically discrete entity, that is, from about 1700 to the establishment of the reservation system, about 1868. It is assumed that certain major concepts are rooted firmly in the culture of the original Oceti Šakowin but that as the Oglalas emerged as a distinct unit, migrating westward, there were some changes in religious ideology and ritual. It is also assumed that after the Oglalas were forced to live on the reservation, additional changes in religion occurred. These latter changes will be treated in Part III.

What follows may be regarded as Oglala theology which was largely understood only by sacred persons, and that it was the responsibility of those persons to interpret the religious concepts to the common people. The sources on which I rely for matters dealing with cosmology and cosmogony are primarily Walker (1917), and secondarily Deloria (1932), Dorsey (1894), Hassrick (1964), and Sword (n.d.). I begin by providing a synopsis of ten myths collected by Walker which relate to the creation of the universe, the establishment of time and space, and the origin of the Oglalas. I then discuss the myth related to the origin of the sacred pipe and the seven sacred rites. General themes related to the culture hero, Inktomi, and other myths are drawn primarily from Deloria, with comparisons from my own field work.

Cosmology

The following myths are presented in the same order in which they were published by Walker. Walker supplied titles for the myths; I have numbered them (M^1, M^2, etc.) for future reference. Taken as a whole, the first ten myths represent a logical sequence of events. However, there is much overlapping of themes between the myths, and for this reason I have summarized them.

M^1. *When the People Laughed at Hanwi.* At one time all people dwelled beneath the earth. The chief of these people was Wazi. He was married to Kanka, a seer, and their daughter, Ite, was considered the most beautiful of women. The daughter was married to Tate and by him had given birth to quadruplet sons who because of the nature of their father and their birth were gods. Ite was also pregnant with a fifth child.

Wazi and Kanka were not content, for they wished the powers of gods. Inktomi, knowing this, promised to give them such powers if they would conspire with him to make people look ridiculous. At first Wazi was afraid, saying to his wife that Inktomi would make people laugh at her. But she concluded that once given the powers of gods, they would not be threatened by Inktomi. Thus Wazi and Kanka agreed to help Inktomi if he would first prove that he would give them powers. To show them good faith, he gave them a charm which would make anyone more beautiful.

Next, Inktomi spoke with their daughter, Ite. He told her that she would be the most beautiful of all beings. He also told her that Hanwi's husband, Wi, chief of the gods, had noticed her beauty and spoken of it. When Ite told her mother what Inktomi had said, she replied that Ite would sit with the gods, and gave her the charm to make her the most beautiful of all beings. Similarly, Inktomi talked with Wi, telling him that Ite was both a wife of a god and mother of gods and should have a seat with the gods. He then talked with Kanka, telling her that Wi would be pleased to see her daughter.

Ite became possessed by her beauty, and she began to neglect her sons. She adorned herself often and one day, while walking with her mother and father, passed before the face of Wi, who noticed her beauty and invited her to the feast of the gods. Before the feast, Inktomi instructed her to take the vacant seat next to Wi because he was tired of his companion, Hanwi, and sought a younger woman.

While the feast was being prepared, Inktomi approached Hanwi, saying that her husband thought Ite was the most beautiful of all beings and had invited her to the feast. Hanwi thus stayed behind to adorn herself. In the meantime, Ite arrived early to the feast and took the vacant seat next to Wi. When Hanwi arrived and saw Ite occupying her seat, she stood behind Wi with her robe over her head. When the people saw this, they began to laugh at Hanwi. Inktomi laughed the loudest. Kanka sang a song of joy, but Wazi was still afraid. Tate left the feast and returned to his own lodge, where he painted his face and the faces of his sons black in mourning over the loss of his wife.

After the feast, Hanwi stood before Škan, who gives movement to all things. Škan asked why she had hidden her face, and she replied because she was ashamed that another woman had taken her place. Škan then asked Wi why he permitted this to happen. Wi replied that Ite's beauty had caused him to forget Hanwi. Škan then asked Ite why she sat in Hanwi's seat. Ite replied that her mother had foretold that she would sit with the gods, that Inktomi had told her she was the most beautiful of women, and that Wi had invited her to the feast. Škan then asked Kanka why she had schemed to have her daughter replace Hanwi. Kanka replied that she had gotten the power from Inktomi, and that Wi had wished to see her daughter. Škan asked Wazi why he had obtained power from Inktomi. Wazi replied that he wanted to do more good.

Škan then assigned the following judgements: Because Wi as the chief of gods had allowed a woman to come between him and his wife, Hanwi would be free to go her own way. Although they both ruled two periods of time, day and night, she would rule a third: the interval between the time she left him and the time she returned. Because Wi had caused her to hide her face, she would always do so when she came near him, and only uncover it when she was away from him. Because Ite had neglected her children, she would bear her fifth child prematurely. He would never grow up normally, and he, along with the other four sons, would live with their father, Tate. Because she was vain, she would go to the world and live without friends. Moreover, she would keep her beautiful face, but would be given another, horrid face and be known forever as Anog-Ite, Double-Face. Because Kanka had obtained her powers fraudulently, she would go to the earth and live alone until she learned how to help people. She would be forever known as the Old Woman, or Witch. Because Wazi did not use his powers appropriately, he too would go to the earth and live alone until he learned to help his grandsons. He would forever be known as the Old Man, the Wizard.

Inktomi laughed at the judgments and taunted Kanka by saying that she would have cheated him and laughed at him, but he in fact had made her and her kindred ashamed. When Škan questioned Inktomi about his reason for making everyone ashamed, Inktomi stated that he was a god and the son of a god—that his father, the Rock, was the oldest of all gods, but because his other parent, the flying god, had no shape, everybody laughed at him. Because everyone laughed at him, he would laugh at them. Škan then told Inktomi that because of his deeds he too must go to the world, where he would live without friends, and that all men and gods would hate him and the sound of rattles would torture him. Upon hearing this, Inktomi laughed, saying that Škan had forgotten to mention the birds and animals, and that Inktomi would dwell with them and continue to make fools of mankind.

As consolation to Tate and his five sons, who still wept for their mother, Škan allowed Tate to live near Anog-Ite, Double-Face, doing with her as he wished. Tate was told to send his elder four sons to the earth, where they would establish the fourth period of time. He continued to mourn, as did Hanwi, who painted her face black. But the people laughed at her no more.

M^2. *When the Wizard Came.* The Wizard was not permitted on the earth, so he traveled around the edge of it, making a trail. He spoke to the stars near the edge, asking each permission to go upon the earth, but they never granted his request. He noticed that some stars never came down to the earth, so he built a lodge under them, hoping that if they did come down they would grant him permission. He finally received a vision in the lodge telling him to go to the edge of the earth, where he would receive a message. There a bright star in the form of a woman spoke to him. She said she was the daughter of the sky, and told him to return to his lodge until the moon was full. Then he would find the sons of Tate, and he should help them with their work. After, he could go upon the earth.

He found the sons of Tate and asked to camp with them. Yata, the first-born and leader of the party, was mean and turned his back on the Wizard; but Okaga, the fourth-born, was kind and offered the Wizard food from a bag which no matter how much they ate could not be depleted. When they were ready to sleep, three brothers wrapped themselves in their robes, but Okaga offered his to the Wizard. The robe was so large that it served both of them. In the morning, the robe was light and new again.

The Wizard asked the brothers where they wanted to go, and they replied that their father had told them to make the four directions on the edge of the earth. Since the Wizard lived there, he offered to show them the way. The Wizard gave the brothers moccasins, which they had never worn before. By wearing these moccasins they could travel from one hilltop to the next. The Wizard bade Yata, the first-born, to go first, but he was afraid. Eya, the second-born, went first and soon was at a distant hilltop. Then Yata stepped forward and was beside Eya. Then Yanpa, the third-born, stepped and stood beside his brothers. The Wizard and Okaga stepped together, going far beyond the three brothers. The Wizard told them that they could travel better under the clouds, and when they did so they moved faster than the birds. They reached the edge of the wood and set up a pile of stones marking the first direction.

When they saw that the sun set on the mountain which marked the first direction, Yata raged, for it was Eya's direction that was created first. The Wizard told Yata that because he was mean and surly and did not follow his father's bidding, his birthright had been taken from him. From here on, Eya would be considered first in all things. Then Yata hid his face and wept.

M³. The Old Woman. There once was an industrious woman whose children were all boys. Her mother gave her a charm which made her more beautiful. There was also a chief who was a brave and handsome man and wanted this beautiful woman, but she would not listen to him. The chief promised the mother that if she could persuade her daughter to listen to him, the mother would be powerful. The mother agreed, and the chief gained influence over the daughter. The daughter began to neglect her children, but grew more beautiful each day. Her husband still loved her and did not scarify her face although she caused him misery. When the mother saw what she had done, she grew old and feeble and wanted to die.

The daughter now boasted that she was more beautiful than the Moon, so the Moon blackened her face and complained to the Sky. The Sky told the chief to move his tipi outside the camp circle as punishment for disrupting the beautiful woman's household, and the woman was given the face of a terrible beast. Sky told the old woman that she would be stronger than a man and would never die. Today she never erects her tipi in camp. She appears withered and feeble, and may appear to young men and women, bringing them good fortune if they deserve it, or misfortune if they do not. She is Wakanka, the Old Woman, the Witch.

M⁴. When Wohpe Came to the World. Before the directions were made, Tate with his four sons and little son dwelled in a round lodge in the region of the pines. At midday, the sun looked into the lodge to see that all was well with Tate. Tate occupied the seat of honor, and his oldest son, Yata, was next to him. The seat of Eya, the second-born, was at the right of the lodge; the seat of Yanpa the third-born, at the left; and Okaga, the fourth-born, was next to the door. The little son, Yum, had no birth; therefore he had no seat, but sat where he chose.

One day when the sons were out traveling, something shiny fell near the lodge. Tate found it to be a young woman who had been sent from her father, the Sky, to find friends. She carried a queer pouch with strange symbols marked on it. Tate invited her to stay in his lodge, telling her not to disclose to his sons who she was. She accepted and began to take over the woman's work Tate had been doing. She cut out clothing from a hide and taught Tate how to wear it.

The brothers returned in the order of their birth. Each one gazed at the woman, left the lodge, and turned his eyes to the

ground. Okaga and Yum returned last and asked why their brothers gazed at the ground. They replied that a witch was in the lodge,
and that their father was wearing a strange garment, and that there
was no food. Yum and Okaga looked into the lodge and the woman
smiled at them. Tate remembered that he had forgotten to prepare
the food, but the woman said that she would do the work and
immediately there was a fire going in the lodge. She put hot stones
from the fire in her cooking bag and told Tate that the food was
ready to be eaten.

Tate called the other sons to come in and eat, but they each
stated that food could not be prepared because there was none,
just as there was no firewood. They thought that the woman was a
witch and that each in turn would be bewitched by her. Finally
they went into the lodge. When they were finally seated, they all
gazed at the ground except Yum, who looked directly into the
woman's eyes. Tate was pleased.

The woman then asked each what his favorite food was. Tate
replied that he wanted tripe, wild turnips, and soup. She produced
these foods from her bag and gave them to Tate, whom she now
called father. Yata said that he wanted boiled flesh and fat, pemmican, and soup. She produced these foods from her bag and
called him brother. Eya stated that he wanted boiled duck, wild
rice, and soup. She produced these from her bag, and called him
brother. Yanpa said that he wanted tripe, flesh, fat, a duck, turnips,
rice, and soup. She produced these from her bag, calling him
brother.

Then she took out from her bag a small platter and bowl and
put into them strange food and drink, the latter having the odor of
sweetgrass. She handed them to Yum and told him to give them to
his brother who sat by the door. Yata complained that he should
have the best food. Okaga looked at the food and drink, but there
was little of it. He put all the food in his mouth, but immediately
there was more food on the platter. So he ate and drank until he
was satisfied.

When it was time to sleep, the brothers went outside and found
a new tipi with four beds in it, each arranged in the appropriate
place. Three brothers lay down, but Okaga stayed outside beside
the water playing his flute. The woman smiled when she heard the
flute and told Yum that he would always be her little brother.

The next morning the woman had filled the lodge with firewood and had prepared the meal. The four brothers entered and Tate told them that it was now time to fix the directions in the world and that this would be the fourth period of time. He said that Yata was the oldest and his direction should be where the shadows are longest at midday. Eya must be where the sun goes over the mountain and down under the world when his day is done. Yanpa must be where the sun comes up at the edge of the world to begin his journey. Okaga must be under the sun at midday.

He told them to prepare for four days and leave on the fifth. He said that the journey would be long and that there would be as many moons in the fourth time as had passed from the time they left the lodge until the time they returned. When they left, Tate mourned for them as he mourned for the dead because he knew they would abide in his lodge no more.

M⁵. How the North Wind Lost His Birthright. The directions moved all over the earth, so the Wind told the Four Winds that they should mark their directions so that they each knew where they belonged. Since the North Wind was the oldest, he should have the first direction which is the farthest from the sun. Each direction should be marked with a pile of stones.

The Wizard met them on their way to the edge of the earth and because the North Wind was mean and cowardly, the Wizard took away his birthright and gave it to the West Wind. When the Four Winds arrived at the place farthest from the sun, they saw the tipi of the Wizard. He invited them in, and all but the North Wind entered. The North Wind claimed that his tipi should be there and asked a magpie to sit on the tipi poles and befoul the Wizard when he came through the door. The magpie did so and to this day is required to befoul his own nest. Then the Wizard told the North Wind that because he had asked the magpie to do that, it would be his messenger forever, and the Wizard would take the first place in the name of the direction of the North Wind. This is why the direction of the North Wind is called Waziyata.

M⁶. How the West Wind Became the Companion of the Winged God. When the Four Winds were fixing their directions, they heard fearful noises on the mountain. All were afraid except Okaga, who offered to go on ahead. If he found danger he would call to them, but if he did not they would follow. He went ahead and came to a level place in the center of which was a round lodge with an opening in the top but no doors. Beside the lodge was a great cedar tree and in it a huge nest made of dried bones. In the nest was an enormous egg. Someone in the lodge was drumming, and someone in the egg was pecking, both accounting for the terrible noise.

As Okaga neared the lodge, a voice bellowed, asking him who dared approach the lodge of the Winged God. Okaga identified himself and explained the mission of his brothers and him. The voice told him to pass, and Okaga called to his brothers that there was no danger. Each in turn passed the lodge and was told to continue. Eya stopped to look at the lodge and the nest. The voice asked what he wished and he answered that he wanted to know who was in the lodge. A swallow flew up through the hole, saying that it was the lodge of the Winged God and that the egg in the nest was his. When Eya said that he would like to see the Winged God, the swallow said that if he looked at the Winged God he would become a *heyoka* and thereafter would have to act in an antinatural manner. But if one saw Heyoka, he need not become *heyoka*. Eya said that he wanted to see both, and at that moment there arose from the lodge a shapeless thing like a cloud of smoke. It had a beak like an eagle with four rows of sharp teeth; its glance was like lightning and its voice like thunder. It had four jointed wings but no legs or feet, and eight toes bearing the talons of an eagle, each talon as long as an eagle's wing. It seized the egg and shook it, and the noise was like the rolling thunder.

It told Eya that because he did not fall down or run away, he would become the companion of the Winged God and help cleanse the world of filthy and evil things. The swallow then said that as long as man had ceremonies for the gods, the West Wind would have precedence over all but one, and that he should establish his direction on the mountain side and it should be recognized as the first direction.

The West Wind commanded his brothers to erect a pile of stones and each choose a bird as his messenger. The North Wind chose the magpie; the East Wind, a crow; the South Wind, a meadowlark; and the West Wind, a swallow. Since that time, the

West Wind travels with the Winged God, Wakinyan, and the swallows fly high in circles.

M⁷. Wooing Woȟpe. Woȟpe dwelled in the lodge of Tate and served him and his sons well. One day they began to argue about her, each wanting her for his own, except Okaga, who said that they should ask her whom she wanted. Each in turn approached Woȟpe, but she looked into the eyes of Okaga, saying that whoever pleased her most would be the one in whose robe she would stand. The brothers, except Okaga, continued to argue as to who should make the first offering.

In order to determine who should have Woȟpe, each brother attempted to influence her. The North Wind went hunting and brought her game, but everything he brought her turned to ice and made the lodge cold and dreary. The West Wind brought his drum and danced and sang before her, but he made so much noise that the tipi fell down. The East Wind sat down and talked with her so foolishly that she felt like crying. Then the South Wind made her beautiful things and she decided to be his woman. This made the North Wind angry because he felt that he should have first choice. The two brothers quarreled, and finally the South Wind told his woman that they should go away and live in peace.

As they were leaving, the North Wind tried to steal her. When she heard him coming, she took off her dress and got under it to hide. When the North Wind saw the dress, he embraced it and everything turned hard and cold and icy. He heard the South Wind coming and fled, but the South Wind could not find his woman, so he went to look for her. Each time he tried, she spread the dress out farther and farther so that he could not crawl underneath.

Again the South Wind returned, but the woman had spread the dress out so far that there was no end to it and he could not get to her. Enraged, the South Wind followed the trail of the North Wind until he came to his lodge, where he was boasting to his other brothers what he had done to the woman. The West Wind and East Wind finally rushed in to help the South Wind. They could not kill their brother, but they bound his hands and feet and left him in his tipi. After that the three brothers vowed that they would never live with the North Wind, and each went his own direction. The little wind was too small to have a tipi of his own, so he stayed mainly with the South Wind, and occasionally with the West Wind. The East Wind was so disagreeable that he did not even visit him.

The North Wind threatened to freeze the woman's dress again, but the three brothers and the little brother tried to warm the dress. When the woman found out what they were doing, she thrust bright ornaments through the dress, and it was again beautiful with green, red, blue, and all other colors. When the North Wind freed himself, he again attempted to freeze the woman's dress, but each time the three brothers with the help of the little brother fought and drove back the mean brother and commenced to warm the dress. Each time the beautiful ornaments froze from the North Wind's touch, and each time the dress was warmed and the woman pushed through the bright ornaments. Thus began the warfare between the brothers that continues to the present.

M^8. *The Wars of the Winds.* (This is largely a recapitulation of M^4 and M^7.) Tate asked the woman her name and she answered that it was Woȟpe. She said that the Sun was her father; the Moon, her mother; and the stars, her people. Okaga made her a dress more beautiful than her own, and she said to Tate, "My father, my journey is ended."

M^9. *The Feast by Tate.* When Woȟpe came to stay with Tate, he decided to give a feast to Taku Wakan and asked his sons whom he should invite. The sons chose Wi, Hanwi, Škan, and Inyan because they were *Wakan tanka*. They along with Tate formed the council and made the rules by which all would be governed. They also invited Unktehi, Unkcegila, Wakinyan, Tunkan, Tatanka, Can Oti, Hohnogica, and Nagi.

The South Wind made the invitation wands, and the West Wind delivered them. When the guests arrived, they each told of their own origins and powers. Inktomi tricked them and lied. Tate gave presents to all, and they all asked what he wished in return. Tate stated that the feast was in honor of Woȟpe and that they should give gifts to her. When asked what she wanted, she requested that no one have power over the Sun and Moon, and it was agreed.

Then they all danced. Yumni, the little brother, was the best and made Yata angry. When the Wašicun danced, Woȟpe danced with them and her hair shone in flashes. Since then, when the Wašicun dance, there are flashes of light in the north (the aurora borealis). Waziya joined in with Yata, and Inktomi gave them a choice of colors. They chose white. When Yanpa did things to amuse the company, Inktomi offered him a color. He chose blue. Then Eya performed and Inktomi offered him a color. He chose yellow. Okaga did things so wonderfully that no one tired of watching him. Inktomi offered him a choice and it was red.

Then Woȟpe asked Okaga to do something for each of the guests. He asked what each wanted the most and it was granted. Unkcegila wanted power in his horns and tail and it was granted (but Inktomi made them brittle). Inyan wanted to be able to resist anything, and it was granted (but Inktomi made him brittle so that he would break into pieces but not be destroyed). The Wašicun wanted to be invisible, and it was granted (but Inktomi deprived them of any form so that when they wanted to communicate with anything they had to assume the shape of something else). The Wakinyan wanted bright eyes and loud voices, and it was granted (but Inktomi made their glances destructive and their voices terrible). Then Takuškanškan said that he wanted power over all moving things so that he could protect them, and it was granted (but Inktomi made him sleepy). The Tunkan wanted many children so that he would be revered and taken care of, and it was granted (but Inktomi said that his children would strive among themselves and forget him except when in trouble). Finally, Iya said that he wanted plenty of food to eat, and it was granted (but Inktomi declared that he would always be hungry and his food would give him pain).

COSMOGONY

The following myth from the Walker collection addresses itself specifically to the origin of the Oglalas.

M[10]. *How the Lakotas Came upon the World.* Inktomi played pranks on the animals, but they were not ashamed, so he longed to play pranks on mankind. At that time there were only the Old Man, the Old Woman, and Double-Face on the earth. Inktomi feared the Old Man and Woman, but Double-Face feared him because he had caused her so much shame and misery.

He appeared before her tipi as a young man but she knew who he was. He often sat with his head bowed as if he were grieving. When she asked why he sat that way, he answered that he was ashamed that he had caused her so much misery and longed to know what he might do to make her happy. Double-Face answered that only being with her people would make her happy. Inktomi said that if she would tell him how he might bring her people to the earth, he would do it. And she said that if the people tasted meat and saw the fine clothing and tipis, they would come. Inktomi told her that he would help her and would never more trick her.

While Double-Face made robes and clothing, Inktomi sent a wolf to a cave that is the entrance to the world. He gave the wolf a pack containing meat and clothes with instructions that when the wolf met a strong and brave man, he should give him the pack and tell him there were more things like this in the world. The wolf entered the cave and soon came upon such a man. The man was Tokahe, and the wolf told him that the pack would make him a leader if he showed it to his people. The man did so, and told the people that there was more in the world. The people tasted the meat and liked it, and his wife wore the clothing, making the others jealous. An old man suggested that Tokahe take three men and go see these things so that the people would know he told the truth.

Tokahe chose three strong and brave men, who accompanied him to the world. There Double-Face, hiding her horrid face, cooked them a fine meal, and Inktomi, appearing as a young man, told them that they were really old, but if they ate meat they would stay young. When they finished, Inktomi gave them gifts of meat, robes, and soft tanned skins, and directed the wolf to lead them back to their people. Inktomi instructed the wolf to stay by the cave entrance, and when the people reappeared, to guide them far from food and water.

Tokahe showed his people the marvelous gifts, but the old chief and an old woman warned them not to go to the world, for there the winds blew cold and the game must be hunted. The chief said that whoever would go would not be able to return to the underworld. Tokahe said that he would lead his people, and six men and their families agreed to go with him. They met the wolf, who guided them through the cave all day. At night their children cried for food, and when they met Inktomi he laughed at them. The Double-Face woman appeared to comfort them, but when they saw her horrid face they fled in terror. In the morning they did not know where to go until they met the Old Man and Woman, who led them to the region of the pines. They taught them how to hunt and make clothing and tipis. Thus Tokahe and his friends were the first people in the world and their children are the Lakotas.

A number of variations of the myth explaining the origin of the sacred pipe have been published (Brown, 1953; Densmore, 1918; Hassrick, 1964; Neihardt, 1932; Smith, 1967; Sword, n.d., in Lakota and English). The following is a synopsis of the story told by Black Elk (Brown, 1953).

M^{11}. *The Gift of the Sacred Pipe.* Once two men were out hunting with bows and arrows when they saw in the distance something wondrous approaching them. As the object came closer, they saw that it was a beautiful woman dressed in white buckskin and carrying a bundle on her back. The woman was so beautiful that one of the men had bad intentions toward her. She told this man to come forward, and as he neared her they were both enveloped by a mist. When the mist lifted, the man was nothing but bones and terrible snakes were eating him.

She told the other man to return to his camp and tell his chief to prepare a great lodge and tell all the people to gather. She had something of great importance to tell them. The man returned and told what had happened. The chief ordered that several tipis be taken down and made into a large lodge. The people dressed in their finest clothes and awaited the appearance of the mysterious woman.

The woman arrived and entered the lodge in a sunwise direction. She bore the bundle in her hands and offered it to the chief, saying that was a sacred pipe and with it the people would send their voices to *Wakantanka*. From her bundle she took the sacred pipe and a round stone, placing the latter on the ground. She took the pipe and offered the stem to the heavens, saying, "With this sacred pipe you will walk upon the Earth; for the Earth is your Grandmother and Mother and She is sacred."

She told the people that the pipe bowl was made of red stone and represented the earth. Carved in the stone was a buffalo calf which represented all four-legged creatures. The stem of the pipe was made of wood and represented all growing things. And the twelve feathers which decorated the pipe represented the Spotted Eagle and all the winged creatures of the air. All the peoples and the things of the universe would be joined with whoever smoked the sacred pipe. The woman then touched the pipe to the round stone, saying, "With this pipe you will be bound to all your relatives: your Grandfather and Father, your Grandmother and Mother."

She told the people to behold the seven circles inscribed on the round stone and that these represented the seven rites in which the pipe would be used. The first large circle represented the rite she would teach them on this day, and others represented rites that would later be revealed to them. She told the chief that through the pipe the people would increase. Then she instructed them in the first rite, which was the ghost-keeping ceremony. In this ceremony the people could send their voices to *Wakantanka* through the soul of a deceased person. The day on which the soul is released to return to *Wakantanka* would be sacred, and on this day four women would be made sacred and in time bear children.

As the sacred woman was about to leave, she addressed the chief, saying that he must always treat the pipe in a sacred manner. "Remember," she said, "in me there are four ages. I am leaving now but I shall look back upon your people in every age, and at the end I shall return."

Moving around the lodge in a sunwise manner, the woman left, but after walking a short distance she sat down. When she arose the people were amazed to see that she had turned into a red and brown buffalo calf. The calf walked on, lay down, rolled, and when it got up it was a white buffalo calf. Again the white buffalo walked farther, and turned into a black buffalo. The black buffalo walked farther away, stopped, and after bowing to each quarter of the universe, disappeared over a hill.

The other variations of the Sacred Calf Pipe myth, or Coming of the White Buffalo Calf Woman myth, as it is sometimes called, agree substantially with Black Elk's account. Sword's is more detailed, stating that when the woman offered the pipe to the chief, she feigned three times before giving it to him, saying that the presentation of the pipe should always be done this way. She also outlined the organization of the camp circle, the duties of the leaders, and taboos related to certain foods. Black Elk notes one contradiction in his own rendition, stating that the Oglalas already had the sweat lodge and vision quest before the woman appeared, but that these should be regarded as two of the seven rites.

INKTOMI

The classic trickster-transformer (Underhill, 1965) or trickster cycle (Radin, 1956) appears in Oglala mythology, featuring the character Inktomi (also Iktomi, Ikto), the Spider, whose deceptions are responsible for the creation of time and space. Stories about Inktomi, as well as other sacred characters, belong to the Oglala genre *ohunkankan,* usually translated as "story, myth, fable" (Buechel, 1970:374), or "just-for-fun-story" (Clark, 1941:1). *Ohunkankan* are contrasted with *wicooyake* 'story, telling', which refer to stories about war adventures or local events reckoned to be "true." It is fair to say that while the Oglalas recognize that *ohunkakan* treat of incredible beings and situations of a bygone era, they do not agree that these stories are in any sense false (although Christian Oglalas might regard them as such). The distinction between *ohunkakan* and *wicooyake* is not one which suggests an opposition between that which is false and that which is true. Rather, *ohunkakan* refers to the domain of the supernatural, while *wicooyake* refers to the domain of man.

Ohunkakan are traditionally told at nighttime, and can be recognized not only by their content but by their formulaic ending *hehanyelo oihanke* 'that is all, that is the end', or simply *hehanyela yelo* (Deloria, 1932). Although there has been no systematic collec-

tion of Inktomi stories for the Oglalas, the following generaliza-
tions of themes contain cognates found in Radin's treatment of
Winnebago and Assiniboin trickster stories (Radin, 1956).

Inktomi is responsible for having named all things and creating
language. He is sometimes called the Mocker (*waunca*, also the
present word for monkey). Most stories find him traveling about
the world communicating with the animals. He is responsible for
their forms and colors, usually given as a result of a misadventure
or as a punishment for deception. He is mischievous and likes to
play pranks on man and the animals, but often winds up the butt of
his own jokes. He is capable of transforming himself into any shape
he desires, most often that of a coyote or a handsome man. At other
times, he treats his own body as if it were foreign: he causes his
hands to fight each other, he roasts his own anus, and he carries his
huge penis in a box. He learns from the mice how to juggle his eyes,
but throws them so high that they become stuck in a tree and he
goes blind.

Inktomi is constantly the subject of social transgressions. He
does not know his kinship terms and argues with others over who is
the oldest. He breaks the mother-in-law avoidance rule by taking
his mother-in-law to war with him, returning with a multitude of
children. He feigns death and returns in disguise to marry his own
daughter. He also transforms himself into a beautiful woman and
marries the son of a chief.

Trickster stories are the favorites of the young people, and it is
through the travails of Inktomi that they learn, by means of pro-
scriptions, the history and culture of their people, and the origins of
the universe.

THE GREAT FLOOD AND END OF THE WORLD

Following are three myths, one related to a deluge which
decimated the Sioux in their original homeland, and two regarding
the end of the world.

M^{12}. *How the Sioux Nation Was Born.* At one time a great flood
visited the western plains. Many tribes came to the prairie hills to

escape from the rising waters. The water continued to rise until it covered all the people. Their flesh and blood was turned into red pipestone.

While the people were drowning, a bald eagle flew by so that a beautiful woman could catch onto its feet and be carried away to a great tree on a cliff above the water. Upon this cliff the woman gave birth to twins. Their father was the eagle. The twins began a new tribe that was strong and brave. The pipestone, the flesh of their ancestors, was to be smoked as a symbol of peace. And the eagle feather was to be worn on the heads of the warriors (Reese, 1941; Lame Deer and Erdoes, 1972).

M^{13}. *The End of the World.* An Indian woman sits in the moonlight making porcupine quillwork. Near her there is a kettle of herbs boiling. As she puts down her quillwork to stir the kettle, her dog unravels her work. As fast as she sews, the dog unravels her work. If she should ever finish her quillwork, the world will end at that instant (Reese, 1941).

M^{14}. *The End of the Cycle.* At the beginning of time a buffalo was placed in the west in order to hold back the waters. Every year the buffalo loses one hair, and every age he loses one leg. When all his hair and all his legs are gone, the waters will rush in and the cycle will end. It is believed that the buffalo currently stands on one leg and is very nearly bald (Brown, 1953).

Chapter 8

RITUAL

THE SACRED PIPE

Before describing the seven rites given to the Lakotas by the White Buffalo Calf Woman, it is appropriate to discuss the sacred pipe inasmuch as it represents the symbol of integration between all rituals. The pipe, under certain circumstances, also represents the total Oglala universe.

After the original pipe was given to the people, copies were made. There were two types, one called an L-shape, the other, used for ceremonial occasions, a T-shape, both terms referring to the shape of the catlinite bowl. The native term for pipe is *cannunpa* (from *can* 'wood' and *nunpa* 'two'). The precise derivation of the term is conjectural; possibly it refers to the manufacture of some pipes in which a piece of ash is split, the pith gouged out, and the two parts glued together. The bowl of the pipe is called *pahu* 'head bone', and the stem is called *ihupa*, from *i* 'mouth' and *hupa* 'tent pole.' The mouthpiece is *oyape* 'to take or hold in the mouth' and the connection between the stem and bowl is *oagle* 'to set, place in'. The stem is sometimes referred to as *sinte* 'tail'. The ideal pipe is made from catlinite found only in the Pipestone Quarry near Pipestone, Minnesota. Its red color is ascribed to its origin in the flesh and blood of persons killed in the great flood.

When not in use, the pipe is carried or stored in a beaded and quilled pipe bag (*cantojuha*, from *cante* 'heart' and *ojuha* 'bag'). The bowl and stem must be separated when not in use, because the pipe is powerful. When joined, the pipe is analogous to a loaded gun. Its average length is eighteen inches, and the width of the stem, flattened on the top and bottom, is approximately two inches. The pipe is usually decorated with plaited porcupine quillwork running for several inches from the mouthpiece toward the bowl. The stem may also be decorated with the head of a mallard and hanging eagle feathers. The bowl may be plain, but is often decorated with lead inlay or carved objects, particularly buffalo. Often there are relief carvings on the stem depicting spiders, turtles, or lizards.

A pipe may be smoked ceremonially or for pleasure, but the Oglalas make a careful distinction. Smaller pipes are often used for the latter. Some smoking pipes were also made from the femur of a deer or buffalo. There are a variety of native tobaccos, but the preferred is *canšaša* 'red wood', which is made from the dried inner bark of the red willow (*Salix* spp.). It is often mixed with scrapings of *canli cahi* 'tobacco mix' (snakeroot).

A pipe used for ceremonial purposes is called *cannunpa wakan* 'sacred pipe', and the filled pipe is known as *opagi* (*opagi* also means "to fill a pipe" and probably refers to the tamping down of tobacco). The pipe was filled ceremonially before religious events and also before war journeys. In each case the tobacco was placed in the bowl and the bowl was sealed with buffalo fat. If the war journey was successful, the seal was broken and the pipe smoked (Wissler, 1912).

There were two ways of offering the pipe. It may either be raised above the head with both hands (*ihupa wogluze* 'to hold onto the pipe'), or the stem of the pipe may be pointed in the direction of the power invoked (*oyaȟpeya*). The latter is analagous to casting out the pipe as a fisherman casts out his line. It is stated that war parties offered common pipes to sacred men in order that they be consecrated and thus serve as war medicine. Most of the men's societies maintained custodians of the pipe whose duty it was to conduct the special ceremonies of the sodalities (ibid.).

The consecration of the pipe was effected in the following way. A sacred person joined the bowl and the stem, applying sputum to the *oagle* to seal it. Sprigs of sage were held in the left hand, on which the bowl of the pipe rested. With the right hand, the sacred person reached into the *cantojuha*, taking out a pinch of *canšaša* between his thumb and index finger. The pinch of tobacco was placed in the bowl with a precise gesture, the right hand being lifted quickly and slowly lowered until the tobacco touched the mouth of the bowl. Each gesture was done seven times; and with each a prayer was offered to the four directions, the zenith and nadir, and the Spotted Eagle, the latter being the messenger of *Wakantanka*. When the seven pinches of tobacco had been placed in the bowl, the sacred person tamped the pipe with a special stick (*icašloka*) and sealed the contents with fat from the heart of a buffalo or a crumpled sprig of sage. In this manner, the total powers of the universe were conceived to be inhered in the pipe, and it was rendered sacred.

When occasion came to smoke the pipe, the seal was removed and the tobacco lighted with an ember or a buffalo chip. The usual arrangement for the pipe ceremony was a circle. The owner of the pipe or presiding sacred man held the pipe for the man on his right to light. After drawing on it and taking four puffs, offering the mouthpiece to the four directions, the owner passed it to the man on his left, who repeated the invocation, passing it to the man on his left until all had smoked. At the completion of the ceremony the owner of the pipe cleaned out the residue with a pipe cleaner (*iglaye*), separated the bowl from the stem, and returned them to the pipe bag.

To smoke or even touch a pipe was regarded as a sacred act and only men and women of integrity could do so. Bonds between groups, vows to *Wakantanka*, and prophecies were validated by means of the pipe, and any transgressions against it would cause the offender or his family to suffer misfortune or even death. Thus the pipe could not be desecrated by word or deed, and it could be handled only by persons properly trained in its protocol. It could not be touched by a menstruating woman, or even placed in her presence. One must be careful never to step over a pipe, or store it improperly when the camp was preparing to move. If a pipe were in any manner desecrated, it was required that a sacred person take it into a sweat lodge, where its power could be renewed with the proper ceremony. If the pipe continued to be inefficacious, it was buried and thus returned to mother earth and the *hunkake*, the ancestors, from whose flesh and blood it had emerged.

The Seven Rites

All ceremonies whose objectives are to influence the supernatural beings and powers are called *wakan wicoȟ'an* (from *wakan* 'sacred' and *wicoȟ'an* 'acts, deeds, way'). The seven rites are those given to the people by the White Buffalo Calf Woman (*Ptehincala San Win*), but they do not represent the total repertory of Oglala ceremonies. Rather, they should be regarded as the central religious theme of Oglala ceremonialism. There are variations to this theme, just as there are varieties of religious practitioners whose specializations differ on the basis of revelationary instructions.

The seven rites, as I reconstruct them, are generalized mainly from the works of Brown (1953), Densmore (1918), Dorsey (1894), Neihardt (1932), Walker (1917), and Wissler (1912) and my own field work. The first two rituals are presented in a logical order, the sweat lodge followed by the vision quest. Although each of them is a ritual sui generis, they both serve as rituals preliminary to the remaining five, as well as to rituals related to hunting, warfare, and life crises.

The Sweat Lodge. The ritual is called *inikagapi* (from *i* 'by means of, on account of'; *ni* 'life, breath'; *kagapi* 'they make, cause'). The ritual is held in a sweat lodge, *oinikage* (from *o* 'in' and *inikage*), also called *initipi* (from *ini* and *tipi* 'dwelling'). The purpose of the ritual is to revivify persons spiritually and/or physically. The ritual must be conducted under the supervision of a sacred person. Any number of persons may participate, the maximum number being determined by the dimensions of the sweat lodge (usually five or six). Both men and women may participate, but not together.

The sweat lodge is constructed in the following manner: Sixteen willow saplings, approximately one inch in diameter at the butt end, are peeled and imbedded in the ground so as to describe a circle approximately six to eight feet in diameter. The saplings are then bent over and tied with rawhide thongs to form a domoidal structure, at the center approximately four feet from the ground to the apex of the roof. The saplings are arranged so that there are four on each side of the lodge, with an entrance on the east.

The earth in the center of the lodge is dug out, leaving a hole approximately two feet in diameter and two feet deep into which hot stones will be placed during the ritual. The earth which is removed is used to form a sacred path approximately eight paces from the entrance. The path runs east and west, and at the eastern end, the remaining earth is molded into a mound called *unci* 'grandmother'. Two paces east of the mound, the ground is cleared for the fireplace, called *peta oihankešni* 'fire without end'. The fireplace is made by placing four sticks running east and west, and upon them four sticks running north and south. Around these sticks more are laid in a tipi fashion. Four stones are placed at the four directions, and then the remaining rocks are piled up over the wood. One man, the fire tender, lights it and maintains it. As the ceremony begins, he hands in the rocks through the entrance by means of two wooden paddles.

When the ritual is about to begin, the saplings are covered with buffalo robes and other skins. The robes are arranged by the fire tender so that when the door is finally closed no light will be admitted into the lodge. In order to begin the ritual, the sacred person takes the pipe and tobacco into the lodge, enters sunwise, and sits at the west side facing the entrance. He places four pinches of tobacco around the hole and then fills the pipe. Sage is placed around the lodge where the participants will sit. The leader then burns *wacanga* 'sweetgrass' and rubs the smoke over his body and the pipe, thus purifying everything in the lodge. After the pipe has been filled, he leaves the lodge in a sunwise direction and walks alongside the sacred path to the earth mound, where he leans the pipe in such a way that the mouthpiece faces the east.

The leader and the participants then remove all their clothing. The leader enters the lodge first, moving sunwise until he reaches the place next to the door. If he has an assistant, he will enter last and take his place on the opposite side of the door. When all are seated, the leader calls for the heated stones. Four stones are placed in the bottom of the hole so that they describe the four directions. Two stones are then laid on them representing the zenith and nadir. Finally one stone is laid in representing the

Spotted Eagle. After the seven stones have been prayed over, the fire tender puts in place the remaining stones, as many as thirty in all. The leader then calls for a bucket of water and ladle, which are handed in to him by the fire tender. The fire tender is then given the command *"Yuȟpa yo!"* (Close it!), and the lodge is sealed.

Once the door is sealed, the leader sprinkles the ladle of water on the hot stones four times, praying to the four directions. Prayers and songs which will coax spirits into the lodge are intoned. The men perspire and slap their bodies. When the spirits enter, the intentions of the participants are made known through the mediation of the sacred person. Each time water is sprinkled on the stones the men cry out *"Ho! Tunkašila!"* (Ho! Grandfather!); and each time a prayer is ended, the men cry out, *"Hau!"*

During the course of the ritual, the door is opened four times. Often the robes are rolled up at the west end also to permit air to pass through the lodge. Each time the door is opened the ladle of water is passed around to the participants, who drink it and pour it over their heads. After so doing they say, *"Mitak oyasȟn"* (*mitakuye* 'my relations'; *oyasȟn* 'all'; 'All my relations'). Each time the door is closed, water is again sprinkled on the hot stones and the prayers and songs are repeated. The pipe is also moved sunwise each time so that the mouthpiece faces a new direction. During the third opening, the pipe is brought into the lodge and smoked. After each person smokes, he says, *"Mitak oyasȟn."* The fourth time the lodge is opened, the participants leave the lodge in a sunwise direction.

The Vision Quest. The vision quest is called *hanbleceya* 'crying for a vision' (from *hanble* 'vision, dream' and *ceya* 'to cry'). It is a ritual primarily enacted by one person, but it must be done under the supervision of a sacred person. A person undertakes a vision quest to gain power or to seek a vision which will help explain unsolicited visions or to help prophesy the outcome of a hunting or war expedition. It may be performed as often as an individual feels that it is required, and it is usually performed the first time during adolescence.

A person wishing to *hanbleceya* obtains a pipe and seeks out a wise sacred man. He tells the sacred man of his intention to obtain a vision. If the sacred man accepts the responsibility of guiding him, the pipe is smoked between the two and a sacred relationship formed. The supplicant then decides on how many days he will undertake the ordeal, anywhere from two to four. Preparations are made, and relatives of the youth and the sacred person participate in a sweat lodge.

The sacred person then takes the youth on horseback to a sacred hill, away from the camp, where he instructs the youth how to behave during the ordeal. The youth wears only moccasins and a breech cloth, and carries a buffalo robe and a pipe filled with tobacco and sealed with tallow.

The sacred person prepares the appointed place on the hill in the following manner: A pit is dug large enough to accommodate the youth. It is covered over with brush, leaving an opening by means of which he will crawl in and spend part of the ordeal. Saplings are imbedded in the earth at the four directions, and they are connected at the ground by means of a string of tobacco offerings prepared in advance by the youth's relatives. The four directional poles are decorated with colored cloth, each color symbolizing one of the four directions.

The youth is instructed to remove his moccasins as a sign of humility. He is told to stay in the pit, but that he may arise at dawn and go to each of the directions and pray. He is also instructed to hold onto the pipe, and that as long as he does so, nothing will harm him, although many things may come to visit him to test his strength and bravery. He may drink no water or eat any food during the *hanbleceya*.

During his stay on the hill, animals and birds will talk with him. He may be visited by the Thunder-beings from the west, or by seductive women. He must pray to the Morning Star (*anpo wicahpi* 'dawn star') when the sun comes up and always listen carefully to the birds and animals, for they will have a message for him. An older man seeking power from *Wakantanka* may be taken spiritually by the spirits to a far-off place where he will be instructed in curing.

After giving instructions, the sacred man leaves the youth and returns to the camp, where he and the youth's relatives pray for the safe return of the youth. At the appointed time, the sacred man returns for the youth and takes him back to the camp, where after another sweat lodge the youth's visions are interpreted by the sacred person.

If a person dreams of thunder or lightning, he must act out his dream in a ceremony called *Heyoka Kaga* 'Clown Making'. He must forever live his life in an antinatural manner. Others who have had similar dreams will upon occasion hold feasts, dancing around a kettle filled with dog meat, plunging their hands into the boiling water to retrieve choice morsels for the elders. If the youth seeks war medicine, he must kill the animal or bird that appeared in his dream and wear or carry a part of it when he goes on a war journey. If he seeks curing power, he must obtain a part of the animal which instructed him and use it in his curing ceremonies. If he does not accept the instructions given to him in his vision, misfortune may occur to someone in his family or to himself. Particularly, if he does not heed the instructions of the Thunder-beings, he will be struck by lightning.

Ghost Keeping. When a person dies, particularly a favorite son (*hoksicantkiye* 'boy beloved'), the parents may elect to perform a ritual called *Wanagi yuhapi* (from *wanagi* 'ghost'; *yuhapi* 'they have, keep'). Although at one time a ghost was kept for two or more years, nowadays six months to a year is sufficient.

Normally, when a person dies his *wanagi* travels south along the *Wanagi tacanku* 'ghost road' (the Milky Way) until it meets the old woman who decides its fate and sends it on to the hereafter or orders it to return to the earth, where it will live as a shade. To "go south" is a metaphor for dying.

If a ghost is kept, however, by means of this special ceremony, the *wanagi* will linger around its relatives until such time as it is ritually released. A ghost is kept so that by the proper rites it will be assured a return to its origin, and because the lingering ghost will help people to be mindful of death. Keeping the ghost also requires that the immediate members of the family go through a great sacrifice, ultimately giving away all their personal belongings to the needy in memory of the ghost.

The ritual is initiated when the family of the deceased calls in a sacred person, to whom they offer a pipe. If he accepts, they smoke, and then the sacred person cuts a lock of hair from the forehead of the deceased. It is wrapped in a new cloth or skin and put away for four days. Four yards of red cloth are then cut in half and the mother offers half to the earth by burying it in a three-foot hole away from camp. The other half is divided into eight parts and each part is given to a man who has successfully kept a ghost at another time.

Once the lock of hair has been cut, the duties of the father begin. There are many restrictions that he must observe lest he cause misfortune to fall upon his family. To demonstrate that he is in mourning (*wašigla*), he must not eat dog meat or any meat scraped from the hide of an animal. He may not cut open the skull of an animal to obtain the brains, and he may not break the ribs of any animal or butcher it. He may not take any weapon into his hands; he may not run, swim, or make any violent movement that disturbs the air. No one may pass in front of him or touch him. He must live separately from his wife, and must never take a child into his arms.

A special tipi (*wanagi tipi*) is made for the ghost. The lock of hair is put into a buckskin bag, and it, along with the pipe used to initiate the ritual and any other objects chosen by the family, is rolled up in a bundle approximately two feet long and six inches in diameter. The father takes the bundle into his arms as if he were cradling an infant and rides on horseback around the camp, thus announcing to all his intention to keep the ghost.

A slender pine pole is then selected and the ghost bundle is tied to it. It is then placed outside the door of the ghost keeper for four days. At the end of this time, three crotched sticks are cut and made into a tripod and placed in the ghost lodge at the *catku*, or place of honor opposite the doorway. The three feet of the tripod are placed at the west, north, and east, leaving an opening at the south where the ghost bundle is tied.

Once the ghost bundle is in the tipi, it requires constant care. Anyone entering the tipi must pass sunwise, always going behind the tripod. The father and mother each day are required to feed the ghost meat and cherry juice, which is buried in a mellowed place in front of the tripod. On clear days, the mother places the bundle out in the sun, but should a strong wind arise, or should there be a portending thunderstorm, the bundle is quickly retrieved and returned to the tipi. If the camp moves, the tripod, bundle, and paraphernalia needed to keep it are packed on a special horse called the *wanagi tašunke* 'ghost's horse' and carefully transported to the new destination. During the entire period of mourning, the family and their near relatives occupy themselves in making articles of clothing, household utensils, and other goods which will be given away on the final day of the ghost keeping.

As the final day approaches, a sacred person is chosen to carve a spirit post *(wanagi glepi* 'spirit place'). The post is dressed to represent the deceased and is erected inside the spirit lodge on the south side. On the day on which the soul is to be released, a special ritual called *wakicagapi* 'they do something for it' is performed. All the family's relatives and friends, and even members from other tribes, assemble at the spirit lodge. A great feast is prepared and the ghost fed for the last time. Women enter the spirit lodge, each in turn hugging the spirit post and lamenting. The articles of clothing and other utensils are then given away to all who are in attendance. The clothing of the family, all its personal belongings, horses, and tipi are given away and the family is left impoverished. Later, relatives and friends give new clothing, a new tipi, and other necessities to the family, permitting them to begin their lives anew.

Sun Dance. The sun dance is called Wi *wanyang wacipi* (from *wi* 'sun', *wanyang* 'to gaze', and *wacipi* 'they dance'; hence "sun-gazing dance"). This is the only calendrical ritual, performed in the summer, usually in June or July. During this time the numerous *tiyošpayes* assemble for the common buffalo hunt, and while they are gathered, certain men who have pledged to dance the sun dance fulfill their vows by praying for the welfare of the entire tribe and by undertaking various forms of sacrifice.

The sun dance site is chosen by mutual consent of the *tiyošpaye* leaders. Many tribes may be invited to participate and each takes its place in the camp circle. During these large gatherings, the circle may be as large as three quarters of a mile in diameter. The maintenance of order in camp is supervised by the *tiyošpaye* leaders, the sodalities, and the *akicita*. The performance of the sun dance and related ceremonies, however, is under the supervision of the sacred persons, from whom one is selected as sun dance

leader. After the camp circle has been established and preparations for the sun dance completed, the ritual itself begins and continues over a four-day period.

On the first day a place in the center of the camp circle is
selected where a hole will be dug and the sacred pole (*can wakan*)
erected. A scout is sent out to find a suitable cottonwood tree
(*wagacan*), which will later be captured by warriors who regard it
as an enemy to be subdued. While the scout is away from camp, as
many men as possible are selected to begin construction of the
sacred lodge (*iyohanziglepi* 'shade'), which is built around the
center hole.

The lodge is constructed of two rows of forked ash posts which
form concentric circles with an opening to the east. These posts are
joined with saplings, and pine trees and brush are laid across them
to form a shaded area where spectators will watch the Sun dance
and participants will occasionally rest. The diameter of the completed lodge is approximately twenty-five yards.

A person is selected to dig the hole for the sacred pole. Dirt
removed from the hole is formed into a square patch of earth to the
west of the pole. The digger is then instructed to follow the sun
dance leader, who walks from the center hole to the east, stopping
every four paces. At each place, the digger hammers a wooden
stake into the ground. The sun dance leader continues pacing until
sixteen stakes have been hammered in, and the sixteenth stake
marks the location of the sacred tipi (*tipi wakan*), where the sun
dancers will receive their instructions and stay for the duration of
the sun dance.

The floor of the sacred tipi is lined with sage (*pejiȟota*); an altar
(*owank wakan*) is constructed from mellowed earth at the west
side; and a buffalo skull whose orbital and nasal orifices are
plugged with sage is placed so that it faces west. During the
ceremonies in the sacred tipi, prayers will be offered so that the
buffalo spirit prevails and the people will be ensured of food over
the coming year.

Offerings of tobacco (*canli wapaȟte*) are attached to the sixteen stakes by the sun dancers, and no one may pass through the
line of stakes, which represents the path of the sun. A sweat lodge is
constructed on the north side of the sacred tipi where the par-

ticipants and their paraphernalia will be purified before the ritual begins.

On the second day the scout returns to camp announcing that he has found an enemy, and a large party of warriors and their female kin ride out to the place where the enemy has been discovered. It is normally located west of camp in such a place that the warriors must cross a small stream to reach it. Once the stream has been crossed and proper prayers intoned to the spirits of the water, the scout points out the cottonwood tree and the warriors rush it, counting coup on it. The sun dance leader then offers the pipe to the tree, touching the stem of his pipe to the trunk in four directions, moving around it sunwise from west to south. Brave warriors then begin to fell the tree, each striking it with an ax four times from each direction. When the tree is ready to fall, virgins are selected to fell the tree in such a way that it falls to the south. As the tree falls, there is a great shout and war songs are sung.

The tree is carefully trimmed and peeled except for the forked branches at the top. Then begins the procession carrying the tree back to the camp. Special carrying sticks approximately two feet long are used to carry the tree so that human hands will not touch it. The sticks are slid under the tree, and twenty to forty men on either side bear it along on the sticks. The procession stops to rest four times along the way, and on the fourth time, men who wish to compete for honors line up to race to the center hole in the sun dance lodge. The first to reach it will be entitled to carry a special banner.

On the third day the sacred pole is painted red on four sides of the trunk, at the base, and at the tip of the branches. Cherry branches are then secured at the fork of the sacred pole to form a cross, which is regarded as the nest of the Thunderbird. Rawhide effigies of a man and a buffalo are suspended from the crosspiece, and a banner of calfskin painted red is similarly tied in place. Other kinds of offerings such as tobacco or small bags of tallow may also be attached to the sacred pole.

At the appointed time, the sun dance leader directs selected men to raise the pole, placing the butt end into the hole. This is done in such a way that the pole is raised in four attempts, a quarter of the way each time with brief intervals in between during which the men rest. On the fourth time the pole is slid into the hole and earth is packed around it so that it stands firm. This action is described as *canpaslatapi* 'to erect a pole by pushing', a term also used synonymously for sacred pole.

Once the pole is in place, the warrior societies dress in their finest clothes and prepare for the *owank onasto wacipi* 'ground-flattening dance.' They load their guns and when the singing begins they dance to the west, firing their guns into the air. They dance back to the sacred pole and fire their guns at the effigies of the man and buffalo, each trying to hit them. The dance is repeated toward each of the remaining directions so that at the end of the dance, a flattened area in the form of a cross has been stamped into the earth. There is great rejoicing over the killing of the man and buffalo effigies, for this represents future success in hunting and victory in war. After the dance, men and women mount their horses and there is a great parade around the camp circle (*uucita* 'parade'). Sexual restrictions are temporarily lifted and the young men and women leave the camp circle and head for the seclusion of the outlying prairie.

During the first three days those men who have pledged to sacrifice themselves in the sun dance meet with their mentors and the sun dance leader for instructions. Each may pledge to dance in one of four ways: *wiwayang wacipi* 'gazing at the sun', *wicapahlo-kapi* 'pierced', *okaške wacipi* 'suspended', or *ptepa yuslohanpi* 'dragging buffalo skulls'. In the first form of the dance, the dancer gazes at the sun from dawn to dusk. In the second, both his breasts are pierced by a sacred person, wooden skewers are inserted, and the skewers are attached to two rawhide ropes, which are tied about halfway up the sacred pole. In the third form the dancer's breasts and the flesh over his scapulae are pierced, wooden skewers are inserted, and he is suspended between four posts, approximately one foot off the ground. In the fourth form, the flesh over the dancer's scapulae is pierced, wooden skewers are inserted, and thongs are attached to one or more buffalo skulls which he will be required to drag around the dance area. In the last three forms, the dancers must sacrifice themselves until the flesh has torn through. If they suffer for a long time, their comrades, female kin, or even children may assist them by adding their

Left: Medicine man praying with pipe before selecting sun dance pole. (All photographs in this section taken at the 1967 Pine Ridge sun dance. From the author's collection.)

Below: Carrying the sacred pole.

Right: Raising the sacred pole.

Below: Medicine man talking to dancers inside the sweat lodge.

Left: Procession of sun dancers leaving the sacred tipi.

Below: Medicine man piercing a dancer.

Above: Dancers saluting the sun.

Below: Dancers leaving the sun dance arbor, led by medicine man, carrying the pipe bag, and his assistant, carrying the buffalo skull.

weight, pulling back against the rawhide ropes. Children may be encouraged to ride on the buffalo skulls to expedite the release.

On the fourth day, before each prepares for his ordeal, the dancers, led by the sun dance leader, who carries the buffalo skull, leave the sacred tipi, walking along the south side of the sixteen offering stakes. They circle the sun dance lodge four times sunwise, and then enter the lodge. They are all barefoot and wear white deerskin kilts around their waists. Wreathes of sage are placed upon their heads and around their wrists. Suspended from their necks are rawhide disks which represent the sunflower. They hold eagle-bone whistles (*šiyotanka*) tipped with eagle down (*wacihin*) in their mouths. As the opening song of the sun dance starts, they bob up and down in a line, blowing on their whistles in time with the drum. During the course of this introductory dance they face each of the four directions.

The dancers may not eat or drink during their ordeal. To test their courage and stamina, an assistant of the sun dance leader holds a paunch of water in front of them as they dance and spills it casually on the ground. Occasionally the dancers may rest, but only after two of them have been selected by the sun dance leader to approach the singers with pipes. They dance up to the singers, holding the pipes in front of them while the head singer kneels in front of them. He stretches out his hands as if to take the pipe, but each time the dancers dance away from him. After he has feigned at the pipe three times, he accepts it on the fourth and the singers immediately stop singing and smoke the pipe. The dancers then retire underneath the shade until the singers have finished smoking, at which time the sun dance leader begins the dancing again.

When it is time to begin the ordeal, a buffalo robe is spread on the west side of the pole, and each dancer in turn lies on the robe. The sun dance leader makes the proper incisions with a steel awl (*tainšpa*) and his assistants tie the rawhide ropes to the skewers. During this period, other people may offer bits of flesh from their arms to *Wakantanka*. Men and women so desiring file up to the buffalo robe, and the sun dance leader or one of his assistants cut half-inch pieces of flesh from their arms. Women whose children have been sick over the winter may have their children's ears pierced at this time as a fulfillment of a vow. The piercing of ears is an act which incorporates children into the tribe, and is particularly auspicious during a sun dance, when the child forms a symbolic bond between himself and the pierced dancers.

After all the dancers have been freed from their ordeal, the sun dance is over. The men, however, are imbued with sacred power as a result of their ordeal and communication with *Wakantanka*, and they may invest some of their power in the sick by placing their hands on them. As the tribal camp circle breaks up, the ritual paraphernalia is given away, but the sun dance lodge and the sacred pole are left intact until they deteriorate from exposure to the elements and thus return to Mother Earth.

The Making of Relatives. The common name for this ritual is *Hunkalowanpi* 'Hunka ritual' (from *hunka*, regarded by most investigators as an exogenic term, and *lowanpi* 'they sing', i.e., a ritual). The ritual is also called *alowanpi* 'they sing on or over', referring to a specific part of the ritual in which wands (*hunkatacannunpa*, literally, *Hunka* "pipes") are waved over the participants (*hunkakazopi* 'wand waving'). An Oglala winter count for 1805 identifies that as the year in which "*tasinte un akicilowanpi*" 'they sang over each other with horsetails', horsetails referring to the manner in which the wands were decorated.

The purpose of the *Hunka* ritual is to create a bond between two people which is stronger than a kinship tie. The two people involved in this fictive relationship are obliged to die for each other if the need arises. One of the two is always older than the other and, after the ritual has established the bond, is referred to by the other as *Hunka ate* 'Hunka father'. The younger is called by the other *mihunka* 'my *Hunka*'. If he chooses, an adult may adopt more than one *hunka* at the same ceremony, and often more than one adult adopts one or more *hunka* at the same ceremony.

One wishing to initiate a *Hunkalowanpi* requests a sacred person to conduct the ceremony. A large tipi is erected in which an earthen altar is made, and upon it are laid a buffalo skull and a rack upon which the pipe and wands will be placed when not in use. Two wands are required, each approximately three feet in length and decorated with horsetails and feathers. In addition, two gourd rattles and another wand, to the end of which an ear of corn is skewered, are set on the altar. When the ceremony is about to begin, the prospective *hunkayapi* ('they call them *hunka*') are symbolically captured by the sacred person and his attendants and led into the tipi. All those who have *hunka* relationships also enter the lodge, and the ritual formally begins.

The sacred person then paints the faces of the *hunka* and waves the wands and rattles over them while he sings an appropriate song. The wand bearing the ear of corn is planted in the altar, reminding the people assembled of their obligation to Mother Earth. Those who are to be *Hunka ate* then sit beside their respective *hunkayapi* and are covered with a robe. The sacred person crawls under the covering with a small bag and the singers are commanded to sing. When the sacred person emerges, he sits at the west of the lodge and commands his assistants to remove the covering. When the cover is lifted, the *Hunka ate* and his *hunka* are sitting next to each other, side by side, with their arms and legs bound to each other, symbolic of their new relationship. With this the ritual ends, and gifts are exchanged between the families of the *Hunka ate* and *hunka*.

Girl's Puberty Ritual. At the onset of a girl's first menstruation, a puberty rite called *Išnati awicalowan* 'they sing over her first menses' was performed. *Išnati* literally means *to dwell alone* (from *isnala* 'alone' and *ti* 'to dwell'), and refers both to the act of menstruation and the isolation in which women lived during their menstrual period. The ritual has also been referred to as the Buffalo Ceremony inasmuch as the buffalo supernaturals guard over a woman's chastity and fecundity. It marks the passage from adolescense to womanhood, and during the performance the girl is instructed by a sacred person, before a large congregation, in her responsibilities to her family and people. The ritual also establishes her relationship with the sacred White Buffalo Calf Woman.

Within several days after the girl's menstrual period, her father requests a sacred person to conduct the ritual. The mother and her female relatives erect a new tipi, and the girl is instructed to place her menstrual bundle in a plum tree to safeguard it from the evil influences of Inktomi. A new altar is constructed, and a buffalo skull, pipe, prayer wands, bowl, and sweet-smelling grasses are placed on it. The sacred person in his role of conductor dresses in a buffalo headdress and wears behind him a buffalo tail. All outstanding men and women are invited to the tipi, but women who are having their menstrual periods are not permitted to enter lest they ritually pollute the sacred paraphernalia or render the ritual inefficacious. When all have been seated, the girl is instructed to sit between the altar and the fireplace, cross-legged like men and children.

The sacred person fills and smokes the pipe and blows smoke into the orbital and nasal orifices of the buffalo skull. He then applies red paint to the forehead of the skull, from which a red line runs perpendicularly back to the occipital region. He then instructs the girl to be industrious like the spider, silent and wise like the turtle, and cheerful like the meadowlark. If she heeds those words, men will pay bride-price for her and she will bear many children. The sacred person then cautions her about evil influences. He tells her that she is now a buffalo cow and he is a bull. The singing begins, and he dances toward her, lowing like a bull during the rutting season. As he dances up to her, he sidles up to her just as buffalo do in their mating ritual. Each time he sidles up to her, the girl's mother places sage under her arms and in her lap. The sacred person then places the bowl filled with water and chokecherries on the ground and tells the girl that this is a buffalo watering hole on the prairie, whereupon the girl bends over and drinks from it in imitation of a buffalo. Once she has consumed some of the water and chokecherry mixture, the remainder is passed around so that all may drink. The girl is then instructed to sit in the sacred place in the manner of a woman, with both legs to one side of her.

She is instructed to take off her dress. The sacred person places it over the buffalo skull, saying that the girl now gives her dress to the buffalo woman and any needy person may come and get it. A needy woman from outside the tipi enters and takes the dress. The mother then parts the girl's hair, permitting it to fall to the shoulders and hang in front, rather than behind, which is the hairstyle of children. The sacred person paints her forehead red, with a red line extending through the part of her hair. The mother is directed to remove the binding which secured the girl's menstrual bundle. At this juncture she is told that she is now a woman and may leave the lodge. All the people then leave the tipi and take part in a feast in the girl's honor.

Throwing of the Ball. This ritual is called *Tapa wankayeyapi* 'throwing up the ball' (from *tapa* 'ball', *wanka* 'upward', and *yeyapi* 'they cause to go'). This ritual was taught to the Oglalas in a vision in which a man saw a little buffalo calf grow into a human. She had a ball made from a buffalo hide covering stuffed with buffalo hair. She tossed the ball to a herd of buffalo standing in the west and they immediately turned into humans, one catching the ball and returning it to her. This was repeated to the four directions, after which time the girl again turned into a buffalo calf.

In the ritual, a young girl stands in the center of a playing field, while large numbers of people stand at the four directions. She throws a round ball which is symbolically painted to represent the universe in turn to each of the four directions, beginning with the west, and each person in that group attempts to catch it. The one who succeeds offers the ball to the four directions and the zenith and nadir, and then returns it to the girl for the next throw.

It is said that the ball represents *Wakantanka* and the teams of competitors represent people scrambling to be close to the spirits in the modern world. In the old days, each person had an opportunity to catch the sacred ball, but today only a few are capable of catching it. The ball is symbolic of knowledge, and people's attempt to catch it represents the struggle of people submerged in ignorance to free themselves.

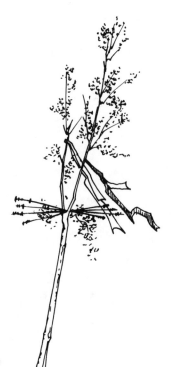

Part III

ALL MY
RELATIONS

Chapter 9

PINE RIDGE

THE RESERVATION

Pine Ridge is a literal translation of the Lakota *Wazi ahanhan,* a name applied to the characteristic topography of the reservation: rolling prairie land broken by whiteface buttes dotted with yellow pine. The Pine Ridge Indian Reservation, as the Oglala reservation is officially called, is located in southwestern South Dakota. The western boundary is marked by the Fall River–Shannon county line, approximately sixty-five miles due east of the South Dakota–Wyoming state line. The western part of the reservation leads to the foothills of the Black Hills through the off-reservation town of Oelrichs. North of Oelrichs are the city of Hot Springs and the Black Hills proper.

The northern boundary of the reservation is marked prominently by the Badlands National Monument and the off-reservation towns of Scenic, Interior, and Kadoka, South Dakota. To the east, Pine Ridge shares a common border with the Rosebud Indian Reservation, home of the Sicangu, the division of the two reservations being demarcated in the north by Black Pipe Creek. To the south, the reservation boundary line is contiguous with the Nebraska–South Dakota state line.

The Pine Ridge Reservation is second in size only to the Navajo Reservation. It comprises a total area of 2,786,540 acres, or 4,353 square miles. It is approximately rectangular in shape, fifty miles north to south and one hundred miles east to west. Its boundaries were established in 1889 (Maynard and Twiss, 1970). The reservation is comprised of three South Dakota counties—Shannon, Washabaugh, and Bennett. The latter is organized with its own government and is therefore referred to as the ceded portion of the reservation. However, there is still federal land held in trust for Indians in Bennett County and its Indian residents are represented on the Oglala Sioux Tribal Council.

The seat of Pine Ridge tribal government and headquarters for the Bureau of Indian Affairs is Pine Ridge Village, located two miles north of the Nebraska state line at the junction of Nebraska State Highway 87 and U.S. Highway 18 in South Dakota. For administrative purposes, the reservation was originally divided into seven districts, the administrative district being called *Wakpamni* (literally, "distribution," i.e., the place where annuities are distributed to the Oglalas, and also the name of the town of Pine Ridge). The other districts were White Clay (additionally the name of a creek, a dam, and an off-reservation town two miles south in Nebraska), Wounded Knee, Porcupine, Medicine Root, Eagle Nest, and Pass Creek. Later, Pass Creek was divided into two districts, Pass Creek and LaCreek, making a total of eight districts.

The Oglala Sioux Tribal Council, which was established as a result of the Indian Reorganization Act of 1934, is comprised of a president, vice president, secretary, and treasurer, and one councilman from each of the eight districts. The tribal council is organized as a bureaucracy which ultimately answers to the superintendent, the resident representative of the Bureau of Indian Affairs; the area director, located in Aberdeen, South Dakota; the commissioner of Indian affairs in Washington, D.C.; and the secretary of the interior. The tribal council is authorized by Congress, with the approval of its superior chain of command, to transact business on behalf of the Oglala people, who elect their duly sworn representatives in reservation-wide balloting every two years.

The eight districts today are comprised of numerous communities which are located primarily along creeks, and are thus known as *wakpala* 'creek' or, properly, *oti* 'community' (from *o* 'in' and *ti* 'to dwell'). After the historical incidents which led to the establishment of the Pine Ridge Agency (the Treaty of Fort Laramie, 1868, and battle of the Little Big Horn, 1876), the roving *tiyošpayes* were eventually required to settle down on the reservation. In 1878–79, when the Oglalas were moved from their agency near Crawford, Nebraska, to Pine Ridge, the seven *tiyošpayes* settled in the following way:

1. The Tapišlecas, Wagluĥes, Itešicas, and Payabyas settled in what is now Wakpamni District.
2. The Oyuĥpes settled in what is now Wounded Knee District.
3. The Wajajes settled in Porcupine District.
4. The Kiyaksas established their homes in Medicine Root District (cf. Powers, 1963:35–36).

In 1887, the Dawes Act (land allotment act) was passed by Congress requiring the allotment of Indian reservations in severalty. In addition to being criticized by the mjority of Oglalas on ideological grounds (the land could not be "owned"), it necessitated a rearrangement of social organization antithetical to the original *tiyošpaye* organization. Individual families within the *tiyošpayes* were required to set up independent households, fairly evenly distributed throughout the seven (later eight) districts, with the exception of districts in Bennett County, where "surplus" lands were bought up by non-Indians. Since 1887 there has been both a reduction in reservation land and an increase in the number of small communities. In 1970, eighty-nine communities were reported for the entire reservation (Maynard and Twiss, 1970).

The total population of Pine Ridge has been estimated at between 13,500 (ibid.) and 15,000 (Deloria, 1974). Population density is approximately 3.1 persons per square mile. Seventy-four percent of the population is Indian, and of the Indian population, 48 percent is full-blood. Approximately 2 percent of the full-blood population is from other tribes, mainly from the adjacent Rosebud Reservation.

Sixty-eight percent of the Oglalas are bilingual, and among the sixty-five-year-old group no full-bloods speak only English. Only 17 percent of all the Indians have no knowledge of their native language, but there is a general apprehension among older people that the young ones are losing their language. Lakota is taught at both the government schools and mission schools, and Lakota bilingual education materials are being developed in a number of subjects. Most courses are taught by native speakers under the direction of a linguist employed by the tribe.

INCOME, HOUSING, AND PUBLIC HEALTH

A 1969 Senate subcommittee on American Indian education found the results of its investigation of contemporary Indian education (and concomitantly employment, alcoholism, suicides, standards of housing, life span, and other measures of statistical value) equally a "national tragedy and a national disgrace" (Kennedy, 1969). The national average statistics for Native Americans are typified by the Oglalas: inordinately high un- or underemployment, inadequate housing, high rates of dropout, grim rates of suicide and alcoholism among young people.

The average income of the Oglalas places them below the poverty level. In 1970, sixty-three percent of Oglala families reported an income of less than $3,000 per annum. There is less income among those Oglalas who regard themselves as full-blood than among mixed-bloods. In 1970, the unemployment rate on the Pine Ridge Reservation was 36.6 percent, roughly ten times the national average. Over one-fourth of the employed Oglalas were employed only part-time (Maynard and Twiss, 1970).

Over half of those employed work for the Bureau of Indian Affairs, Office of Economic Opportunity, the Oglala Sioux Tribe, or the Public Health Service. Others earn an income in light industry and road construction. The only industry on the Pine Ridge Reservation today is the Moccasin Factory located in Pine Ridge Village. At one time Wright-McGill produced fishhooks on the reservation, but their last factory closed in 1968. Over one-third of the mixed-blood work force, and 3 percent of the full-bloods are self-employed, mainly at ranching. Still others are engaged in seasonal harvesting, mainly potato and beet picking in Nebraska. Indians who own their own land as a result of the Dawes Act lease their unused land mainly to white ranchers, but Indian ranchers have first bid on open land. Oglala cattlemen pay a rate of $20.50 per head of cattle annually. Non-Indians bid on land not used by Oglalas and often pay two or three times the rate paid by Oglalas (ibid.).

Unearned income (aid to dependent children, aid to the disabled, aid to the blind, old-age assistance, and BIA general assistance) is most prevalent among full-bloods. Many Indian families are eligible to receive commodities such as flour, lard, powdered milk, canned meats and fruits, and, occasionally, beef.

Most housing on the reservation is regarded as substandard compared with general conditions in the United States. Thirty-three percent of the houses are log cabins, many of them built about 1868. They were originally constructed with dirt floors and sod roofs, but many have been renovated by adding a stucco veneer, wooden floors, and shingled roofs. Typically, the log cabin has one room in which there are a central wood stove for heating and cooking, enough beds to accommodate the residents, table and chairs, and miscellaneous cupboards, shelves, bureaus, and other household needs. Only 40 percent of homes have inside plumbing; drinking water is pumped from a local well or is hauled from a more distant one. A bucket containing drinking water is normally found indoors, as is a so-called slop bucket, used for garbage. Outdoor privies are the norm, even where there is running water.

Except for the brick government buildings, the remainder of Oglala housing is of frame construction, often with several rooms. Contemporary dwellings have been made available by the federal government and are occupied mainly by mixed-bloods. Prefabricated houses from the former military base at Igloo, South Dakota, have recently been made available to the Oglalas at a minimal price. These "Igloo houses" are first offered to welfare families or to those with a minimal income, much to the consternation of Oglalas who work for the Bureau of Indian Affairs or some other government agency, but who cannot afford the more luxurious modern homes. The argument over who is more entitled to new housing is only part of a larger on-going debate between full-bloods and mixed-bloods over manifest favoritism by the federal government.

Oglala homes are usually regarded as overcrowded; however, statistically the modal home of two rooms houses 1.81 Indians per room. This does not take into consideration the size of the room or use of outdoor space, summer tents, or outdoor cooking arbors, which are integral to most Oglala households outside the reservation towns.

Since the establishment of the reservation, medical facilities have been made available to the Oglalas. Originally, physicians who also served in other administrative roles were assigned to the districts. In 1930, the Bureau of Indian Affairs opened a hospital on the north ridge of Pine Ridge Village. In 1955, the medical care of Indians came under the jurisdiction of the U.S. Public Health Service, Indian Health Service branch. The Public Health Service still maintains the Pine Ridge hospital and out-patient clinics and some field service to the local communities. In 1965, a mental health program was inaugurated which provided somewhat limited psychiatric care and administered a research program in mental health.

Health problems, particularly among the full-bloods, are found among 33 percent of the people. Statistically, the Oglalas have twice as many mental and physical disabilities as non-Indians. The most common medical problems are arthritis, diabetes, and heart trouble, but long-term disabilities often go untreated or only partly treated. Among the full-bloods, there is the myth that the white physician is capable of curing any illness immediately by the dispensation of an appropriate medication. Oglalas who require long-range medication often discard their prescriptions once they feel relief from their immediate symptoms, only to suffer a relapse, sometimes fatal.

Inasmuch as the medical staff is temporary, there is little opportunity for close doctor-patient relationships to develop. The effectiveness of the medical staff is always being questioned by the full-bloods, particularly by native practitioners and ritual specialists. Many full-bloods ignore the Public Health Service, and when they are obliged to consult a physician, travel to private doctors in nearby Nebraska towns. There they may receive consultation and treatment without waiting in the long lines at the Pine Ridge Hospital, and they also feel that their association with the off-reservation doctors is more personal and, therefore, beneficial.

CHRISTIAN INFLUENCES

The two leading Christian denominations on the Pine Ridge Reservation are the Roman Catholic and Episcopalian. The former, called *Sapa un* ('to wear black', hence the "Black Robes"), claims the largest Christian membership, nearly 45 percent of the

Christian Oglalas. The latter, called *Ska un* ('to wear white', hence "White Robes"), claims 38 percent of the Christian Oglalas; however, it has more full-bloods among its constituency than the Roman Catholic (Maynard, 1969).

This distribution has emerged from historic circumstances. The Episcopalians, in 1875, were the first to establish a mission on Pine Ridge. The Holy Cross Episcopal Church is still maintained at Pine Ridge Village; however, unlike the Roman Catholic Church, it does not provide educational facilities on the reservation. In addition, there are twenty-eight other churches scattered throughout the reservation. Episcopal clergymen are augmented by lay leaders, most of whom are Oglalas, and preach in the native Lakota. Like other missionaries, the Episcopalians translated readings and psalms into the native language and continue to use it today to attract more members. Not only have the Oglalas been exposed longer to the Episcopalians, but their use of the native language appears to have some effect on reaching more full-bloods.

Although Jesuits have proselytized among the Sioux since their first contact in the seventeenth century, it was not until 1888 that the Holy Rosary Mission was established by German Jesuits on the Pine Ridge Reservation, four miles north of Pine Ridge Village. The mission was originally a gift of Katharine Drexel, daughter of a Philadelphia philanthropist, and during its early development was known as Drexel Mission. Like the Episcopalians, the Jesuits translated Christian scripture into Lakota, but in addition developed other literature of a more scholarly nature. Particularly significant is the work of Eugene Buechel, S.J., who wrote the first grammar of the Lakota dialect as well as a Lakota-English dictionary published posthumously (Beuchel, 1939, 1970).

The Presbyterian Church reaches approximately 11 percent of the Christian Oglalas; and the Body of Christ Church, somewhat over 1 percent. The remaining Christian sects, including the Native American Church, or "Peyote Cult," each claims less than 1 percent of the Christian Oglalas. These include the Church of Jesus Christ of Latter Day Saints (Mormons), Seventh Day Adventist, Church of God, Lutheran, Gospel Missionary Union, Congregational, Methodist, and Baptist (Maynard, 1969).

The early attitudes of the missionaries toward the Oglalas is reflected in the work of the Jesuit Louis Goll; for example: "The Sioux tribes even prior to the advent of the Catholic missionaries believed in God, in one God only. There is among them no trace of real polytheism, no trace of idolatry" (Goll, 1940:14). Ritual specialists were characterized in the following manner:

> While there was very little real worship of God, there existed a good deal of superstition among the Sioux. Clever and cunning men, called medicine men, wielded a baneful influence over the people, making them believe that they had seen visions or had had significant dreams after going through certain rites of fasting. After such a dream, the medicine men would tell, for example, where the hunters could find buffaloes. Of course, the medicine men had previously located the animals. [Ibid.: 15]

These attitudes persisted through the 1950s. Native religion was regarded by missionaries, particularly the Roman Catholics, as the work of the devil. This had an interesting effect on the Oglalas: at the same time missionaries were attempting to eradicate all signs of native religion, the Oglalas were positive that it worked. Those who subscribed to more than one religion, mainly native religion and Christianity, were regarded as transitional. Even medicine men attended Catholic mass, participating fully in holy communion—according to priests, a sure sign of their Catholicism.

At one time, like the Episcopalians, the Roman Catholics sponsored a laiety called the St. Joseph and Mary Societies. These societies were made up of catechists who conducted Catholic rituals in the absence of priests. Originally there were twenty-nine chapels distributed throughout the Pine Ridge communities, but because of a shortage of priests, regular masses were conducted at only a few of them. The catechists, in lieu of regular attendance by the itinerant priests, conducted prayer services, maintained the chapels, and served as liaisons between the church and Catholic laymen. As more Oglalas were consolidated into merging communities, the number of Catholic chapels decreased, as did that of sodality members. Without the presence of the church in the remote areas of the reservation, native religion continued to flourish as it had before, but without the overt criticism of the visiting priests.

Through the 1940s it was taken for granted by missionaries and anthropologists that native religion was on the wane. But even Macgregor reported during his research at Pine Ridge that "the acceptance of Christianity was at first and continues to be to some extent today, an acceptance of the deity of the conquerors and a search for his power, without complete abandonment of the old beliefs" (Macgregor, 1946:92, cited in Maynard, 1969:1).

It should be noted here that whether or not the Oglalas accepted the deity of their conquerors or completely abandoned their native religion, there has never been any empirical evidence to favor one or the other. The Oglalas had in fact accepted the technology of the white man and had succumbed to his political authority. But to what extent they accepted his deity must go challenged. What was not reported by the missionaries or by anthropologists is that during the 1940s, and conceivably since the missionaries first came in contact with the Oglalas, Oglala medicine men were challenging the white man's god. But the missionaries were not aware of the Oglala polemics against Christianity, because they could only be "superstitious." At the same time missionaries were working out conversion strategies that would make Christianity somehow analogous to native religion, medicine men were discussing how Christianity was ambiguous in its own terms. Young Oglalas forced to go to mission schools were required to cut their hair, and then, much to their astonishment, were given a picture of a hirsute Jesus and his disciples (Deloria, 1969:109). The Catholics preached against the evils of alcoholism, but allowed their priests to drink wine at mass. When the medicine men explained the notion of praying over minute packets of tobacco offerings to the spirits, the Catholics (and anthropologists) reported it as a form of saying the rosary, and a diagnostic of Christian elements in native religion.

During the 1950s, younger Jesuits attempted to provide a scheme of Christianity that was even more relevant to the Oglalas. With a decline in membership as well as in the number of local chapels, missionaries began to redesign the ritual in such a way that it would become more appealing to potential adherents. The work of the Reverend Paul Steinmetz, S.J., is instructive, and typical, at least on the Northern Plains reservations, of relevant models for Indian Christianity.

Steinmetz, who was parish priest at the Sacred Heart Mission in Pine Ridge Village, began participating in local native ceremonies, much to the consternation of his superiors. His objective was to create a more relevant connection between native religion and Catholicism. He designed a new church in Pine Ridge Village, one whose symbolism would reflect Oglala beliefs as well as Catholic. He also initiated the use of the sacred pipe as a part of the mass. He writes:

> The Pipe is a type of Christ because it is the instrument of the mediator in the Sioux religion just as the Sacred Humanity is the instrument of Christ the Mediator in our Christian Religion. Christ fulfills the Pipe rather than destroys it since He does in a more perfect way what the person praying with the Pipe does in an imperfect way. The Pipe, then, is the great Sioux foreshadowing of Christ in his Priestly Office. [Steinmetz, 1969:20]

Steinmetz went on to employ and publish prayers to be used with the sacred pipe. Little did he know at that time that the practicing ritual specialists among the Oglalas, the same medicine men who sat in the front pew at his church every Sunday, were greatly impressed by the fact that he, a Jesuit priest, had finally seen the light! While the Jesuits were creating a new relationship between Christ and the flock, the Oglalas were asserting that the priests were at last recognizing the potency of *Wakantanka* and the efficacy of the sacred rituals first brought to the people by the Sacred Buffalo Calf Woman.

Chapter 10

POLITICAL DISCONTINUITY

TRADITION VERSUS BUREAUCRACY

During my earlier visits to Pine Ridge in the 1950s, the town of Pine Ridge (since called Pine Ridge Village) served as a geographic symbol of the dichotomy between Indians and whites. The town was roughly divided in half by U.S. Highway 18, the west side representing the federal government, the Bureau of Indian Affairs, the jail and courthouse, the distribution center for annuities, the tribal office, and the Oglala Community High School, one of the many boarding schools operated by the BIA. The east side was the town proper, consisting of the frame and stucco homes of Pine Ridge residents, the *ieska,* or mixed-bloods. The east-west division was somewhat mediated by a square block of churches, service stations, a drugstore, pool hall, two cafes, and a supermarket. The town had its own hotel, Gerber's, a barber shop, and a post office. Eventually these landmarks changed hands and the corner hallmark, the Gates Store, was torn down and ultimately replaced by the more modern Billy Mills Hall, which now houses the post office and serves as a town meeting hall as well as a center for teenage "white" dances and indoor powwows.

On "office day" (Monday), the horses and wagons, and some automobiles, made their way into Pine Ridge over miles and miles of wagon roads leading from the small communities in the districts. On Saturdays, the people came into town to shop and gossip. The grandparents, men with long braids and women in long dresses, sat along Highway 18, changing their positions with the sun, watching a steady stream of "odd" cars from out of state coming to a full stop in front of the Gates Store, only to start up again for the Black Hills or Badlands to the north and west: white tourists perhaps amused with the tranquillity of the small Indian town and the quaintness of its residents, pictures of another era in their tall hats and braids, some still wearing moccasins.

This geographic distinction changed slowly in the 1960s. The population grew from three hundred to perhaps one thousand. Many of the residents were really transients, moving back and forth from their homes in the country to dilapidated shacks on the east side. New housing projects like the North Ridge Estates, a senior citizens' home opposite the expanded public health facilities; the Moccasin Factory; and a spate of trailer homes began to change the complexion of Pine Ridge.

Although the geographic distinction was less clearly defined, the ideological split between Indian and white was still keenly felt. It was not only between Oglalas and non-Oglalas, but between what was later to be formally called sociological full-bloods and mixed-bloods (Macgregor, 1946:25) or country Indians (Wax, Wax, and Dumont, 1964; Kemnitzer, 1968) and their urban or town counterparts. Although formalized by anthropologists, the distinction was clearly a part of the Oglalas' emic model of the Pine Ridge Reservation. The traditional Oglalas, those who lived in the country in the small communities, some of which still bear the names of the original *tiyošpaye* leaders, represented a culture separate not only from that of the white man, but from that of the mixed-bloods, the offsprings of the (predominantly) French and Indian marriages of two generations ago. To these traditionalists, the west side of town still represented the seat of power and authority, exemplified by the Oglala Sioux Tribal Council, incorporated in 1936 as a result of the Indian Reorganization Act of 1934 (McNickle, 1973). The council, in theory, represented the interests of all Oglalas, but over the years it was the mixed-bloods who commanded the power invested in them through the local superintendent, the Bureau of Indian Affairs, the Department of the Interior, and Congress itself.

Power and authority were, and still are today, expressed in economic terms. It was the mixed-bloods who got the jobs with the Bureau of Indian Affairs and other federal agencies. The discontent over full-bloods' being rejected for jobs was often reflected in such statements as "If you have an Indian name, don't even apply for the job." The traditionalists still feel that "real Indians" are discriminated against by their mixed-blood tribesmen, a notion held over from the time when the sons of French traders and Indian mothers were regarded as the most educable inasmuch as they were bilingual (and because they "inherited" the economic rationale from their fathers).

There are other than economic distinctions which are not so sharply defined and which cannot be correlated with the Indian or European sound of surnames. Many full-bloods in fact hold government jobs; and many mixed-bloods live like traditional Oglalas when they leave their government jobs in the afternoon, returning to an "Indian" household. The Indian–non-Indian, or full-blood–mixed-blood distinction is more profitably analyzed as a continuum. Most Oglalas live in the midrange of the scale despite the composition of their names, or their source (or absence) of income. At the ends of the continuum we find traditional Oglalas at one extreme and the bureaucrats at the other. Most people move back and forth along the continuum situationally: in dealing with matters of kin, it is more profitable to be Oglala; in dealing with matters of economics, one switches to his "white" side.

Pine Ridge Village cannot really be regarded as an Indian community. There is an absence of any traditional ties between its residents and preexisting *tiyošpayes* because its residents are primarily mixed-blood. The tribal council members, however, who are representative of their districts and communities indeed have direct ties with *tiyošpayes*. Their allegiance to *tiyošpaye* leaders of generations ago is based on current kinship ties. And herein lies the predicament and paradox: bureaucratic leaders are given the constitutional responsibility of acting on behalf of all Oglalas (that is, all *tiyošpayes*), when their kinship responsibilities lie primarily with their respective *tiyošpayes*, exclusive of all others. The federal government has ignored the traditional *tiyošpaye* leaders in favor of a centralized, bureaucratic government. This more than anything else has led to the political problems of the Pine Ridge Reservation. According to one government official, the lack of recognition of local leadership, and the establishment of a tribal council may account for the political factionation that is the hallmark of Pine Ridge. He writes: "In the view of most technicians, and particularly that of the representatives of those federal agencies concerned, Pine Ridge has long been considered a 'trouble spot' in terms of social and political disorganization" (Feraca, 1966:1).

The social and political disorganization of course stems from the same dilemma faced by all colonized people: to what extent can a traditional society function under a superimposed bureaucratic structure? But underlying this question is one of more practical importance to the Oglalas. They ask not so much who represents the leadership of the reservation, but rather, just who the real Oglalas are.

The descendants of the *tiyošpaye* leaders, the traditional Oglalas, are not unaware of their de facto loss of power and authority. The Oglalas have become accustomed to changing their life style since the beginning of the reservation period. Each new administration brought changes, as did each agent in charge of Pine Ridge. In 1881, it was decreed by the federal government that the Oglalas must curtail the sun dance, and the "last" was held near the bald-face buttes in northern Nebraska easily observable from the present sun dance grounds. The Oglalas were powerless to reverse this federal mandate, but the institution of the sun dance was not easily abdicated. It was held out in the hills away from the white people until after the passage of the Indian Reorganization Act of 1934, when it was formally reinstated.

Although some were afraid that the assassination of Crazy Horse at Fort Robinson (Crawford), Nebraska, in 1877 heralded the final downfall (Sandoz, 1942), that notion was premature. In 1889, the Oglalas living at Pine Ridge, as well as other Northern Plains tribes, heard that somewhere in the west the sun had died, and that a new messiah who favored the Indian over the white man awaited them. There was a new religion underway, one called by the whites the ghost dance craze (see particularly Mooney, 1896), which would herald a new day for the downtrodden Indian. The messiah preached that a time would come when the earth would be overturned, and the white man with it. The old Indians who had died and the buffalo would return again, and the old life would be resumed.

The Oglalas sent emissaries to Walker Lake, Nevada, to meet with the new prophet, a Paiute Indian named Wovoka. He himself had "died" and had communicated with the deceased. There he was told of a new Indian gospel, one which stated: "Jesus is now upon the earth. He appears like a cloud. The dead are all alive again. I do not know when they will be here; maybe this fall or in the spring. When the time comes there will be no more sickness and everyone will be young again" (Mooney, 1896:23).

The Oglalas adapted the *Wanagi wacipi* 'ghost dance' to their own modes of cultural expression. They planted a sacred tree and the adepts danced around it, falling into trances. During the trances the dancers visited with the deceased and came back to life to sing songs about their visions. Although warned by the prophet not to fight with the white man, the Oglalas donned sacred ghost shirts (*ogle wakan* 'sacred shirt') which were believed to be impenetrable by the white man's bullets.

Not only the Oglalas but other Sioux became involved in the ghost dance religion. Sitting Bull, leader of the Hunkpapas on the Standing Rock Reservation, became a ghost dance leader. He was invited to Pine Ridge to meet the prophet, but when he requested a pass from his agent, the latter, fearing hostilities and another uprising, commanded his Indian police force to arrest the old man. On December 15, 1890, a detachment of police under the command of Lieutenant Bull Head attempted to arrest Sitting Bull, and during the fracas the Hunkpapa was killed (Vestal, 1932).

Some of Sitting Bull's followers joined Big Foot's band of Mnikowojus who were planning to travel to Pine Ridge and participate in a large ghost dance. Warned of his arrival, the Pine Ridge agent sent Colonel George A. Forsyth and, ironically, remnants of Custer's Seventh Cavalry, to intercept Big Foot and his followers. On December 29, the interception took place on Wounded Knee Creek, sixteen miles east of Pine Ridge Agency. The old chief was suffering from pneumonia, but he and his 106 men, and 250 women and children were required to halt and set up their tipis. They were surrounded by nearly 500 men and four Hotchkiss guns, strategically located on a slight rise over the grassy plain. The next morning, the Indians were disarmed and routed out of their tipis, where the soldiers tore apart their belongings looking for concealed weapons. Shocked at the indignity, an old man cried out that the people should resist, and a shot rang out. Immediately a command was given to fire and the Hotchkiss guns exploded their shells in the huddled group of Indians lined up in front of their tipis. Trying to flee for their lives, Indians ran for cover along the creek bed, but within the hour 40 men and 200 women and children had been massacred. Some bodies were found as far away as three miles from the point of interception. A blizzard blew, and the frozen bodies of the Indians were buried unceremoniously in a common trench. Forsyth was charged with misconduct, but 23 of his men received the Medal of Honor for "heroic action" at Wounded Knee.

The year 1890 also signaled another event. The federal government required all Oglalas who were currently ghost keeping to release their souls on an appointed day (Brown, 1953).

ACCULTURATION AND DECULTURATION

The Oglalas at Pine Ridge never quite recuperated from the grim horror of Wounded Knee. It has been only within the past decade that most of the survivors have died, and their children still live to retell their families' involvement in the massacre. It is not surprising that members of the American Indian Movement, when appealed to by the traditional faction of the Oglala Sioux Tribal Council to intervene in local political matters, selected Wounded Knee as the site for their seventy-one-day protest in 1973–74. A year earlier, approximately two hundred young adults destroyed the Wounded Knee museum adjacent to the battlefield. Indian photographs were torn, artifacts destroyed or stolen, and the interior of the museum vandalized. It was as if the young Indians were destroying that what was symbolic of their oppression and despair; the only Indians that white people knew were the Indians in books, photographs, and museums (cf. Douglas, 1970:xi–xvi).

Despite the outcome of the ghost dance movement and the ongoing pressure by the federal government to transform Oglalas into white men, neither military strategy nor congressional legislation was capable of eliminating tribal identity. Visitors to the reservation were prone to judge the seat of power, Pine Ridge Village, as typical of the acculturation process to which the Oglalas were inevitably resigned. But out in the districts this resignation was hardly apparent, although deculturation was anticipated to be the lot of even the country Indians.

As Feraca states:

> Despite the ill effects of the allotment system and ongoing decultura-
> tion, the Oglala have tenaciously held to the modified form of the
> traditional band. Called communities by Whites, the Lakota equiva-
> lent is still *tiyošpaye*. These groups continue to maintain their struc-
> ture and identity despite what might be regarded as overwhelming
> odds to their disfavor. Communities were rarely considered as such in
> administrative programming; indeed the identity or existence of
> many was unknown except to day school teachers and a few field
> workers. [Feraca, 1966:6]

Part of this tenacity may be ascribed to a set of values which the traditionalists recognize as *Lakol wicoȟʼan*, commonly glossed as "the Indian Way" (from *Lakol*, attenuated form of *Lakota*, 'In-dian'; and *wicoȟʼan* 'act, deed, way'). The Indian Way is a set of beliefs which ranks certain values as superior to the white man's. This notion of superiority should not be taken as a new phenome-non, nor should it be interpreted as merely a psychological com-pensation for the reality of white dominance. The Oglalas and other Sioux have always regarded themselves as superior not only to the white man, but to other tribes. According to Walker:

> Those who speak certain dialects and conform to certain customs and
> usages are Lakota. The Lakota are allied against all others of
> mankind, though they may war among themselves. They are *oyate
> ikce* (native people), and are *ankatu* (superior), while all others of
> mankind are *oyate unma* (other-people), who are *ihukuya* (con-
> sidered-inferior). This is the relation of the Lakota to all others of
> mankind, and if any refuse to acknowledge this relation they are
> *tokoyapi* [*sic*] (considered-enemies), and should be treated as such.
> [Walker, 1914:97]

The traditional Oglalas, despite their superiority, are not oblivious to the predominance of the white man's technology on the reservation and off. Many are anxious to receive new housing and new meeting places for their communities. When lease money comes due, the old people buy new cars for themselves or finance cars for their children and grandchildren. At small feasts and larger celebrations, participants are harangued by the elders about the necessity of education for the younger generation. Light industry is welcome because it means the young people will not have to leave the reservation for employment. A high priority is placed on buying new clothing—straw hats and Stetsons, boots, flashy shirts and Levis, leather belts with western buckles—all in anticipation of entering school, participating in a powwow or rodeo, or taking an off-reservation trip to visit urban relatives and friends. But the extent to which acquiring the white man's technology has made the Oglalas more Western must be seriously questioned. These manifest forms of so-called acculturation or deculturation have been offered in the past as indicators of culture change without examination of the extent to which Western technology has in fact become "Indianized," that is, to what extent traditional Oglala values have been applied to culturally intrusive elements of Euro-American design. But there are indications that the Oglalas have adapted intrusive element to their own value system rather than adopt a new value system along with the intrusive elements. A rereading of anthropological and missionary literature provides some corroboration.

CONTINUITY

If we examine those manifest aspects of political power at Pine Ridge, it is clear that there is political discontinuity with respect to native Oglala sociopolitical organization. But if we investigate other kinds of values, the less obvious ideational systems in conflict on the reservation, another kind of conclusion may be drawn.

One of the major ambiguities recorded for the Oglalas, as well as other tribes, is the apparent ambivalence with which Indians practice Christianity and native religion simultaneously. Although Christian missionaries have always required a definite distinction between the two, most Christian Oglalas have not. If we examine the earlier missionary literature, it becomes apparent that missionary zeal was often the major cause of misunderstanding or ignoring the existence of two religious standards.

Writing for the period following the Wounded Knee massacre, Goll states that

> the early missionaries found that the Fourth of July celebrations among the Indians were often occasions for reviving harmful practices. The reason was not hard to find. The Indians could hardly be expected to take an interest in the speeches and fireworks of that day. They could not speak of liberation but of subjugation.... When the Indians gathered together...all the old customs, especially the vicious "give away," were revived. [Goll, 1940:39]

Goll continues by saying that Bishop Marty found a way to prevent this "misfortune" by establishing the first Catholic congress in July 1891. It was held on the Standing Rock Reservation, and Christian Indians had to travel a great distance on their "pilgrimage." A description of the moving camps is instructive. Here I paraphrase Goll (ibid.: 39–43).

When Indians traveled in those days, the whole family went—by horse and wagon. A caravan of forty or fifty wagons made the journey, and stopping places were predetermined by "officers" who assigned camping grounds to the travelers from the same districts. During the stops, officials took care of the horses and women prepared the evening meal. All gathered around the missionary's tent for the evening prayer. The people then retired and were awakened at dawn by the camp crier. The wagons were loaded and the caravan proceeded. Upon arrival at the congress meeting, officials assigned camp grounds to the travelers "in such a way that the entire assembly formed a large circle." The formal welcome was held after supper "in a bower made of branches cut in the woods nearby." The hosts sat on one side and visitors on the other, and while singing, persons would walk around the circle shaking hands with each other. Between 1900 and 1914, no fewer than three thousand persons attended annually. During the congress, confessions were held, baptismal instructions were given, and Indians were confirmed. Marriages were also "rectified." All received Holy Communion in the bower, and sermons were preached.

Goll attributes the success of the Congress as follows:

> No doubt, the question occurs, How were all these people, three
> thousand for many years, taken care of whilst at the congresses? The
> Indians' answer is very simple: *the guests eat at the table of the hosts.*
> The guests one year will be hosts some other year. And if a locality
> cannot afford to be host,—well, the congress cannot be held there. It
> would require a complete change of the law of hospitality among the
> Sioux, if visitors had to provide board for themselves.... When peo-
> ple are willing to be hospitable to visitors out of friendship, why
> should they change their attitude when religion is added to
> friendship? [Ibid.: 43; italics added]

Although Goll does not give the native terms for the "officials," he
might very well have been describing the traditional methods of
moving and forming a summer camp for the buffalo hunt and sun
dance. The hosts at whose table the travelers ate were at least
partly represented by the missionaries themselves. The standard
strategy of enticing people to mass, even to this day, is to provide
breakfast after the services. The missionaries found to their con-
cern (and to the Oglala's amusement) that when they eliminated
the feast, the congregation did not come.

In describing the catechist sodalities, the St. Mary and St.
Joseph Societies, Goll is somewhat more specific about the roles of
the laymen:

> The Jesuit Fathers introduced these societies in their missions....
> One man, elected and approved for that purpose, led in a kind of lay-
> service.... This finished, the president ("grandfather") gave a well-
> thought-out address.... The St. Mary Society also had its program.
> The president ("grandmother") would address all present.... The
> fight against old Indian customs and superstitions kept the meetings
> of the St. Joseph and St. Mary Societies animated. [Ibid.: 37]

The use of *grandfather* and *grandmother* could not have been
more appropriate. What Goll regards as the fight against old Indian
customs and superstitions, however, is rather one-sided. The present-day sacred persons continue their side of the debate over the
efficacy of Christianity vis-à-vis native religion.

Although during subsequent field work, Macgregor was of the
opinion that native religion was dying out, as were the native prac-

titioners, he conceded that the acceptance of Christianity was without complete abandonment of native beliefs. He states: "The Dakota also accepted Christianity because it was the one part of the white man's life in which the Indian was accepted as an equal" (Macgregor, 1946:92). He points out that the missionary use of native terms, such as *Wakantanka* for God, made it relatively easy for the old Oglalas to "understand" Christianity, as did the concepts of the asceticism, the torture of the crucifixion (similar to the sun dance), charity (the highest form of status), and virginity. Even the offering at church was analogous to the give-away. Macgregor's discussion of the Episcopal and Catholic convocations held during his field work in 1942–43 resemble Goll's earlier observations:

> These gatherings are held annually, but since they include all the Sioux reservations, Pine Ridge is the meeting place only one in every seven or eight years. Although, of course, no Indian ceremonial is part of these meetings, the summer gathering of friends and relatives from different parts of the reservation and the camping in tents given the convocations some of the social functions of the old Sun dance. [Ibid.: 97]

At the community level, Macgregor provides more insight:

> Individuals in rural communities all tend to join one church, especially if there is any common bond of band origin. It was noted that, in many families, a Catholic or Protestant has joined the church of the other upon marriage. In one family a Catholic mother became an Episcopalian, but her Episcopalian daughter became a Catholic upon her marriage. [Ibid.:97-98]

Here we see an analogy between marrying out of one's *tiyošpaye* and marrying out of one's denomination.

Finally, Macgregor notes:

> Without detracting from the work of early and contemporary Pine Ridge missionaries, it can be said in all fairness that much of the significance which Christianity holds has come from its interpretation by the Dakota in terms of their former religion. Similarly, the church organizations have become significant as they have supplied a center around which band organizations and integration could continue.

[But] under the *pressure of the churches,* the increasing knowledge of modern medicine, the fear of white criticism, and the general
process of assimilation, the old religious practices seem bound for
extinction. [Ibid.:102–3; italics added]

Thus the missionaries contributed a great deal to sustaining
earlier forms of Oglala social organization by providing a
framework similar to the *tiyospaye.* On the surface it did, in fact,
appear that the old religious institutions were bound for extinction,
but both the very pressure exerted by the churches and the sanction by other whites of missionary activities enabled Oglala social
organization to persist under the guise of denominational
membership.

Chapter 11

CONTEMPORARY RELIGION

INTRODUCTION

Given the religious alternatives available to the Oglalas, we find a correlation between full-bloods and native religion on one end of a scale, and the mixed-bloods, non-Indians, and Christianity on the other. The Native American Church has never made much headway on the Pine Ridge Reservation. Feraca's statement that his "estimate of ten percent of the full blood Oglala being peyote members is to be taken with reservation" (Feraca, 1963:52) is probably accurate.

Part of the problem of religious identity is solved by regarding adherence to a Christian sect or the Native American Church as membership, that is, one joins or is born into it. Conversely, native Oglala religion has no membership or formal leadership. Oglalas participate in native religion as their individual needs arise; their participation is situational. Given the preceding evidence that church membership is organized along *tiyošpaye* lines, Christianity may be regarded as a means of satisfying social needs; it enables the older sociopolitical form of organization to persist under another guise. Native religion, on the other hand, enables people to identify themselves and each other as Oglala.

The same distinction between Indian and white man appears at another level of social organization, the treatment of health problems. The Oglalas believe that certain kinds of sicknesses are "white man's disease." Such medical problems as heart trouble, diabetes, tuberculosis, glaucoma, and venereal disease are reckoned to have been brought to the New World by the European. If they are white man's diseases, they must be treated by the white man's doctors and in his facilities. Indian sickness, those illnesses from which Indians suffered prior to the white man's arrival, are curable by native practitioners. Indian sickness is caused by disharmony between common man and the supernatural beings and powers.

In either case, the diagnostic expert is the Oglala sacred person. People who are inexplicably sick seek the expert opinion of the sacred person. If the sickness is diagnosed to be a white man's disease, the patient is instructed to go to the hospital or to a white doctor off the reservation. If it is diagnosed as an Indian disease, the sacred person himself may perform a ritual, or he may recommend a specialist in matters related to the nature of the disease. If the patient lives or is cured by either the white doctor or the sacred person, the sacred person is given credit for making the proper diagnosis. If the patient dies, however, the white doctor is criticized for administering his brand of medicine inefficaciously.

At still another level of social relations, an Oglala who has troubles over drinking, his family, finances, business transactions, theft of property, or the education of his young may in fact seek out counsel from a wide number of federal bureaus with offices on the reservation. Alternatively, he may seek solutions for all these problems from the sacred persons, for they are expert not only in matters of faith and health, but in all matters of day-to-day living. Not only do the sacred persons preserve the myth and ritual of their people, but they assume the responsibilities to their people once held by the now politically powerless *tiyošpaye* leaders.

THE ORGANIZATION OF OGLALA RELIGION

In the view of the Oglala sacred persons, Christianity is factionated: there are ideological debates among the various Christian sects, differences in their rituals, songs, prayers, churches, and vestments. Oglala religion, on the other hand, is unified. There are in fact many variations of ritual, depending on the nature of the supernatural power imbued in each of the native practitioners. But despite the ritual inconsistencies, the rationale for Oglala religion, embodied in the cosmology and cosmogony, is consistent.

Although there is no Lakota word for religion, the idea of mediation between common man and *Taku wakan* is organized around participation in a number of calendrical and noncalendrical events which are still an integral part of Oglala life. These events include four of the original sacred rites brought to the Oglalas by the White Buffalo Calf Woman, which I discuss in this chapter, and variants of a curing rite known as *Yuwipi*, which I discuss in the next. The following descriptions of the rituals are taken from my own field data.

The Memorial Feast. The ritual known as *wokiksuye kicagapi* (*wokiksuye* 'memorial'; *kicagapi* 'they make for him/her') is conducted approximately one year after the death of a loved one. The Oglalas believe that the *nagi* (ghost) of a person lingers near the place where he died and for one year attempts to lure loved ones away. The presence of the spirit is often manifested in the form of a child crying or cock crowing. As an immediate precaution for preventing death in the family, a gun is shot off or incense (*wazilya*) is burned to frighten the spirit away (cf. Bushotter, 1887–88). Cedar (*ȟante*) or sweetgrass (*wacanga*) is most frequently used.

After a person dies, a close relative may elect to perform the duties of a mourner (*wašigla*), which last for one year. During this period the mourner must refrain from attending social functions such as powwows, feasts, or any other secular rituals. He regards the spirit as being nominally alive: it is talked to and ritually fed every day. A place is set at the table for the spirit, and meat and water are offered it. At the end of the meal, the meat is buried or burned and the water cast on the ground. The task is arduous and dangerous, for once a person elects to feed the spirit, he must not forget his daily obligations lest the spirit become angry and potentially harmful to the mourner or someone else in the family.

Much of the mourner's time is spent with close relatives preparing items for the give-away that will accompany the final memorial feast. The usual items consist of star quilts, quilt tops, hand-decorated linens, beadwork, or other craftwork. Money is saved during this time for the purchase of other give-away items such as blankets, shawls, shoes, and other personal needs. Relatives of the mourner are expected to help out by contributing to the manufacture of goods and accumulation of money and foods which will be distributed during the memorial. Those who have helped out the most will receive recompense at the final give-away.

Memorial feasts may be held in a mourner's home, a community house, or a church. When it is held under the auspices of a denominational sect, the memorial feast is often regarded as a Christian ritual. However, sacred persons participate as well as lay catechists. Prayers and psalms are sung in Lakota, but the structure of the ritual otherwise resembles a memorial feast held in the country without Christian intervention.

Prior to the assigned day, a relative of the mourner or the community announcer (*eyapaha*) informs the people in the community, as well as relatives living in other parts of the reservation, that the memorial feast will be conducted. The feast is known colloquially as "memorial dinner" or simply "dinner." In Lakota it may be called feast (*wohanpi*), or, more formally, memorial feast (*wokiksuye wohanpi*).

On the assigned day, as many as three hundred to four hundred relatives and friends journey to the memorial feast. At the more traditional feasts, old-time foods are served. The men may hunt for venison, and the families often donate dog meat for the enjoyment of the older people. Men do the cooking outdoors over large iron grills placed over pit fires. Pies and pastries are usually prepared indoors by the women. Fry bread (*wigli un kagapi* 'they make it with grease'), pemmican (*wasna*), and fruit soup (*wojapi*) are usually served along with store-bought bread, crackers, coffee, potatoes, and sweet breads.

The memorial feasts I have attended always begin on a light sociable note despite the eventual seriousness of the event. People arrive about noon and spend the day chatting and smoking with their friends and relations. During the summer, the feasts are normally held outdoors in an arbor. In the winter, if the assembly is not too large, they may be held inside the community houses. The people sit in a large circle, inside of which the family has set up a table with the various foods that will be distributed to the guests. As the food is prepared, it is passed out among the guests by servers making their way around the circle as many times as required to distribute all the food. As at any other feast, the visitors bring their own knives, forks, spoons, bowls, and cups. In addition, they bring *wateca* buckets (*wateca* 'leftovers') for whatever they cannot consume on the spot.

After the people have been fed, the spirit may be ritually fed for the last time. Following are notes I made at a memorial feast held in the Red Cloud Community in August 1967 at which an Arapaho man conducted the ceremony for a mourner to whom he was related. The fact that an Arapaho conducted an Oglala ritual should not be regarded as unusual. The Oglalas regard the Arapahos as particularly religious people. Also, some Oglala sacred persons travel to Wind River, Wyoming, to conduct curing rituals for Arapaho families.

> When the feast ended, an old Arapaho man related to Mrs. AML's son-in-law was given some *wasna*. The son-in-law directed the people out of the yard to the gumbo road out front. The old man held a piece of fried bread in one hand and the *wasna* in the other. He raised both hands over his head, fists clenched, and then lowered them slowly and deliberately in front of him. The son-in-law placed both hands on the old man's right shoulder, then drew his hands toward himself as if he were squeezing some vital force out of the old man's arms. As the young man's hands passed over the older man's arms he took the *wasna* and fried bread from the man's hands and walked several paces to the north, where he stooped down, dug a small hole in the earth with his fingers, and placed the food in it. He then repeated the operation four more times, each time taking more of the food from the old man's hands, then walking to the east, west, south, and finally to the center of the circle at the feet of the old man, where he placed the last bite of food. This concluded, the spirit of Mrs. AML had been fed for the last time, and it was released.

Following the ritual feeding of the spirit, the family sponsoring the memorial feast prepares the give-away. The give-away (*otuȟ'an*) is a traditional Oglala institution found in a number of sacred and secular contexts. When a person dies, his next of kin give away everything the deceased owned in life, as well as their own personal property. This custom is still an integral part of the funeral rituals, even those held in Christian churches. Once all their personal belongings have been given away, the donors are rendered destitute (*unšike*) and their neighbors and relatives will take pity on them. Usually within the year, at future give-aways, the original donors will become the recipients of goods and money, and eventually the original personal property that they gave away will be replaced.

The give-away associated with the memorial feast is a thanksgiving (*wopila*) in which the mourner and his or her family acknowledge the help received from neighbors and kin during the one-year period. A table is set up in the middle of the circular shade or community house and the gifts placed on it. The mourner and close kin stand around the table and select gifts to be given to specific people, whose names are announced by an announcer. As each person's name is called, he or she approaches the table, receives the gift, and shakes hands with all the members of the family (possibly as many as a half-dozen relatives stand at the table, but the mourner is the central focus). After all the gifts have been handed out, the announcer asks the people to shake hands with the mourner and close kin, upon which they form a line which passes in front of the table, each in turn shaking hands with the mourner and his or her family. Often a picture of the deceased is placed on the table or is carried around periphery of the shade for all to see, and the participants view the deceased for the last time. At this point in the memorial feast, the tenor has changed from the initial one of sociability to one highly pitched with emotion. Men and women begin to cry openly as they pass the family and shake hands. The mourner begins to weep, and the people embrace him or her and offer condolences. The mourner often collapses and has to be carried away before all the people have filed by. With the final shaking of hands, the memorial feast is concluded.

The Sweat Lodge. The homes of traditional Oglalas are marked by the presence of a sweat lodge (*initipi*) located a few yards from their dwellings. The sweat lodge ritual (*inikagapi*) has not changed over the years. It is conducted by a sacred person at the request of any member of the community; normally five or six participate perhaps once a week during the spring and summer. The sweat lodge is held separately for both spiritual and physical health purposes and in conjunction with other rituals such as the vision quest, sun dance, and curing ceremonies. Although the description of the ritual in Chapter 8 obtains well for the Oglalas today, I would like to add some personal details about the ritual which I acquired as a participant and observer during my field work.

The sweat lodge ritual is regarded as an ordeal, but its serious nature is often obfuscated by an air of joviality among the participants. There is an implicit feeling that Oglalas can withstand the sweat lodge better than a non-Indian. Numerous stories are told about white men who could not withstand the heat and interrupted the ritual by either standing up in the lodge, thereby tearing off the coverings, or by simply running out of the lodge when it became too hot. The intense heat and steam created by sprinkling water on the white-hot rocks are also a focus of humor. A man will tell his brother-in-law, "Wait till I get you in the sweat lodge; I'll dump the whole bucket on the rocks." This can be understood fully only by those who have gone through the ordeal. Even before water is sprinkled on the rocks, intense heat is created by the rocks as they are handed into the lodge. It is intense enough to make it impossible to lean back against the willow frame without scorching one's back.

When the rocks are handed in, there is always the possibility that sparks may fall on one's knees because of the limited room in which to sit. When the door flap is closed and the first water is sprinkled on the rocks, there is a sudden rush of steam, analogous to opening the door of a blast furnace. The first time I entered a sweat lodge, I was instructed by the sacred person to put my face on the ground in the sage bed where I could breathe more easily. With five or six participants this is impossible. Some of the jokes allude to this cramped situation, and one participant will chide another, saying, "You always want to sit next to the door so you can get out in a hurry." Others are jokingly accused of lifting the lodge covering a few inches so that fresh air can blow in.

To emphasize the alacrity with which participants prepare for the sweat lodge, some will state that more tarps and blankets should be placed on the framework so that no heat will escape, while others suggest that there are not enough rocks. Given that one begins to sweat profusely even when the first rock is handed in, the effect of thirty rocks can be imagined. I had first thought that my evaluation of the intense heat was part of my own cultural conditioning, and was somewhat relieved when the sacred person, after we both left the lodge, laughed and said, "Too hot!"

The job of fire tender (colloquially called the janitor) is equally arduous. Some of the rocks weigh as much as twenty-five pounds and must be maneuvered carefully through the door flap so that none of the participants are burned. Today a pitchfork is used. The rocks are laid one by one at the edge of the center hole, where they are received by the sacred person or his assistant with wooden paddles and are laid carefully, in the proper ritual manner, in the hole. It requires perhaps twenty minutes to hand in all the rocks.

Once the door flap has been closed, the sweat lodge is dark except for the glow from the heated rocks. The sacred person prays to the spirits of deceased men, animals, birds, and other cosmological forces, addressing them as *Tunkašila,* Grandfather. He prays for the welfare of the people, for participants' special concerns such as financial needs, family and health problems, and important decisions that have to be made with reference to business transactions with the federal government. The sacred person addresses the spirits and is addressed by them. Occasionally songs are sung in a loud voice by all. One recurrent theme is exemplified in the following song:

> *Wankatakiya hoyewaye lo.*
> *Cannunpa kin yuha hoyewaye lo.*
> *"Mitakuye ob wani kte ca lecamun welo,"*
> *Eyaya Tunkašila cewakiye lo.*

> I send a voice above.
> With the pipe, I send a voice above.
> "I do this because I want to live with my relatives,"
> Saying this over and over, I pray to Grandfather.

After each round of prayers and songs, the participants say, *"Mitak' oyasin"* (All my relations). Some may take into the sweat lodge prayer offerings of tobacco (*canli wapaȟte*), usually a string of seven minutely wrapped bundles of tobacco. The offerings, one for each of the four directions, the zenith and nadir, and the Spotted Eagle, are either left tied to the willow frame of the sweat lodge or later taken to the person's home and hung in a tree. They are usually wrapped in red cloth.

The Vision Quest. The objective of the vision quest (*hanbleceya*) is still primarily to receive power. Most sacred persons embark on the quest at least once a year, usually in the spring, but anyone may conceivably undertake it, especially if they intend to make an offering to the supernaturals. The general description of the vision quest in Chapter 8 still applies to the present-day ritual. I will focus on the nature of the vision.

Ruby discusses the following vision for an Oglala who later became a sacred person; I offer the following paraphrase of his report (Ruby, 1955:50–52):

In 1939, Willie Wound suffered from hepatitis and was told that he would not live. Upon leaving the hospital he had a vision of the Great Spirit, who promised to help him if he would undertake a vision quest for four days in the midst of a raging storm. Willie Wound agreed, and despite protests from his family and friends went to a mountain with only a pipe and some tobacco. On the mountain, a storm raged around him except at the spot where he sat. He stayed there for three days with no food or drink. On the fourth day a giant appeared telling him that the Great Spirit would come presently. Soon a white form which he discerned to be the bones of a human shrouded in a white mist appeared, stating that it was the Great Spirit. Willie Wound lit the pipe and offered it to the white mist, but when the pipe touched the mist it felt as if it were striking a hard object. The mist spoke, saying that he should become a medicine man and that the powers of the lightning and thunder would enable him to cure people. The cloud vanished and Willie Wound felt strong. He returned home and became a medicine man.

Zimmerly elicited the following information about visions from Pete Catches, an Oglala sacred man who has participated in and directed the annual sun dance:

It's like this: it isn't like a dream. At night you go to bed and think hard on something. Like say, just anything, a car probably. Think hard on it, worry about it, and in a dream you will dream about a car. It's not like that, the visions come, whether you're thinking about a car, a horse will appear, or something, different, you know what I mean. It's like looking out in space and suddenly somebody shows you a picture. It's like that. [Zimmerly, 1969:60]

The Oglala sacred man George Plenty Wolf, who was trained by the famous Horn Chips and in turn trained Pete Catches, told me about his vision (Powers, 1971:25-26):

> Plenty Wolf spent four days on the butte. Nothing happened for the first two days, but on the third night he was confronted by a beautiful woman who tried to tempt him. But he held tightly to the pipe and prayed. During the remainder of the third and fourth nights he was visited by a coyote which yelled loudly at him to frighten him. But Plenty Wolf continued to pray with the pipe. Finally, he was visited in quick succession by the spirits of a stone, two mourning doves, a white owl, and a rattlesnake. They instructed him to go back and make a rattle such as the kind used in Yuwipi ceremonies, and to add one rattle every five years that he practices until he had attained four.

The following visionary experience was told to me by an Oglala named Tail in 1972. Tail is not a sacred person, but has embarked on vision quests all his life. Tail had been instructed to go to a butte near Porcupine, northeast of Pine Ridge. He stayed there for two days. On the morning of the second he watched the "old man dancing" (the rays of the sun appearing on the horizon). The sounds of nature were magnified: the steps of the ants were so loud he had to hold his ears. The birds talked to him and he could understand their language. Suddenly out of the west the clouds began to roll in. He had been instructed not to be afraid, but to hold onto the pipe and point it at anything threatening. Tail knew that there was something near him: two deer, one black-tailed, the other white-tailed. They came toward him to tempt him, but he held his pipe in front of himself, and the two walked around him and disappeared. The clouds began to open up now and he could see the horses of the Thunder people (the *Wakinyan Oyate*) coming toward him. He could not see the *Wakinyan* because they were hidden in the clouds, but they drove horses before them, each of which was connected to the clouds by leashes made from lightning. In front of the horses were the *akicita*, also called the *Wakinyan wayaka* 'Thunder slaves'. The horses and the men were slaves of *Wakinyan* because they had been struck by lightning. They came to test his bravery, and he was instructed to hold the pipe toward them and it would protect him. He was afraid, but he did as the sacred person had instructed him and the clouds parted, going past on either side of him.

Since the turn of the century, many sacred persons have had visions related to World Wars I and II and the Korean and Vietnam wars. They see flags, guns, tanks, and airplanes, all of which are signs for them to pray for peace in the world. Often the sacred persons are carried away from their vision pits to other places and are left in awkward positions. Plenty Wolf went on a vision quest on a butte near the community of Slim Buttes, east of Pine Ridge Village. During the night the spirits came and took him to Devil's Tower in Wyoming. They returned him the next day and left him hanging by a rope over the side of the butte.

The Sun Dance. A number of descriptions of the sun dance have been published (Brown, 1953; Densmore, 1918; Dorsey, 1894; Feraca, 1963; Fletcher, 1882; Nurge, 1966; Riggs, 1893; Schwatka, 1890; and Walker, 1917). I have personally attended fourteen sun dances at Pine Ridge. Between the literature and my own observations it becomes obvious that no two sun dances have been performed quite the same since 1950 and perhaps they never were (see Nurge, 1966, on this same point).

The sun dance was officially banned in 1881 but was not discontinued until after the 1883 dance. During John Collier's administration as commissioner of Indian Affairs (1933-45), and under the Indian Reorganization Act of 1934, the sun dance was officially reinstated. However, sun dancing was probably being done as early as the 1920s (Feraca, 1963). Since there are no statistics regarding the sun dance for this period, it is possible that the sun dance, in fact, never ceased to be performed. Certainly not enough time elapsed for the dance to be forgotten, although until 1960 it was performed without the immolations that are so often associated with the dance.

When the Oglalas were traveling about after game, the site of the sun dance varied from one year to the next. Since about 1955 it has been held in a large sun dance arbor located on the east edge of Pine Ridge Village, one-half mile north of Highway 18. Most of the rituals described for the sun dance in Chapter 8 still obtain, but the

overall length of the sun dance has been cut. This is partly due to
the fact that in 1934 the administration of the sun dance was
assumed by the Oglala Sioux Tribal Council. The council appointed a sun dance committee whose responsibilities corre-
sponded roughly to those of the seven chiefs, the *wicašayatanpi*,
and *wakicunze*, that is, the officials who administered the earlier
tribal camp circles. The duties of the *akicita* were assumed
primarily by the tribal police force. Aside from its religious function, the tribal council saw opportunities over the years (with en-
couragement from the Bureau of Indian Affairs) to transform the
sun dance into a tourist attraction. This required advertising and
promotion and a fixed calendrical date in order to entice tourists
onto the reservation, particularly from the neighboring white
towns and the Black Hills–Badlands area, which had already been
established as a thriving tourist attraction.

The crass commercialism of the sacred rite has been the subject
of criticism by traditional purists, and the tribal council has been
accused of sensationalizing the "torture" of the sun dance in an
attempt to draw more tourists. The commercialism has also tended
to underscore the extant factionalism between the full-bloods and
mixed-bloods, at least politically and economically. In other ways,
the sun dance tends to mediate between traditional and non-
traditional tribal members. Indianness and whiteness are concepts
which are quite disparate throughout most of the year. However,
during the sun dance, the two concepts come face to face on the
sun dance grounds. Given that one's predisposition is to finding
signs of acculturation and deculturation, the sun dance perhaps
becomes an important testing ground. Up through 1972, it was
performed only on the first two mornings of the four-day celebration, the remaining two days and nights being devoted to secular
dances. The sacred tree was usually selected on the day before the
dance and hauled into the grounds on a truck. The dancers'
costumes were made from commercial cloth, cardboard, and
women's shawls, and the men sometimes blew on five-and-dime
toy whistles (Feraca, 1963:17). Indians—and anthropologists—
have regarded these adaptations and others as indisputable signs of
religious degeneration.

Some resident Oglalas, as well as visiting anthropologists and
missionaries, have regarded the contemporary sun dance as a

measure of religious syncretism. In describing the life of an Oglala sacred man who said that Christianity had a profound influence on his present Indian philosophy, Zimmerly states that "syncretism is evident throughout this paper and is a feature of virtually all contemporary Sioux religious practices" (Zimmerly, 1969:50). However, he does not give any examples of syncretism except to the extent that Christianity has influenced the native religious perspective of his informant.

Feraca cites an Oglala informant as considering the sun dance thoroughly Christian from its very beginnings. According to Feraca:

> He is by no means alone in this belief, citing the similarity between crucifix and Sun dance pole, and equating the sufferings of the dancers with the Christian concept of penance. [The informant] assured me that the late Father...a Jesuit beloved by the Sioux, had often repeated his belief that the Sun dance was an approach to Christianity. [Feraca, 1963:15]

Such assertions appear to be similar to those expounded by other missionaries like Goll, particularly in assuming a priori that mere contact with Christianity is capable of bringing about a change in religious philosophy. No clergyman, at least, thought that the sun dance, as a prime example of "paganism," could exist except within a Christian ideology.

The rift between the tribal council and traditionalists was somewhat assuaged in 1960 when the council permitted an Oglala to resume the immolative features of the sun dance. The man had been living off the reservation, working as a plumber's assistant in an urban area. His niece had contracted polio and he had vowed that if she recuperated, he would be pierced. As it turned out, the niece recovered and the man fulfilled his vow. In August 1960 he was laid in front of the sacred pole on a buffalo robe and his breast was pierced by a sacred person. The dancer, with a skewer through his breast, was attached to the pole by means of a rope, and he danced until the flesh broke through. Since 1960, one or more dancers have been pierced each year. In 1972, thirty were pierced, most of them younger members of the American Indian Movement.

Chapter 12

RELIGION AS
AN INSTITUTION

MEDIATION OF THE SUN DANCE

Each year the sun dance becomes an arena in which the traditionalists and bureaucrats air their factional differences. From the traditionalists' point of view the reinstitution of the immolative features of the sun dance might be regarded as partly contrived. As more dancers pledged to be pierced in the 1960s, the sun dance committee of the tribal council increasingly placed emphasis on the flesh offerings in their tourist publicity. The Oglalas regard the very manner in which the piercing is treated by the committee as ludicrous. During the sun dance, the price of admission increases, as does the monetary charge for permission to take photographs (still photography being cheaper than motion pictures), on the day of piercing. However, the tourist population has probably not increased substantially vis-à-vis the Indian attendance at recent sun dances.

But what is often regarded by observers of the ritual as a caricature of the "real" sun dance reflects only the attitudes and innovations of the committee, tribal council, and federal government. Traditional Oglalas who participate in or observe the sun dance have a completely different perception of the ritual: it is religious despite the commercial overtones the council chooses to give it. That there are factional disputes over the propriety with which the tribal council operates the sun dance cannot be denied. But the creation of factions over the sun dance is more typically Sioux than it is Euro-American, judging from what we know about conflicts over Oglala leadership during prereservation and early reservation periods. At sun dance time, the bureaucratic faction of

Oglala society becomes analogous to a *tiyošpaye* whose leadership is being contested, in this case not by another *tiyošpaye*, but by the entire traditional Oglala faction. Thus the sun dance itself becomes a powerful mediating force between the traditional and the modern.

The sun dance satisfies social as well as religious needs of the traditional Oglalas. Each of the communities is in theory represented at the camp ground which encircles the sun dance shade and sometimes comprises as many as ten thousand spectators, mostly Oglalas or Sioux from other reservations. People return to the same camping areas year after year. Campsites are reserved; people know where they and their neighbors and relatives belong in the modern camp circle. Even if they live only a mile away from the sun dance grounds, they still pack up their tents and bedding and camp out. Some may spend weeks preparing for what eventually lasts only four days.

This rather brief calendrical event is not the sole means by which Oglalas assert their religiosity. Although the girl's puberty ritual (*Išnati awicalowan*), and sacred ball game (*Tapa wankaye-yapi*) have not been performed since the 1920s, other rituals which are interrelated with the vision quest and sweat lodge are performed regularly in the outlying communities throughout the year. One such ritual is *Yuwipi*.

Yuwipi

A significant amount of research has been done on *Yuwipi*, a religious institution which Macgregor has called "the only continuing cult of the Dakota religion" (Macgregor, 1946:98). Macgregor is the first to mention *Yuwipi* by name, but other investigators, mainly Cooper (1944), Densmore (1910, 1918, 1932), Dorsey (1894), Ray (1941), Wallis (1947), and Wissler (1912), have mentioned *Yuwipi*-like rituals, all of which include the diagnostic features of Wallace's "shamanic cult institutions" (Wallace, 1966:86). The conscious investigation of *Yuwipi* as a genre of curing rituals under which is subsumed a number of variants has been undertaken primarily by Feraca (1961, 1962, 1963), Fugle (1966),

Howard (1954), Hurt and Howard (1952, 1960, 1961), Kemnitzer (1968, 1970), Powers (1971), and Ruby (1955).

Inasmuch as detailed ethnographies of *Yuwipi* rituals are available (see particularly Kemnitzer, 1968, for a comparison of two rituals, and Powers, 1971, for a translation of an entire ritual), I will concentrate on its broader features and focus on the relationship between *Yuwipi* and other community rituals, and the ritual specialist and his clientele.

Broadly speaking, *Yuwipi* is a generic term which includes a number of variants of curing rituals, all of which are held in darkened rooms and are conducted by specialists known locally as *Yuwipi wicaša* 'Yuwipi man'. The term *Yuwipi* is glossed by most investigators as "they wrap him up," indicating a special feature of the ritual in which the *Yuwipi* man is wrapped in a quilt (*wicaȟpi šina* 'star quilt') and bound with leather thongs. During the course of the ritual, spirits of humans, animals, birds, and inanimate objects enter the room and inform the *Yuwipi* man how a patient's sickness may be cured. While the spirits are present, people other than the patient may also make their requests known to the spirits, addressed as *Tunkašila* 'Grandfather' through the medium of the *Yuwipi* man, who regards himself as *ieska* 'interpreter'.

A more adequate gloss of *Yuwipi* is "they roll it up," *yuwi* signifying the action of rolling up an object such as a ball of yarn. The term may very well refer to the action of tying up the *Yuwipi* man: his hands and fingers are first bound together; the quilt is placed over his head and wrapped around his body; the quilt is then tied by means of a long leather thong or rope, which is placed around his neck and then twined around his body in such a way that there are seven half hitches between his neck and his feet. Sage is placed at each of the seven junctures. The term also refers to the disposition of the rope and tobacco offerings after the spirits have untied the *Yuwipi* man: the rope and offerings are left next to him rolled up like balls of yarn.

Just when the term *Yuwipi* came into fashion is difficult to determine, partly because missionaries openly regarded the ritual as the work of the devil, and it is possible that curing ceremonies of the *Yuwipi* genre were simply being held out in the districts away from the criticism of non-Indians. Properly, *Yuwipi* is an attenuated form of *Yuwipi lowanpi* 'they sing *Yuwipi*', or '*Yuwipi* sing', "sing" being synonymous with "ritual." One informant told me that during her youth (in the 1920s) people would ask, "*Yuwipi lowanpi ekta ni kta he?*" ("Are you going to the Yuwipi sing?") This was simply reduced to *Yuwipi ekta ni kta he?* ("Are you going to the Yuwipi?"), the former being "too much to say." *Yuwipi* meetings, or "spirit" meetings as they are often called in English, also may be referred to as simply *lowanpi* 'sing'. In addition to identifying the nature of the ritual, *Yuwipi* is often used as a synonym for "spirit" in a sense such as "*yuwipis* (spirits) always come to the meetings."

The *Yuwipi* Man

One or more *Yuwipi* men live in each of the districts of the Pine Ridge Reservation, and their clientele is found distributed throughout the numerous communities. They are *wicaša wakan* 'sacred persons' and derive through visions their power to cure Indian sickness, give counsel on family matters and business affairs, and find lost objects. Throughout the year they conduct rituals upon request from patients who approach them with a sacred pipe and ask them to perform their services. If the *Yuwipi* man accepts the case, the pipe is smoked and a time arranged for the ceremony. It is stipulated in all transactions between patients or their families and the *Yuwipi* man that upon a successful cure, the patient must pledge to sponsor a thanksgiving ritual (*wopila*) within one year after the initial ritual has been performed. The thanksgivings are directed to the supernatural beings and powers which have effected the cures, and should the patients ignore them, harm might befall their families or themselves. In practice, thanksgiving rituals are not structurally different from curing rituals, and a patient suffering from some malaise may well be treated at someone else's thanksgiving.

To maintain his power, a *Yuwipi* man must go on a vision quest at least once a year. When not conducting rituals or officiating at the sun dance, he prays with the pipe for the welfare of the people. His instructions have been given to him by the supernaturals and he must do as they bid. However, he must be cautious about the misuse of power, for he is vulnerable to the whims of malevolent spirits. He must observe all the restrictions related to the use of the sacred pipe, and he must keep herbal medicines and other paraphernalia in a place safe from menstruating women.

In addition to curing rituals, *wapiya lowanpi*, and thanksgivings, *wopila lowanpi* (or *wopila wohanpi* 'thanksgiving feast'), the *Yuwipi* man also conducts the sweat lodge rituals and prepares candidates for the vision quest. As part of the curing variant, he may also conduct meetings for the purpose of ensuring the safety of Oglalas who are leaving the community or reservation to go to school, into the military, or on trips to visit friends and relatives.

There are two other kinds of rituals that *Yuwipi* men conduct which they regard as "emergency meetings." One is called an *Inktomi lowanpi* 'Spider [the culture hero] sing', and the other *okile lowanpi* 'hunting [literally, 'to search for'] sing'.

Spider sings are often attenuated. Less time is required for the preparation of the meeting, fewer kinds of paraphernalia are used, and they often require less elaborate food preparation. Spider sings are conducted for people in trouble with the law or the federal government, or at the request of relatives who seek immediate solutions to the problems of the persons in question. They are also conducted for the purpose of investing patients or other clientele with a personal spirit called *wašicun tunkan* (*wašicun* 'an immortal, innate power' and *tunkan* 'stone'). Each "*tunkan*" is manifested in the form of a small, round stone which is found near ant hills. It is placed in a small buckskin pouch lined with sage. When a personal spirit is given to a layman, the stone is named after a person who is deceased, and the deceased person's spirit is said to inhere in the stone and may be called upon in time of need. This particular variant of a Spider sing is called *caštun* 'naming' (literally, 'to give birth to a name', from *caš*, attenuated form of *caje*, 'name', and *tun* 'to give birth to').

Hunting sings are held less frequently today. Originally, a person who believed that property had been stolen from him would request a *Yuwipi* man to find it for him. The *Yuwipi* man, through the intercession of human or animal spirits or sacred stones (see especially Densmore, 1918:204, for the use of stones in finding lost objects), would in a matter of days name the thief, or the place where the stolen property could be found. *Yuwipi* men are reluctant to perform the ritual today because they believe that their divination will ultimately involve the local police and other federal authorities, and they do not want to be responsible for sending another Indian to jail or prison.

Some sacred persons, although they are in a minority, reject the notion of being regarded as *Yuwipi* men and prefer to be called *wapiya wicaša* ('curer' [although all Yuwipi men technically are also *wapiya wicaša*]). Specifically, they refer to themselves according to the source of their visionary power. If it is derived from the eagle or the bear, for example, they are known as *wanbli wapiye* 'eagle curer' or *mato wapiye* 'bear curer'. They resemble more the members of *woihanblapi* 'dream cults' reported by Wissler (1912).

Even those who regard themselves as *Yuwipi* men do not perform identical rituals by any means. Some are regarded, mostly by their own clientele, as being superior to others, and there is a continuing debate about the efficacy of aging *Yuwipi* men. Although they are not permitted to receive money or payment outside the usual reciprocation of the give-away, most *Yuwipi* men earn the reputation (from outsiders) of charging their patients exorbitant fees. When a *Yuwipi* man becomes old, even the members of his own community begin to question his power. If he becomes ill or feeble, it is regarded as a sign that his power is waning. Most *Yuwipi* men abdicate their ritual specialization when they reach their late sixties or early seventies simply because they lose their following. At the same time, a younger *Yuwipi* man, possibly someone from another community (read *tiyošpaye*)begins to attract the attention of the old man's clientele and soon becomes known for his great curative powers. Slowly the old *Yuwipi* man retreats from community activities and the younger one assumes his responsibilities.

The *Yuwipi* Ritual

Following is a rather generalized description of a *Yuwipi* ritual, or "sing." Most rituals begin with a sweat lodge, conducted by the

Yuwipi man joined by five or six participants. The sweat lodge begins about sundown in a lodge adjacent to the house in which the *Yuwipi* is held.

While the men are in the sweat lodge, the women are busy preparing the meal which will be served after the *Yuwipi*, while other men are preparing the ritual site. *Yuwipi*s are held in a one-room house or in a larger house in which a room has been partitioned off from the rest. The site must be ritually sealed: windows and doors are closed, and tarps draped over them and often nailed in place. The room must be sealed in such a way as to ensure total darkness once the meeting has begun. Furniture is removed except for some types which are too awkward to handle, but even these are ritually treated, usually by placing sage on them to render them attractive to the spirits. Metal and glass in particular are covered or removed.

Once the sweat lodge is over, the men dry off and move into the house. The laymen arrange blankets and pillows around the outer perimeter of the room on which to sit. They leave the center of the room vacant, and it is here that the *Yuwipi* man will prepare the sacred altar, called the *hocoka* 'camp circle'.

The construction of the altar constitutes one of the major indices of variation between *Yuwipi* men, one which becomes particularly important in the subsequent analysis. The altar is constructed in the center of the free space on the floor, and is delineated as a square. The square is demarcated at least quadratically; that is, four coffee cans containing earth are placed at the four directions of the altar (northwest, northeast, southeast, and southwest corners). Into these cans are placed *wanunyanpi* 'offerings', colored cloths attached to slim willow canes (*sagye*). Most often the directional color symbolism is expressed by black for the west, red for the north, yellow for the east, and white for the south. Similar colored offerings, it should be noted, are also tied to the top branches of the sun dance pole and appear as demarcations of the vision quest site.

To the four, some *Yuwipi* men add a fifth container, located between the west and north, in which a single or as many as five canes are placed, each bearing a colored cloth or personal object such as eagle feathers, shells, sacred hoops (*cangleška wakan*), roots, and other symbolic objects. Again, some *Yuwipi* men employ seven cans, one for each of the four directions, one personal offering, and two representing the zenith and nadir. Green represents the earth, and blue, the sky. Some younger sacred persons assert that the four essential colors red, white, black, and yellow also symbolize the four races of man.

Connecting the cans and offerings is a string of minute tobacco particles called *canli wapaȟte* 'tobacco bundles'. Each bundle is made by placing a pinch of tobacco in a square inch of cloth and tying it to a long cotton string. The final strings contain on the average four hundred such bundles and represent the number of spirit helpers that the *Yuwipi* man employs in the ritual. Although the construction of the altar varies widely, the number of tobacco bundles is rather consistent. When the spirits finally enter the meeting, they take the essence of tobacco. Each time a *Yuwipi* man names a sacred stone, his total number of spirit helpers is reduced by the number of names he has given away to his clientele. When his power eventually begins to wane, it is attributed to the fact that he has given away too many of his helpers and there are not enough left to assist him. *Yuwipi* men often refer to these tobacco offerings as rosaries because each offering is prayed over as it is attached to the string. This has led some to conjecture that the tobacco offering is a sign of Christian influence. However, tobacco offerings of this kind predate the Christian missionaries.

Another variation in altar decoration is the manner in which certain ritual objects are arranged in the center of the *hocoka*. Most *Yuwipi* men construct a circular earthen subaltar upon which they draw various symbolic designs: the sun, moon, morning and evening stars, pipe, four directions, spider, lightning, or face (*wicite*) of the person to be cured. Around the altar is a short strand of tobacco offerings, and alongside it the *Yuwipi* man places rattles (*wagmuha*), sacks of Bull Durham, sacred stones, the pipe and pipe bag, a bed of sage, an eagle bone whistle, and other paraphernalia he needs to conduct the ritual in accordance with his vision.

Before the altar is completed, the clientele enter the room and take their seats around its periphery. At least one lead singer is required, although eventually everyone in attendance will join in the songs that play an integral part in the *Yuwipi* ritual. The *Yuwipi* man's assistant hands each adept a sprig of sage, which is placed behind the right ear so that the "spirits may know them." The door is closed, usually nailed shut, and covered with a tarp. One light is left on in the room, and is extinguished at the command of the *Yuwipi* man to ensure that the room is entirely dark. Once that is ascertained, the light is turned on again and the *Yuwipi* man fills the pipe: four pinches of tobacco for the four directions, two for the zenith and nadir, and one for the Spotted Eagle. Once filled, the pipe is capped with a sprig of sage.

Here I will outline the gross features of the *Yuwipi* ritual (for a detailed analysis of the ritual grammar, see Kemnitzer, 1968) by dividing it into ritual events which correspond to actions and sets of songs employed to accompany each action. For the musical part of the ritual, there are seven sets of songs, each classified by the Oglalas. In the variations of *Yuwipi* which I witnessed in 1967, 1968, 1972, and 1974, there were consistently seventeen songs distributed over the seven ritual sets. A set is determined not only by the action, but by the lack of a pause between songs accompanying each ritual event; that is to say, in each set, one song flows into the next; between sets songs are separated by discourse. Before the ritual begins, the *Yuwipi* man removes his shoes and shirt and takes his place in the center of the *hocoka,* facing west. His assistant closes off the sacred place by laying sprigs of sage end to end from the end of the string of *canli wapaȟte* at the northeast can to the can at the southeast direction.

Set 1. With the light still on, the *Yuwipi* man begins the *hanbloglaka* 'vision talk', in which he explains the source and nature of his power. He then fills the pipe while the lead singer, beating on a small tambourine drum, begins the *opagipi olowan* 'filling the pipe song'. After the pipe has been filled, the *Yuwipi* man's assistant and one of the singers wrap the *Yuwipi* man in a quilt and tie him. They lay him face down on a bed of sage. This action is called *wicapaȟtepi* 'they bundle him up'.

Set 2. The light is extinguished and the singers begin the *tatetopakiya olowan* 'toward the four winds song', also called *wicakicopi olowan* 'they call them song'. This is a particularly interesting song in that it has seven verses, the first addressed to *kola* 'friends', a term used to address spirits, the other six directed to each of the four winds, the zenith, and the nadir in the following way:

> Friend, I will send a voice, so hear me.
> Friend, I will send a voice, so hear me.
> Friend, I will send a voice, so hear me.
>
> In the west I call a black stone friend.
> Friend, I will send a voice, so hear me.
> Friend, I will send a voice, so hear me.
>
> In the north I call a red stone friend.
> Friend, I will send a voice, so hear me.
> Friend, I will send a voice, so hear me.
>
> In the east I call a yellow stone friend.
> Friend, I will send a voice, so hear me.
> Friend, I will send a voice, so hear me.
>
> In the south I call a white stone friend.
> Friend, I will send a voice, so hear me.
> Friend, I will send a voice, so hear me.
>
> On earth, I will call a spider friend.
> Friend, I will send a voice, so hear me.
> Friend, I will send a voice, so hear me.
>
> Above, I call a spotted eagle friend.
> Friend, I will send a voice, so hear me.
> Friend, I will send a voice, so hear me.

This is regarded as the most powerful of all songs because it is directed at the entire universe and requests the spirits of all the directions to enter the meeting place. It is followed by three more songs, called *wocekiye olowan* 'prayer songs'. On the fourth, the spirits arrive, and their presence is indicated by the sometimes violent shaking of rattles, thumps on the floor and walls, and the emission of the blue sparks (*peta*) from each place the rattles strike.

Set 3. During this set the singers sing another *wocekiye olowan*, after which there is a lengthy discourse by the patient and other clientele. It is during this portion that the *Yuwipi* man communicates with the spirits that are present and determines the proper cure for the patient(s). Among the prescribed remedies are placing tobacco offerings (a strand of seven *canli wapaĥte*) on a sacred butte or in a sweat lodge, simple prayers offered to the spirits, or "doctoring" by the spirits in which they touch the patients on the affected parts of the head or body. Often a *Yuwipi* is held in conjunction with a vision quest, and during this set the *Yuwipi* man may request the spirits go to the sacred butte where the supplicant prays and report on his progress.

Set 4. During this segment, those who wish to be doctored stand up in the darkness and hold on to the nearest flag offering with their backs facing the sacred place. The singers sing *wapiye olowan* 'curing songs' while the rattles dance and touch those who wish to be cured.

Set 5. After the patients have been cured, the singers begin a series of *ceĥohomni olowan* 'around the kettle songs', commonly known as kettle dance or pot dance songs. This set is sung only if traditional dog meat is going to be served as part of the subsequent feast. The kettle dance was originally performed as part of the *Heyoka Kaga* 'clown makers', and during the dance the contraries danced around a kettle full of boiling dog meat, thrusting their hands into the kettle and exclaiming that the water was too cold. The meat was eventually distributed to the older people attending the ceremony. The kettle dance songs sung at the *Yuwipi* are the same as those sung for the present version of the kettle dance. They are omitted when dog meat is not served.

Set 6. During this set there are four songs sung, two while the *Yuwipi* man is being untied by the spirits (*wicayujujupi olowan* 'they untie them song'), one while the people dance (*wacilowan* 'dance song'), and one (unclassified) when the spirits pick up the tobacco offerings.

Those clientele who wish to dance simply stand up in the darkness and dance in place. Some of the spirits also dance while the others are untying the *Yuwipi* man. As the spirits untie him, sparks are emitted from the seven junctures in the rope where sage has been placed. As they pick up the tobacco offerings from the long string of *canli wapaȟte*, sparks are emitted rapidly along the perimeter of the sacred area where the offerings were placed.

Set 7. During this set, two songs are sung while the spirits depart. The songs are called *wanagi kiglapi olowan* 'spirits go home song' and *inakiyapi olowan* 'quitting song'.

In all there are seventeen songs in the seven sets. After the spirits have departed, the lights are turned on and the *Yuwipi* man is found in the middle of the altar, which has been mostly destroyed. The quilt which enveloped him is neatly folded next to him, and the thongs which bound him as well as the long string of *canli wapaȟte* are rolled up, either near him or in the lap of one of the participants. The earthen altar is obliterated and the other ritual paraphernalia disheveled. The freeing of the *Yuwipi* man and the condition of the altar are attributed to the spirits, who have now returned to the west and to the place between the sky and the earth where they live until they are summoned by the *Yuwipi* man. The light is turned on and the filled pipe is smoked by everyone.

Women and children may either smoke or touch the pipe. After each of the participants smokes or touches the pipe, he says, "*Mitak' oyas'in*" (All my relations). A bowl of water is then handed around to each participant, who drinks and again says, "*Mitak' oyas'in.*" The *Yuwipi* man's assistant is required to finish whatever water remains in the bowl. With this the formal part of the ritual is over.

The door is opened and the women bring in the food, which is distributed to all the participants, who are expected to take home with them any leftovers. The *Yuwipi* man and his assistant pick up the ritual paraphernalia and place them in a suitcase or other container. Often the flag offerings and *canli wapaȟte* are given to the patient or one of the other adepts. The flags may later be cut up to make star quilts which are especially efficacious in curing rituals or in herbal curing. The star quilt made from *Yuwipi* offerings is especially helpful when placed over the head and used in conjunction with inhalants. The people eat the food together and the atmosphere is congenial. After the meal, the person on the south side of the door says, "*Mitak' oyas'in*," and each in turn repeats the formula, ending with the *Yuwipi* man. This concludes the *Yuwipi* ritual.

RITUAL RELATIONSHIPS

The prayers and songs employed in the *Yuwipi* rituals are the same as those used in the sweat lodge and in preparation for the vision quest. At the local community level, these three rituals, despite their variations, are related structurally and functionally. The sweat lodge is both a ritual preliminary to the vision quest and *Yuwipi* and a ritual in its own right. Often a *Yuwipi* meeting is held at the same time a person is on a vision quest so that the participants may together pray for the safety of the lone supplicant. *Yuwipi* men themselves must embark on the vision quest to maintain their powers.

The pervasive theme in these three rituals is one of unity, especially among kin. The formula *"Mitak' oyas'in"* conveys more than the simple gloss "All my relations." It signifies the desire to live harmoniously with one's relations. This idea is further enunciated in the recurring song text *"Mitakuye ob wani kta ca lecamun .velo"* (I do this [take part in the ritual, the songs, and the prayers] so that I may live with my relations). The rituals bridge the gap not only between the relatives living in the community but with the deceased, who reappear as spirits at the rituals. There is communication over time and space, and the remedies for curing the symbolic illness of the present are made available through the wisdom of the past. The *Yuwipi* man and other sacred persons serve only as intermediaries; the knowledge comes from another time and another place, both irrevocably Oglala.

At a tribal level, the rituals of the sun dance are in many ways replications of the community rituals. Again, the vision quest and the sweat lodge are integral to the success of the sun dance, only now the participants symbolize the unity of all the communities, not just one. The sacred persons from the outlying districts come together and perform their services collectively for the people. Together these four rituals symbolize the life and continuity of the

Oglalas. It is through these rituals that the Oglalas recognize themselves as distinct from the white man and other non-Oglalas.

Religion has conciously been separated from other aspects of contemporary Oglala social organization because those other aspects have become the domain of the white man. Religion has become an institution which is synonymous with Oglala identity. That the memorial feast is regarded as transitional and does not fit into the structure of other Oglala rituals is understood best perhaps because it is a celebration of death and departure from the community and tribe. The ritual still displays characteristic traits of the ghost-keeping ritual, but it survives because it underscores the old sociopolitical organization of the *tiyošpaye,* now subsumed under such appellations as Catholic and Episcopalian, rather than *Itešica* or *Kiyaksa.*

The Oglalas bemoan their fate in a white man's world. The honor song to the old chief Red Cloud, still sung today at large celebrations, says it poignantly:

> *Maȟpiya Luta, Lakotamayaši na*
> *Iyotiyewakiye lo.*
> *Oyate kin heyakeyape lo.*

> Red Cloud, you told me to be an Indian
> But it's hard to do.
> That's what the people are saying.

Part IV

CONTINUITY AND CHANGE

Chapter 13

STRUCTURAL REPLICATION

INTRODUCTION

The objective of social structural studies is to understand social relations with the aid of models. In this chapter I will apply a structural approach to Oglala social relations, specifically with regard to language, sociopolitical organization, family organization, ritual, and myth, and demonstrate by the use of models how all these aspects of social organization are structural replications of each other.

Whereas Lévi-Strauss regards various ways in which elements of a myth are combined as analogous to language in that they are comprised of *constituent units* (Lévi-Strauss, 1963:206-7), I will expand the notion of constituent units to explain structural relationships between myths, rituals, and other aspects of social organization.

At the level of language, for example, I regard the Siouan dialects spoken by the Oglalas and their antecedents (Lakota, Nakota, and Dakota) as constituent units of Siouan language. At the level of sociopolitical organization, I will analyze native terms, and particularly the semantic range of etymology of these terms and their relation to Siouan dialects, as constituent units of sociopolitical organization. Similarly, under family organization, I will treat birth-order names as constituent units, for reasons which will become obvious later. Finally, I analyze myth and ritual, dividing them likewise into constituent units for the purpose of constructing a single model which will account for the structural replication of all aspects of social relations under analysis.

Here I should reitereate Lévi-Strauss's statement that constituent units (in his treatment of myth) are not isolated relations,
but "bundles of such relations, and it is only as bundles that these
relations can be put to use and combined so as to produce a meaning" (ibid.:207). The purpose of my analysis is to demonstrate how
these bundles of relations have persisted over time and space. In
this sense, my approach corresponds more closely to that of Leach
(1970) in that I provide an analysis which takes into consideration
both synchronic and diachronic processes. Historical documenta-
tion from the early travelers and missionaries among the Oglalas
and other Sioux provides the basis for examining diachronic
transformations. My own ethnography, and ethnographic documents, provide the basis for examining synchronic transformations. By identifying those properties in the structures which
underlie Oglala social relations, and which remain invariant after
undergoing a variety of transformations, I will explain how the
Oglalas preserve their identity over time and space (cf. Maranda,
1972:330–33). In Chapter 14, I will examine these transformations
with respect to ritual use of time and space. In Chapter 15, I will
analyze the symbols which serve to synthesize the ethos of the
Oglalas and which distinguish them from non-Oglalas and non-
Indians.

SIOUAN: CONSTITUENT UNITS OF LANGUAGE

At initial contact, the Oceti Šakowin spoke three Siouan
dialects, Lakota, Nakota, Dakota. The dialects are mutually intelligible, the major difference lying in the initial phoneme of each
dialect term. There are other differences, exemplified in consonantal clusters, as table 4 illustrates.

TABLE 4
COMPARISON OF CONSONANTAL CLUSTERS IN DAKOTA, NAKOTA, AND
LAKOTA

DAKOTA		NAKOTA		LAKOTA	
mn	md	mn	md	mn	bl
hn	hd	kn	kd	gn	gl

SOURCE: Modified after Boas and Swanton, 1911.

We may infer from table 4, as well as from other historical material, that Dakota is more closely related to Nakota than either is to Lakota. This suggests that Nakota has only recently separated from Dakota, while Lakota has been separated for a longer period of time. Dakota appears to be the oldest, not only historically, but linguistically, insofar as we find Dakota elements in Lakota but not the reverse.

Nakoda, the dialect spoken by the Assiniboins after they split off from the Nakota-speakers, is not mutually intelligible to the other three, suggesting a relationship farther removed than even that of the Lakota-speakers. What is critical to note here relative to the dialects is that at contact time four politically discrete units of the Oceti Šakowin spoke Dakota; two spoke Nakota; and one spoke Lakota.

SOCIOPOLITICAL ORGANIZATION:
CONSTITUENT UNITS OF THE OCETI ŠAKOWIN

At this level of sociopolitical organization we find the following kind of correlation between discrete political units and their dialects:

Oceti Šakowin

Mdewakanton			Yankton		Nakota
Wahpeton	}	Dakota	Yanktonais	}	
Sisseton					
Wahpekute			Teton	}	Lakota

If we examine the etymologies of these native terms, we find that in addition to dialectal relationships, there are other kinds, mainly:

1. The Dakota-speakers all bear names which are toponymic: they are names of villages.
2. The Nakota-speakers bear names (actually one is diminutive form of the other) which are positional: they distinguish a specific place in a camp circle, i.e., the ends.
3. The Lakota-speakers bear a name which is distinguishable from those of both Dakota- and Nakota-speakers in that it implies neither toponymy nor position, but rather fissiparousness (see above, Chapter 2, for etymologies).

The seven constituent units of the Oceti Šakowin have in common the suffix *ton* (*tunwan*), 'village', except for the Wahpekutes,
whom we know to have split off from the Wahpetons. We also
know from historical records that the Yanktonais divided from the
Yanktons sometime after the Assiniboins, and as a result of European contact the Tetons and Yankton-Yanktonais began migrating
onto the prairies and plains, where their life style assumed an
equestrian, nomadic subsistence pattern.

In terms of structural replication, we find a relationship
between the constituents of the Oceti Šakowin at the level of both
dialect and etymology of political terms, that is:

> Dakota: toponymic
> Nakota: positional
> Lakota: fissiparous

THE TETONS: CONSTITUENT UNITS

According to early traveler and missionary reports, the Tetons
began to divide into smaller politically discrete units about 1700.
Again we find the Tetons establishing what Hyde has called the
ideal camp circle of seven members (Hyde, 1937). There is also
some indication that the Yanktons and Yanktonais are dividing into
seven constituents each, but data are sparse.

What is interesting about the Teton migration is that it occurs in
two waves, the Oglalas and Sicangus leading the migration, and
the Hunkpapas, Sihasapas, Mnikowojus, Itazipcos, and Oohenunpas following. To put it another way, one wave divides into two
constituent units, the other wave divides into five. Then in turn, on
the basis of what we know of the Oglalas and Sicangus, they each
divide in half (northern and southern Oglalas; upper and lower
Sicangus). Finally, and here we have data only for the Oglalas, the
Oglalas themselves divide into seven *tiyošpayes*.

Aside from the commonality of the Lakota dialect, which is
shared by all members of the Tetons, there are other relations
which bear strong resemblance to the manner in which the constituents of the Oceti Šakowin are related to each other, mainly:
1. The Sicangus, Sihasapas, Itazipcos, and Oohenunpas bear
   names for which there are legendary rationales associated with

warfare and famine. The stories are in the form of myths, but they are historical in content and episodic in nature.

2. The names of the Hunkpapas and Mnikowojus are both toponymic and positional. *Hunkpapa* is derived from the same radical as *Yankton* and means "end of the camp circle," while the second term means "to plant beside a stream" and suggests toponymy.

3. The term *Oglala*, like its counterpart at another level of abstraction, suggests fissiparousness: the Oglalas became divided over conflict between leaders.

Thus the manner in which the constituent units of the Tetons are related to each other replicates the manner in which the Oceti Šakowin are related to each other. Stated another way, the idealized heptadic structure is further divided into tetradic, dyadic, and monadic components.

THE OGLALAS: CONSTITUENT UNITS

Again on the basis of what we know from early nineteenth-century reports, the Oglalas divided into seven *tiyošpayes*, each of which was comprised of three hundred to four hundred people. Up until the reservation period these *tiyošpayes* were nomadic, but after the Treaty of Fort Laramie, they were forced to settle on reservation land. At the time of the establishment of the reservation, the seven *tiyošpayes* reflected internal components of the heptadic structure in the following manner:

1. The Kiyaksas, Oyuȟpes, Payabyas, and Tapišlecas bear names which suggest fissiparousness, at least at a metaphoric level: "to sever by biting"; "throw away"; "to cause to go to the head of the circle" (or, "pushed aside"); and "split liver."

2. The Itešicas and Wagluȟes are related on historical grounds (the second separated from the first) and on the basis that neither term suggests fissiparousness (Bad Face and Loafer).

3. Finally, *Wajaje* is an exogenic term and means Osage Indian (it is also the term used by the Osages to refer to themselves). It is monadic in that it is unique. I suggest that the term is a cognate to the Lakota *wocaje* 'class, kind', and that both are related to *oceti* 'fireplace'.

FAMILY ORDER AND BIRTH ORDER

I have already discussed the metaphoric extensions of the birth-order names (see above, pp. 38-39). The most reliable series of names is that recorded by Wallis for the Dakotas. The Riggs series is incomplete, and Walker's series must be questioned on the grounds that his term for seventh male and female child is really the Lakota term for "twins." Yet looking at Wallis's series for females, we find that the first four names are nonduplicative, the fifth and sixth are diminutive forms of the second and third, and the seventh is a diminutive form of the fourth, generating the series A B C D $B^1 C^1 D^1$.

The birth-order names almost comply with components of the heptadic structure but fall short in D^1, which according to my analysis should be unrelated to the tetrad and dyad. I call attention to birth-order names, however, because at other levels of abstraction the heptadic structure is not always apparent or extant. For example, in ritual, many components are comprised of numerical structures which are on the order of five or six. What I think is important is that in these particular ways of ordering systems, the first four, that is, the tetradic component, are universally similar. The replication may not extend to a heptad, but when it does, it is usually divided into tetradic, dyadic, and monadic components.

THE CONSTITUENT UNITS OF RITUAL

At the macrolevel of ritual it is difficult to discern anything but gross structural relations. This is partly due to the fact that sacred persons conduct their own particular variations of rituals, and two are rarely similar at the macrolevel. The seven sacred rituals are not analyzable at another level of abstraction, although at the micro-level, there are a number of constituent units of ritual which are replicated between the seven sacred rituals and form tetradic, dyadic, and monadic components. These units consist primarily of directional symbolism, color symbolism, the filling of the pipe, offering of tobacco, flag offerings, and the heating of stones for the sweat lodge. At this level of analysis, again, the heptadic structure is not always extant, but when it does appear, it is similar to that of the constituent units of language and sociopolitical organization in the following ways:

In contemplative or verbal prayer, offerings are made to the four directions, the zenith and nadir, and the universe. The order in which the prayers are offered differs somewhat from one sacred person to another but usually is (1) zenith, (2) west, (3) north, (4) east, (5) south, (6) nadir, (7) universe, or center. Interestingly, the Four Winds are never separated from each other, and they are always invoked in the order described above, beginning with the West Wind. Different attributes may be associated with the seven directions, for example, the Spider or Mother Earth with the nadir, and flying things with the zenith; and the four directions may be addressed by appealing to the animal and bird helpers which live in their respective quarters. Color symbolism always corresponds with directional symbolism, but not all sacred persons agree just which are the appropriate corresponding colors. In most cases, the correspondence is as follows (where seven components are present): zenith, blue; west, black; north, red; east, yellow; south, white; nadir, green; universe, special color or multicolor.

In filling the pipe and making tobacco or flag offerings, the directions are appealed to in the same order. However, in filling the pipe, the monad is often referred to as the Spotted Eagle, the messenger of *Wakantanka*, while in the flag offering, the monad is represented by the sacred person's personal altar, often a multicolored flag, but more frequently a cane which supports various personal objects from which he derives power.

There are other heptadic structures found in ritual. For example, at one time there were apparently numerous songs for the sun dance, but today only seven songs are sung, continuously and concatenatively for the duration of the dance. The *Yuwipi* song appearing above (p. 151) is certainly not typical of the format of Oglala songs, sacred or secular. But it is regarded as the most powerful of all *Yuwipi* songs, and its structure complies with the tripartite component of the heptad. In Chapters 14 and 15 I will discuss other ways in which constituent units of sociopolitical organization, ritual, and myth are related on the basis of the ritual conception and use of time and space, but first I will consider the important relationship between myth and the other aspects of social organization analyzed above.

THE CONSTITUENT UNITS OF MYTH

Here I focus on the Walker collection (M^1–M^{10}, Chapter 7), which are by far the most elaborate of the Oglala myths, and for purposes of this analysis the most explicatory. The outstanding feature of M^1–M^9 is the creation of time and space, recounted in the metaphor of kinship and marriage. The supernaturals behave like people, and it is because they succumb to human emotion such as passion, greed, pride, and desire for power that order must be created out of an otherwise amorphous world. Order is created through punishment administered by Škan to the transgressors, giving shape and substance to the universe and permitting the eventual appearance of mankind in M^{10}.

In M^1 we find the Sun and Moon married; they have a daughter, Falling Star. The Old Man and Old Woman are likewise married; they have a daughter, Face, who is married to Wind. They have

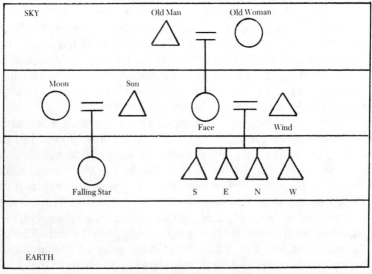

Figure 1. The First Period

four sons, the Four Winds, and Face is pregnant with a fifth child. In this, the first period, time and space are undifferentiated. Figure 1 illustrates the genealogical relationships between the mythological characters having human attributes.

In the same myth, Inktomi, the Old Man, and the Old Woman conspire to encourage the Sun to leave his wife, the Moon, and marry Face. Metaphorically, the Sun and the Moon separate, thus establishing the second period by differentiating day and night. Curiously, in the Lakota, both day and night are expressed by *wi*, which must be qualified, i.e., *anpetu wi* 'daylight *wi*' (sun) and *hanhepi wi* 'dark *wi*' (moon). Figure 2 illustrates the reassemblage of mythical characters in the second period.

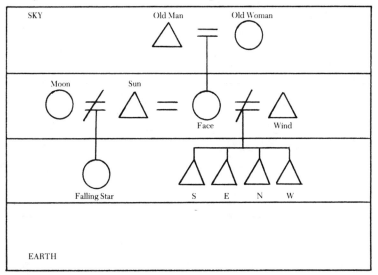

Figure 2. The Second Period

As a result of this rearrangement, certain members of the pantheon are punished. The Sun is ostracized, the most severe form of Oglala punishment, and the Moon is given her separate domain. The division of solar and lunar domains actuates the third period, the month. The Old Man and Old Woman are also ostracized; they are sent to dwell in the world and are to be known forever as the Wizard and the Witch. Their daughter, Face, is similarly sent to the world; she is given a second, horrid face, and is thereafter known as Double-Face (*Anukite* 'face on both sides'). If Face's relationship with Sun is regarded as an adulterous affair, then by mid-nineteenth-century Oglala standards she has received the proper punishment: her face has been disfigured. Cutting off the nose of an adulterous wife was a standard punishment in buffalo-hunting times. Figure 3 illustrates the reassemblage of mythological characters in the third period.

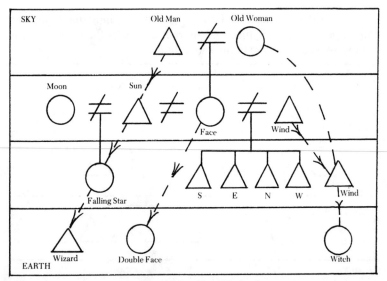

Figure 3. The Third Period

In addition to punishments, there are some rewards given to members of the pantheon. Wind is given custody of his four sons, and the five are sent to the world to establish the four directions. Metaphorically, the Wind's lodge is the universe, and each of the four brothers marks a quarter of the universe. A fifth son is born to Face, and he too goes to live in the world. But because of her transgression, the young son has an ambivalent status: he lives with his father in the world, but he is assigned no permanent direction. The young son's name is logically Yum, or Yumni, a contraction of *wamniomni*, the Lakota term for whirlwind.

The establishment of the universe and the four directions is accomplished in the fourth period, the one in which the Oglalas currently live. The fourth period represents the establishment of the year and the union of time and space. In Lakota, the term for both season and year is *omaka,* which is derived from *maka* 'earth', and which expresses this dyadic concept in a single term quite succinctly. Figure 4 illustrates the fourth period. The time-space dimensions correspond to earth-sky dimensions, and both are mediated by Falling Star, who eventually comes to live in the lodge of the South Wind. The mediation between earth and sky, or properly, supernaturals and humans, is later mediated by the White Buffalo Calf Woman, who brings the seven sacred rites to the Oglalas and who is equated with Wohpe, the Falling Star.

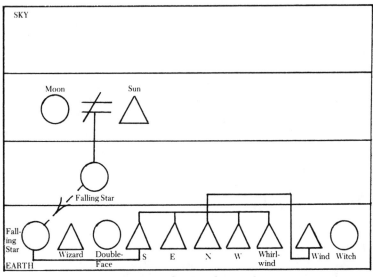

Figure 4. The Fourth Period

What is structurally similar in the cosmology is the rearrangement of mythological characters who are known to have specific relationships with each other. In the realm of the sky, the Sun and Moon remain, each within its own domain and each distinguishing between day, night, and the month. But at the terrestrial level, seven of the male characters and two (later three, with the arrival of Falling Star) females comprise the total constituents for the formation of time and space. If we focus on the seven male characters, their relationships appear to replicate the tripartite components of the heptadic structure found at other levels of analysis. The four winds are related to each other collaterally and consanguineally, that is, they are siblings. The Old Man and Wind are related to each other generationally and affinally, that is, one is the father-in-law, the other, his son-in-law. The fifth son, Yumni, although normally considered a sibling of the Four Winds, is a special case insofar as his growth has been retarded and he has been assigned no specific direction in the universe. According to the myths, he moves about, staying for short periods with his brothers. He does not like the North Wind, who is mean and surly; the East Wind is lazy; most of his time is spent between the West Wind and the South Wind, the latter of whom he particularly likes. This is to say, metaphorically, that the little brother, the anomalous sibling, moves about with the seasons in the same manner as the nomadic hunters did in their search for buffalo.

The structural replication in terms of tetradic, dyadic, and monadic components of a heptadic structure seems apparent here, particularly when the myths are compared with the constituent units of language and the Oceti Šakowin level of sociopolitical organization, where we find the following relationships:

> Dakota: Mdewankanton-Waȟpeton-Sisseton-Waȟpekute: West-North-East-South
>
> Nakota: Yankton-Yanktonais: Old Man-Wind
>
> Lakota: Teton: Yumni

Even the very structure of *Wakantanka* is a variation of this peculiar heptadic structure. There are sixteen aspects of *Wakantanka*, each of which is divided hierarchically into four classes:

1. *Wakan Ankatu* (Superior)
   a. Wi
   b. Skan
   c. Maka
   d. Inyan

2. *Wakan Kolaya* (Associate)
   a. Hanwi
   b. Tate
   c. Woȟpe
   d. Wakinyan
3. *Wakan Kuya* (Subordinate)
   a. Tantanka
   b. Hunonpa
   c. Tatetob
   d. Yumni
4. *Wakanlapi* (Godlike)
   a. Nagi
   b. Niya
   c. Nagila
   d. Šicun

Half of the sixteen aspects (superior and associate) are regarded as *Wakan Kin*, while the other half (subordinate and godlike) are *Taku Wakan*. Thus we find a tetradic component which subsumes the sixteen aspects of *Wakantanka*; a dyadic component which subsumes the tetradic; and finally, the monadic component, *Wakantanka*, of which all other divisions are aspects.

Table 5 summarizes the tetradic, dyadic, and monadic components of the heptadic structures discussed in this chapter. I shall treat the less conspicuous structural replications in the next chapter.

TABLE 5
SUMMARY OF HEPTADIC STRUCTURES

	TETRADIC COMPONENT	DYADIC COMPONENT	MONADIC COMPONENT
	Four (Dakota)	Two (Nakota)	One (Lakota)
LANGUAGE			
Dialects	Four (Dakota)	Two (Nakota)	One (Lakota)
SOCIOPOLITICAL ORGANIZATION			
Oceti Šakowin	Mdewakanton, Wahpeton, Sisseton, Wahpekute	Yankton, Yanktonais	Teton
Teton	Sicangu, Sihasapa, Itazipco, Oohenunpa	Hunkpapa, Mnikowoju	Oglala
Oglala	Kiyaksa, Payabya, Tapisleca, Oyuhpe	Ite Sica, Wagluhe	Wajaje
BIRTH-ORDER NAMES			
Dakota Male	Tcaske', Hepo, Hepi, Watca'to	Hake, Tatco	——
Female	Wino'ne, Ha'pe, Ha'psti, Wiha'ki	Hapo'na, Hapstina	Wihakeda
Lakota Male	Cacke, Hepan, Hepi, Catan	Hake, Hakata	Cekpa
Female	Wi-tokape, Hapan, Hepistinna, Wanska	Wi-hake, Hakata	Cekpa
RITUAL			
Directional Symbolism	West, North, East, South	Sky, Earth	Universe
Color Symbolism	Black, Red, Yellow, White	Blue, Green	Special
Pipe Filling	West Wind, North Wind, East Wind, South Wind	Wakantanka, Mother Earth	Spotted Eagle
Tobacco Offerings	West Wind, North Wind, East Wind, South Wind	Wakantanka, Mother Earth	Spotted Eagle
Flag Offerings	West Wind, North Wind, East Wind, South Wind	Wakantanka, Mother Earth	Personal
Heated Stones	West Wind, North Wind, East Wind, South Wind	Wakantanka, Mother Earth	Universe

TABLE 5 (*continued*)

	TETRADIC COMPONENT	DYADIC COMPONENT	MONADIC COMPONENT
MYTH			
Periods of Time			
First	West, North, East, South	Old Man, Wind	Sun
Second	West, North, East, South	Old Man, Sun	Wind
Third	West, North, East, South	Wind, Yumni	Sun
Fourth	West, North, East, South	Old Man, Wind	Yumni
Aspects of Wakantanka			
Superior	Wi, Skan, Maka, Inyan	Wakan Kin	Wakantanka
Associate	Hanwi, Tate, Wohpe, Wakinyan		
Subordinate	Tatanka, Hunonpa, Tatetob, Yumni	Taku Wakan	
Gods	Nagi, Niya, Nagila, Šicun		

Chapter 14

TIME AND SPACE

The Unity of Time and Space

The Lakota language does not employ separate lexical categories to differentiate between time and space; the two concepts are inseparable. All temporal statements in Lakota are simultaneously spatial ones, and the reverse is true. For example, in everyday Lakota one asks, "When is Pine Ridge from here?" (*Letan Pine Ridge tohan hwo?*), that is, "How far is it to Pine Ridge?" Another term, *tehan*, signifies both "long time" and "long distance," depending on the context in which it is used. The demonstrative pronouns *le* 'this' and *he* 'that' form the base for most Lakota words for time and space. To these radical elements are added suffixes which designate location, motion, direction, and relative position, e.g., *letu* 'right here' (no other possible place); *lehantu* 'right now' (no other possible time); *lel* 'here'; *lehanl* 'nowadays'; *letan* 'from now on, from here on'; *hetu* 'right there' (no other possible place); *hehantu* 'right then' (no other possible time); *hel* 'there'; *hehanl* 'then'; *hetan* 'from then on, from there on'.

The inseparability of time and space figures prominently in Oglala cosmology. In M^1 this union is accomplished only when the temporal-spatial relationships of the celestial world are complemented by the same relationships in the terrestrial world. Through the metaphor of social transgressions related to kinship behavior, the day, night, and month are created in the upper world; and as a result of reward and punishment for these behaviors, the four directions are created in the lower world. The upper and lower worlds are mediated by the concept of season and year since both are the same term in Lakota. This is to say that the Oglalas measure time in accordance with spatial manifestations: spring, summer, fall, winter and their corresponding physiographies.

These corresponding physiographies are metaphorically expressed in the myths as personality traits of the Four Winds. The North Wind is mean and surly, his touch is icy and cold, and he kills everything with which he comes in contact. The West Wind is noisy and boisterous; his direction represents the home of the Thunder-beings, the lightning and thunder. The East Wind is lazy and disagreeable. He likes to lie about the tipi all day. The South Wind is friendly and industrious. He likes to copy things in nature and makes toys for little Yumni, the Whirlwind.

The winds were also born in a certain order, but when it came time to fix the directions, their birth order was rearranged. In M^2, the North Wind is afraid to go with the Wizard over the mountain tops. The first to move to a new direction is the West Wind, who is then followed by the North Wind, East Wind, and South Wind. As a result, the West Wind is considered first in all things. This myth (and also M^4 and M^5) creates the following transformation:

Initial Order of Birth	Final Order of Birth
North-West-East-South	West-North-East-South

In M^4 when again the Four Winds are told to fix their directions, the relationship between time and space becomes clear when the Wind tells his sons to prepare for a journey to their respective locations. Metaphorically, the Wind's lodge is the universe, and each of his sons leaves the lodge and travels around its perimeter. The journey will be long and Wind mourns for them, but each will return in order as he left, and the time required to complete the journey will mark the fourth period. Extending the metaphor, each wind returns to the lodge during his appropriate season, and only one season is in the lodge (universe) during one particular temporal segment. The movement in and out of the lodge is further described in the metaphor of warfare between the four winds in M^8 (and also M^4 and M^7), in which they fight over Falling Star, the North Wind causing her dress to freeze and ornaments to drop off, only to be countered by the South Wind, who creates new ornaments for her dress. In an attempt to hide from the North Wind,

Falling Star hides under her dress, spreading it farther and farther to escape his icy touch. Here the spreading of the dress is a metaphor for the creation of land, and the ornaments which push through it are the foods upon which the Oglalas depended at another period of time, one in which they engaged in agricultural pursuits in Minnesota.

These creative powers of the South Wind are again enunciated in M⁴ when Falling Star gives food to each of the brothers and the Wind. Each requests food which is rather typical of Oglala diet of the Minnesota period as well as today (with the exception of duck, fish, and wild rice). But the South Wind is given a platter of food which has the aroma of sweetgrass (that is, metaphorically, a sacred food) which cannot be depleted no matter how much he eats. The South Wind, in the same myth, plays a courting flute after the meal while his brothers retire. This is also suggestive of virility as a special case of creativity.

But first I would like to emphasize certain spatial relationships and relate these to social relations and ritual. In M⁴, the four brothers are given specific instructions about where to place their directions. The North Wind goes to where his shadow is longest at midday, the West Wind to where the sun goes over the mountain when the day is over, the East Wind to where the sun comes up at the edge of the world to begin his journey, and the South Wind to where he is under the sun at midday. These are obviously instructions which specify relations between the brothers during a given day as well as their relative relations over a given year. Figure 5

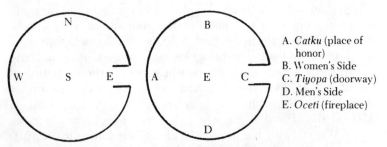

Figure 5. Placement of the Four Directions in M⁴

Figure 6. Floor Plan of Tipi

A. *Catku* (place of honor)
B. Women's Side
C. *Tiyopa* (doorway)
D. Men's Side
E. *Oceti* (fireplace)

illustrates the placement of the four directions in M[4]. Figure 6 shows the floor plan of an Oglala tipi. If we compare the two illustrations, we see that the *catku*, or place of honor, is located at the west; the women's side is at the north, or on the left (from the perspective of the *catku*); the *tiyopa*, or doorway, is at the east; the men's side is at the south, or right (again viewed from the *catku*); but in figure 5 the South Wind has its place in the center, that is, in that part of the lodge normally occupied by the fireplace (figure 6). Given what we know about the wars of the winds, shifting of seasons, and emphasis placed on agriculture in the myths, it seems logical to assume that figure 5 illustrates a particular kind of relationship necessary for food production, i.e., sun (East Wind), warmth (South Wind), and rain (West Wind, the home of the thunders). Similarly, it is logical to place the seat of honor at the west in recognition of the first-honored direction, the doorway at the east where the first light is emitted, and the fireplace in the center for maximum heat. The sun is literally over the fireplace (roughly) at midday, inasmuch as the tipi is open at the top to permit the escape of smoke from the cooking fire. The fireplace itself is a shallow pit; and as we shall see, the idea of placing the South Wind, which symbolized creativity, not only of food but of humankind, in this particular spatial relationship agrees with other rituals and myths in which creativity or revivification is related to concavities in the earth.

As we saw in the previous chapter, there is a relationship between activities among celestial beings and terrestrial ones. This relationship is analogous to that between time and space; and if in the latter case the relationships are interdependent, then this is also true of earth-sky relationships.

The myths are (expectedly) rather vague in defining just where many of the supernatural activities take place. However, there is linguistic evidence that points toward an undifferentiated earth-sky relationship, at least at an earlier period, one no longer recorded in the data. Although it is pure speculation, it is interesting to examine a number of lexical items constructed on the radical element *ma*, which appears to give rise to concepts related to creativity and generation, as the following list demonstrates:

maka 'earth' (*ma* and *ka* [*kan*], an ancient *ma*)
maȟpiya 'sky, clouds, heaven' (possibly *ma* and *ȟpiya* 'shaped by
      wind pressure')
magaju 'rain' (*maga* 'cultivated field, goose' and *ju*, radical element
      found in "to plant" and "to separate, break into pieces")
maga 'cultivated field, goose' (*ma* and *ga* [?])
maya 'river bank, lake shore' (*ma* and *ya* [?])
mama·'woman's breast' (reduplicated form of *ma*)
maȟtani 'old field' (*maȟ*, contraction of *maga* and *tani* 'old')
makagna 'a long time' (*maka* 'earth' and *ogna* 'in')
maku 'chest' (*ma* and *ku*[?])

I do not include in this list *mni* 'water', but it might be
worthwhile to speculate further that *mni* is derived from *mani* (*ma*
and *ni* 'life, breath') since other Siouan-speakers use *ni* as the term
for water. But I believe the list, even without *mni*, provides for
what might be considered the primary ingredients for time, space,
and being in Oglala society, given what we know about the above
relationships in mythical terms. I should point out here that there is
a specific relationship between cultivated field, rain, and goose
which might not be obvious. The connection is explicit in the
Oglala term for the month of April, *Maga agli wi*, 'month when
geese return home', i.e., the month before planting.

To pursue what I regard as a transformation from an undifferentiated earth-sky relationship to a differentiated one, I will
now examine aspects of myth and ritual which demonstrate the
contrast between earth and sky, and the mediation between the
two. The obvious starting place is M⁴, in which the Falling Star,
daughter of the Sun and Moon, comes to the earth and eventually
takes up residence with the South Wind. In the battles that ensue
over her, she constantly takes refuge beneath her dress, which is
metaphorically the earth itself.

In M¹⁰, Double-Face, the Sun's mistress and mother of the Four
Winds, is lonesome for her people, whom we find living in a subterranean world. She beseeches the culture hero, Inktomi, to find
them, resulting in the eventual population of the earth. But the
population occurs in a typical Oglala fashion. Tokahe, the first man,
follows the Wolf (*sunkmahetu* 'underground dog') along with
three other men (the initial tetradic component) to the earth, where
he is met by Inktomi, Double-Face, the Old Man, and the Old

Woman, who introduce the subterranean people to cultural things: preparation of food, clothing, and shelter. He then returns to his subterranean world and again appears with six other men and their families, the perfect heptadic structure. Although it is Inktomi and the Wolf who actually serve as the mediators between the subterranean people and the terranean supernaturals, it is Double-Face's anguish over being separated from her people that causes the initial transformation. That sky people are living in a subterranean world should not be regarded as ambiguous inasmuch as human and supernatural persons are not yet distinguished. Moreover, the source of life (*šicun*) comes from supernatural regions of the sky where it awaits the birth of humans so that it may inhere in them.

When the subterranean people have emerged and are imbued with life, they are again visited by a woman, the White Buffalo Calf Woman, an analogue of Falling Star, who gives them the seven sacred rites. These rites allow them to communicate with the supernaturals through the medium of a sacred person. The White Buffalo Calf Woman is of the sky (she arrives in a mist), but she is also of the earth (she turns into a white buffalo calf). It is through her arrival and bestowal of sacred things upon the people that the distinction between earth and sky is finally attained. The gross features of the differentiation between time and space, and earth and sky may be written as a series of transformations:

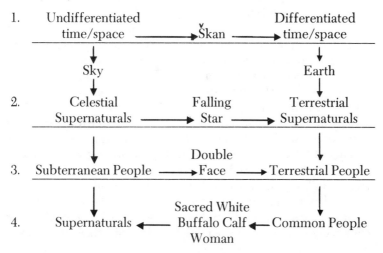

These transformations may be read:

1. Through the mediation of Škan (sacred language for *Taku-škanškan* 'energy, power which causes things to move') undifferentiated time and space are transformed into differentiated time and space, recounted as punishment and reward resulting from social transgressions.
2. Through the mediation of Falling Star, who is part sky (the Sun and Moon are her parents) and part earth (the South Wind becomes her husband), a relationship is created between the sky and earth in the metaphor of kinship.
3. Through the mediation of Double-Face, who is part sky (before differentiation of time and space) and part earth (after differentiation), the subterranean (sky) people populate the earth.
4. Through the mediation of the sacred White Buffalo Calf Woman, who is identified with the sky because she is Falling Star, and who is also of the earth because she turns into a buffalo, the common people may communicate with the supernaturals.

All the above transformations occur at the level of myth. Similar transformations also occur at the level of ritual and social organization.

THE RITUAL USE OF SPACE AND TIME

In contemporary Oglala religion we find the contrasts between darkness and light, ignorance and knowledge, sacred and profane not only verbalized, but dramatized. Each ritual essentially is a re-creation of Indian time and space. Through ritual, a profane dwelling is transformed into the entire Oglala universe during the *Yuwipi* meeting. The sacred persons still pray to the four directions in the order in which they were born: west, north, east, south. The placing of tobacco representing the four winds, zenith, nadir, and Spotted Eagle in a sacred pipe renders the pipe powerful because it contains the entire universe. When it is lighted, life and breath are invested in the universe; and when it is smoked, the universe passes through one's own body and is sent back to *Wakantanka*. The construction of an altar contained by flag offerings and demarcated by tobacco offerings is also a re-creation of time and space in an Indian sense. The sweat lodge is the lodge of the wind, the universe itself; and in the vision quest, a common man submerges himself in the pit so that he may be reborn in the same manner as Tokahe, the first man.

The sacred knowledge that energy is finite and is in constant flux between sacred and evil influences flows through all of Oglala ritual. It is only through sacred ritual that harmony can be achieved and the universe restored to its proper balance. This harmonious balance is dramatized in all of the rituals. The famine of winter is offset by the abundance of summer. In ritual language those who are ill "walk through winter in darkness" (*waniyetu opta aiyakpa omanipi*). The ignorance of darkness is contrasted with the knowledge of light which comes forth every morning in the form of *Anpo wicahpi* 'Morning Star'.

In sacred and profane life, an Oglala still enters the tipi or sacred grounds in a clockwise direction as was prescribed by the White Buffalo Calf Woman. Under profane circumstances he enters from the east, the doorway and source of light. He moves to the south, where he faces death, symbolized above by the direction of the spirit path. He proceeds to the west, where there is darkness and the unpredictability of the Thunder-beings. He finally turns to the north, the land of his forefathers and thus the land of spirits.

But under sacred circumstances, the clockwise circle is filled with positive signs. He first acknowledges his own ignorance and the shortcomings of common man by facing west, the place where out of darkness come the generative powers of rain. He then turns to the north, where there is life and breath, and where the Buffalo People reside, the source of his food. Proceeding to the east, he faces knowledge rather than turn his back on it. And finally, he moves to the south, where the profane symbols of death are replaced by the sacred generative powers of sun and warmth.

In the profane world, a man's spirit is diffused outwardly toward the evil influences of the Four Winds. In the sacred world, it is the benevolent spirits of the Four Winds which are diffused inwardly and inhere in the supplicant himself and in all for whom he prays.

The ideas of accretions and depletions of energy, and the contrasts between darkness and light, are apparent in the seven sacred rituals and in the use of the sacred pipe. Accretions are often symbolized by those things found above the earth; depletions are symbolized by those things below the earth. The following examples from the seven rituals will serve as illustrations:

1. In the sweat lodge, the surplus earth from the hole into which the heated stones will be placed is fashioned into a mound called the sacred hill (*paha wakan*). The ritual is conducted in two phases, light and dark.

2. In the vision quest, a man is placed on a sacred hill and a pit is dug where he will stay while crying for a vision. The dark-light contrast is found at two levels: he must stay for at least a full twenty-four hours (day and night) or any combinations of day and night not exceeding four days and four nights. At another level, the pit is dark, above the pit is light.

3. In the ghost-keeping ritual, the dead body is wrapped and placed on a burial scaffold or in a tree. The spirit is fed for the last time by placing food in the ground. Here, wrapping is symbolic of darkness, metaphorically a return to one's subterranean origins. The depression in the earth into which food is placed is offset by the accretion of the burial scaffold.

4. During the initial sun dance rites, a hole is dug for the sacred pole and the earth is used to construct a sacred altar. The piercing of the dancer's flesh and the attachment to the sacred pole is regarded by Oglala sacred persons as a symbol of ignorance. By facing the sun and eventually breaking through the flesh, the dancer receives knowledge. Piercing is metaphorically expressed as dancing in darkness. The pole is a living tree where the nest of Thunder-beings is recreated.

5. In the Hunka, the candidate is covered with a buffalo robe during the initiation and emerges from it after the relationship between *Hunka Ate* and *mihunka* has been made final.

6. In the girl's puberty ritual, the initiate removes her dress and it is placed over the buffalo skull. She is told to sit in the manner of a woman, and the dress is removed from the skull and given away to a needy person. The transition from prepuberty to woman-

hood is contrasted ritually in terms of darkness and light vis-a-vis the buffalo skull, which is the source of women's power.

7. In the sacred ball game, the ball itself is regarded as *Wakantanka*. The throwing away of the ball represents ignorance, and the players' scrambling to catch the ball represents mankind's attempt to seek knowledge.

In the *Yuwipi* meeting, the *Yuwipi* man is wrapped in a star quilt, which is a metaphor for death. The lights are then extinguished. After his ritual death and communication with the spirits, the lights are turned on, and he is found unwrapped by the spirits.

The sacred pipe itself is a symbol of darkness and light. The powers of the universe are placed in the pipe bowl and the pipe is plugged with sage. When the pipe is lighted and smoked, the tobacco is transformed into smoke which rises, carrying the messages and prayers of the people to *Wakantanka*. Symbolically and logically, fire becomes the mediating agent between death and life, not only in the pipe ceremony, but in the sweat lodge, where profane stones are heated and thereby invested with *ni* 'breath, life'. Table 6 summarizes contrasts between dark and light, depletion and accretion, earth and sky, and ignorance and knowledge at the level of ritual and myth.

Aside from the binary contrasts revealed in the ritual use of space and time, sacred space is distinguished by another feature, circularity. The *cangleška wakan* 'sacred hoop' is the symbol of Oglala solidarity. Miniature hoops, made from a willow frame onto which a cross representing the Four Winds is attached, are worn as hair ornaments or carried in the hand at sacred and secular dances. They are also found as a design motif on beaded and quilled articles. The formation of some kinds of dances, e.g., the round dance, is also symbolic of this unity.

Figures 7–11 represent schematic drawings of ground plans of sacred lodges, or sacred space, compared with the sacred pipe (overview). All have a striking similarity, even when the circle is not described, but implied (fig. 8). Figure 7 is an overview of a sacred pipe. Figure 8 is the ground plan for both the vision quest and the sacred ball game. In the case of the former, the center of

TABLE 6
CONTRASTS IN RITUAL AND MYTH

Ritual	earth/depletion/ darkness/ignorance	sky/accretion/ light/knowledge
Sweat Lodge	hole for heated stones; dark phase	sacred hill; light phase
Vision Quest	vision pit; nighttime	sacred hill; daylight
Ghost Keeping	body wrapped; ghost fed	burial scaffold
Sun Dance	hole for sacred pole; piercing; ignorance	sacred altar; sacred pole; freeing; knowledge
Hunka	candidate covered with robe	candidate emerges
Girl's Puberty Ritual	skull covered with dress	skull uncovered
Sacred Ball game	ball thrown away	ball caught
Yuwipi	man wrapped in quilt; dark phase	man unwrapped; light phase
Pipe	pipe filled; plugged	pipe smoked; message communicated

MYTH

M[1]	subterranean people	celestial supernaturals
M[1]	Hanwi (shaded sun)	Anpetu wi (light sun)
M[2]	Brothers and Wizard sleep under robe	Brothers and Wizard walk over mountain tops
M[6]	Thunderbird baby in egg	Thunderbird nest in tree
M[7]	Falling Star hides under dress (earth)	Ornaments (food) grow above earth
M[11]	Man with bad intentions enveloped in mist	Man with good intentions given instructions
M[12]	People covered by water (turn to pipestone)	Woman gives birth to twins on cliff

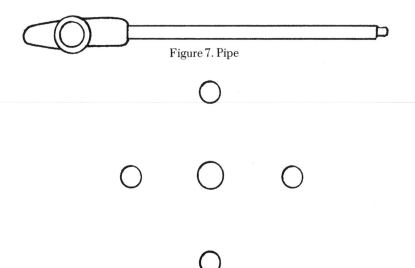

Figure 7. Pipe

Figure 8. Ground Plan for Vision Quest and Sacred Ball Game

the diagram represents the vision pit, and in the latter, the place from which the sacred ball is thrown. The smaller circles designate the four directions, which are marked by sacred flag offerings in the vision quest and by shallow pits in the sacred ball game.

Figure 9 represents the sweat lodge and path to the sacred hill. The center of the sweat lodge marks the hole in which stones are heated. Figure 10 is the ground plan for a secular tipi, as well as for the lodges used in the ghost-keeping, *Hunka,* and girl's puberty rituals. In each case the center marks the position of the fireplace. Figure 11 represents the sun dance lodge on the left, the path made from sixteen tobacco offerings, and the sacred tipi to which the path leads. The center of the sun dance lodge is where the sacred pole is erected; the center of the sacred tipi is a fireplace.

Figure 12 shows a rather generalized plan for a Yuwipi meeting. The small circles represent cans of earth into which canes bearing flag offerings are placed. The circle within the rectangle represents the sacred altar made from earth, usually from a mole's burrow. The line connecting the cans is the long string of *canli wapaȟte* 'tobacco bundles' which delineates the sacred part of the

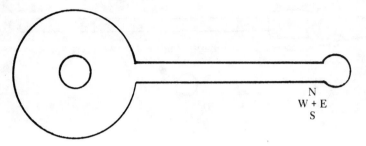

Figure 9. Sweat Lodge and Sacred Hill

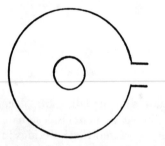

Figure 10. Ground Plan for Tipi, *Hunka*, Ghost-Keeping, and Girl's Puberty Ritual

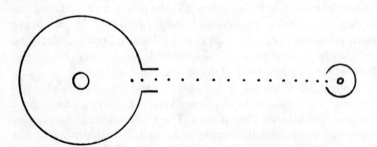

Figure 11. Ground Plan of Sun Dance Lodge and Sacred Tipi

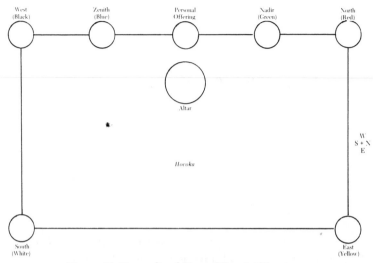

Figure 12. Generalized Plan of *Yuwipi* Meeting

meeting place from the profane. When the tobacco bundles and ritual paraphernalia are laid in place, the closed-off area is regarded as a re-creation of the Oglala universe.

But not only space is transformed from a profane state to a sacred one; time also undergoes a transformation in the sacred rituals. Anxiety over the future of the Oglalas is reduced by calling on the powers of the past, which are conflated with the present. The *Yuwipi* man calls upon his spirit helpers, as many as four hundred, to aid his diagnosis of sickness. This number curiously corresponds to the average number of people living in the mid-nineteenth-century *tiyošpaye*. As intermediary between the common people and the supernaturals, the *Yuwipi* man is simultaneously intermediary between the supernaturals and the common people. Stated another way, he mediates between two *tiyošpayes*, forming a link between the dead and the living, the past and the present, the nomadic hunter-gatherer people before white contact and the community-dwelling Oglalas living under white dominance. Through the mediation of the sacred persons the present world is in continuous communication with the old.

Chapter 15

SOCIAL RELATIONS

NATURE AND CULTURE

Since the seminal works of Durkheim and Mauss (1903) and Lévi-Strauss (1949), it has been generally accepted in social anthropology that man orders his universe in such a way that cultural things are analogous to natural things. Man perceives uniformity in the natural universe: certain celestial and terrestrial phenomena recur predictably through time and space. But as Leach has noted, within this larger framework of repetition man perceives a contradiction in that life itself is nonrepetitive (Leach, 1961). Man has essentially two conflicts to resolve: his rather indeterminate position between nature and culture, and his need to reconcile the irreversibility of death.

In the preceding two chapters I have focused on the logical continuity with which Oglala social structure is replicated synchronically and diachronically. At each level of abstraction there is a conformity which rarely varies: a heptadic structure emerges at each level and is comprised of a tetradic, dyadic, and monadic component. Moreover, concepts related to how the Oglalas perceive time and space are also structurally replicated. Specifically, Oglala ritual focuses on transforming the profane into the sacred by manipulating physical space in some manner: the finiteness of energy and the harmonious balance between accretions and depletions are manifested in rituals which recall man's relation to the earth and sky. The excavation of sacred ground is contrasted with constructs that reach out to the sacred sky.

In this chapter I will deal with the rules and regulations that are used to order consciously Oglala social relations. Like religion and other aspects of sociopolitical organization, these rules are rationalized in the mythical and ritual world. In the nature-culture dilemma in which man finds himself, if the natural world is logically ordered, then the social world also must be logically ordered, and it is in myth that we find this logical reflection.

In myth, the creation of time and space is consciously effected by Škan, the energy behind everything that moves. The rewards and punishments in M^1 are the basis for ordering not only mythical relations, but real ones. If we reconsider M^1 (cf. figure 1, p. 166 above), there is an interesting relationship between the generations. There are two groups of mythical persons: the Sun, Moon, and Falling Star on one side; Old Man, Old Woman, Wind, Face, and the Four Winds on the other. For the sake of analysis let us regard the Old Man and Old Woman as the older generation; Sun, Moon, Face, and Wind, the middle generation; and Falling Star and the Four Winds, the younger generation. In the first period, the two groups are related in a striking way: the Sun-Moon dyad and the Old Man-Old Woman dyad has each given birth to a daughter. In order for Wind to marry Face, he must move to her residence, that is, he must establish matrilocal residence. Until the birth of the Four Winds, consanguineal relations appear as females, affinal relations as male.

But we know that the mid-nineteenth-century Oglalas had a cognatic filiation principle, as they still do, with a mild tendency toward patrilocal, then neolocal residence. If we look further along M^1 during the second period (figure 2, p. 167 above), what becomes apparent is a reconciliation between matrilocality and patrineolocality. Give the assemblage of mythical characters in M^1 and, at the level of social relations, society's striving to perpetuate itself, the Oglala myth maker must somehow conflate the two groups in figure 2 so that there will be a guarantee of continuity through time. The only manner in which the two mythical groups can align themselves is to generate a new union between man and woman based on what the Oglalas regard as the proper rules of marriage, namely, (1) one marries a person of his or her own generation, and (2) one marries outside the group. If the message being communicated in the first period is that residence is matrilocal, then we must also add (3) matrilocal residence, as part of the propriety of marriage, at least for this mythical period of time.

Considering rule (1), generationality, there are two possibilities of aligning the two groups: Falling Star may marry one of the Four Winds; or there can be an annulment of marriage in the middle generation whereby Sun is free to marry Face, or Wind is free to marry Moon.

If we consider the exogamous principle, rule (2), then the above also obtains. But if we introduce rule (3), then we must eliminate Falling Star's marrying one of the Four Winds (at this mythical period) because the winds cannot be separated; in the fourth period they will be fixed in space in relation to each other. That leaves us with the possibility of the middle generation's effecting an alignment, which they do in the second period. Sun leaves Moon for a younger, more beautiful woman, Face. But in the myth, it is Face who comes to the Sun's lodge and takes Moon's place, not the reverse. Thus, the principle of matrilocality does not obtain in either generation; nevertheless, the annulment and remarriage take place. Mythically speaking, matrilocality is transformed into patrilocality. At the level of social relations, men and women are free to annul marriages, but there may be repercussions if the arrangement is not satisfactory to all parties. The arrangement is certainly not satisfactory to Moon, who is ridiculed, the most typical kind of Oglala reprimand, and one certainly not suited for this occasion. As a result, Škan punishes Face, who is given a second, horrible countenance, the proper Oglala treatment for adulterous wives.

In the first and second periods, then, matrilocality is transformed into patrilocality. After the Four Winds have been established in the lodge of Wind, they are visited by Falling Star, who lives with Wind (the father) and after her marriage to South Wind, takes up residence with him. Stated another way, patrilocal residence gives way to neolocal residence.

Whereas rules of marriage and residence are rather clearly reflected in the myths, descent provides a more difficult problem. We know that during contact time the Oglalas were cognatic, and that at present the cognatic principle is maintained and supported through contact with non-Indians, as is neolocality as an ideal

residence pattern. While the myths alone do not suggest matrilineality, if we examine certain relationships between myth and
ritual, an earlier, matrilineal descent system is implicit.

ATTRIBUTES OF THE WINDS

In the fourth period, we find the Four Winds establishing the
directions of the universe. The oldest wind is the North, who eventually in subsequent myths is relegated to the position of second-
born, and the West Wind is regarded as primary in myth and ritual.
Each of these two winds has characteristics which are underscored
in myth and ritual, and which, if analyzed carefully, reveal certain
attributes which reflect social relations on the order of descent.
Combined with other linguistic evidence, there is a rather con-
vincing argument for the presence of matrilineality at an earlier
period before European conquest. I shall first examine the attributes of the Winds, and then follow with a linguistic analysis.

In M^5 the Wizard took away the North Wind's birthright
because the latter was mean and cowardly. In anger the North
Wind told the magpie to befoul the Wizard, and from that time on
the magpie has been the messenger of the North Wind. The Wizard
is also known as *waziya*. In Lakota, north is *waziyata* 'toward the
pine', *wazi* meaning "pine" and presumably relating to Minnesota
as the place of pines. The North Wind is also associated with the
winter, *waniyetu*, which may be glossed as the "time and place of
life (breath)." The messenger magpie is called *unkcekiȟ'an* (*unkce*
'defecation, flatulence' and *kiȟ'an* 'stormy'). In ritual, red is the
color associated with the north. Red is *ša* and is etymologically
related to *šan* 'vagina'. The buffalo come from the north (*tatanka*
'buffalo bull'; but *pte* 'buffalo cow' is used as the generic term for
buffalo in ritual). Since *ni* 'life, breath' is regarded as an aspect of
soul, the north is also the place of the *ni*. Now south is normally
regarded as the direction of death, and spirits travel along the
wanagi tacanku 'ghost road' (Milky Way) until they meet the old
woman who determines the final course they will take. The
Oglalas regard the north-south axis as analogous to the east-west
axis. In the case of the latter, the sun rises and travels toward the
west through the sky. When it reaches the west, it goes under the

earth and returns to the east. Similarly, the *wanagi* travel along the Milky Way to the south and, when they arrive, return to the north under the earth.

The total range of the North Wind's attributes may be summarized as old, female, life-giving, and eternal. Implicit is an association between the north and matrilocality, because of the relation between the Old Man (Wizard) and the Wind, who married his daughter, Face.

In M⁵, because the West Wind was brave and did not run away from the terrible Thunder-being, the two would be companions. The messenger of the West Wind became the swallow, and from then on the West Wind would help the Thunder-being rid the world of filthy and evil things. In Lakota, West Wind is *wiyoȟpe-yata* 'toward the place where the sun falls over, or falls off'. The West Wind is associated with autumn, which in Lakota is *ptanyetu* 'time and place of change'. *Ptan* is a radical element in such words as *yuptan* 'to change [a tire, record, etc.]'; *yaptan* 'to change [the conversation, the song]'; and *kaptan* 'to roll over'. The swallow messenger of the West Wind is *pšica* 'to jump' (also called *upijata* 'forked tail'). The term *icapšipši* refers to flocks of birds which disband suddenly when frightened; *pšica kinye s'e* is an idiom meaning "in the manner of flying and jumping" and is used to describe a crowd of people milling about, bumping into each other.

In ritual, the color associated with the west is black (which is *sapa*, and is etymologically related to *šapa* 'dirty'). The West Wind is the companion of the Thunder-being, or Winged People, *Wakin-yan Oyate* (from *wakinyan* 'flying things', i.e., lightning; and *oyate* 'people'). The voice of the *Wakinyan* is thunder (*wakinyan hotun*, from *wakinyan* and *hotun* 'to produce a sound, voice'). It is thus the source of rain, and it is the rain that rids the world of filth. "Dirty," then, is not an attribute of the west, but an attribute of the evil it sets forth to change. The forked tail of the swallow is symbolic of lightning. In design motifs, lightning is depicted by a zigzag line ending in a bifurcation.

In summary, the West Wind is disorderly, but capable of creating order out of chaos, cleanness out of filth, through the process of change. It is contrasted with the East Wind, which is masculine; thus the west has some female characteristics.

If we regard the exchange of birth-order positions of the North and West Winds as a metaphor for an exchange of their attributes, then we find the transition accounts for the change from matrilocality to something else. But the something else becomes clear only when in another myth Falling Star comes to the lodge of the Wind and meets the South Wind.

The South Wind is an especially strong male character; he has all the attributes of an Oglala husband: he is brave, he fights with the North Wind in order to protect Falling Star. He is industrious: he makes ornaments for her dress (metaphorically, planting in the earth) and toys for his young whirlwind companion. He plays the courting flute for Falling Star while the rest of his brothers sleep. He and Falling Star are eventually married, and they move away. The series is then complete: matrilocality→ patrilocality→ neolocality.

The focus on change particularly underscored in the attributes of the West Wind may also be extended to account for other kinds of change aside from residential ones. There is a change in subsistence patterns; agriculture gives way to nomadic hunting-gathering. There are internecine wars between the Oceti Šakowin and the Algonquian-speakers, who have been armed with guns by the white man. Most interestingly, there is a decided change in the geographic movement of the Siouan-speakers. In prehistoric times, the constituents that will form the Oceti Šakowin have traveled north from the Ohio Valley. In historic times, they disperse, migrating west through present Iowa and South Dakota. From a migratory perspective, north and west are exchanged as primary directions, and the myths have rationalized this rearrangement in the metaphor of the brotherly exchange.

But the reassemblage of the winds does not account for the postulated presence of matrilineality among the forerunners of the Oglalas. For this kind of change, we must consider mythical and linguistic evidence of another kind.

THE WOMAN IN THE MOON

As we know, the separation of the Sun and Moon, that is, the differentiation between day and night, resulted in a distinction between two kinds of *wi, anpetu wi,* a light *wi,* and *hanhepi wi,* a shaded, or dark, *wi*. But when the Moon is rewarded by being given her own domain, the undifferentiated term *wi* is retained, and signifies month. Thus, *wi*, month, is female, and appropriately so inasmuch as the Moon is isolated from the Sun during the month, just as women are isolated from men during their menstrual period, when they retire to the *išnatipi* 'menstrual lodge' (lit., 'they live alone'). But Face is also sent away from the Sun as punishment because she has sat in the place of the Moon. It appears that there are a number of metaphors here which are rationalizations for social relations. First, the man does not have sexual relations with a woman who sits in the place of the Moon, that is, during her menstrual period. Second, the disfigurement of Face is more than just the prescribed punishment for an adulterous wife; it is symbolic of the double nature of woman: she is both wife and mother, she is touchable and untouchable, clean and polluted. Her ugly side must not be viewed by men, nor must it be allowed to view sacred objects lest they be rendered profane.

At still another symbolic level, although I have postulated an annulment of the previous marriages between Sun and Moon on one hand, and Wind and Face on the other, the acquisition of a second wife was permissible in Oglala society. But polygynous marriages were usually reserved for chiefs, that is, men of means. Properly they took a younger wife as their second, but it was necessary for the chief to maintain order in his own lodge between the wives, usually by establishing separate tipis for each wife and her children. Under no circumstances, however, could a man steal another man's wife unless he was prepared to face the consequences. Wife stealing appears to have been practiced at an earlier period, however, as evidenced in the literature for other Siouan-speakers (particularly the Crows, [Lowie, 1935]).

Aside from the multisymbolic nature of the Moon, there are other kinds of evidence which more strongly associate the Moon with feminine characteristics. Although it has not received previous attention from anthropologists, there is a correspondence between *wi* 'month' and *wi* (*win*) 'female'. *Win* is employed as a female marker in proper names to distinguish women from men. It is now glossed as "Mrs." inasmuch as Oglala women take their husband's surname in accordance with American law. In prior times, however, *win* was affixed to women's names even though wives retained their own name after marriage.

In M[13], the woman who sits in the moonlight doing quillwork and stirring her kettle, and whose completion of the tasks signifies the end of the world, is known as *Hokewin* or *Hokewinla*. Dorsey (1894) glosses this as Turtle Man, a man who lives in the moon with his hands outstretched. But the form is clearly feminine. There are two radical elements in *hoke*, *ho* 'pertaining to a camp circle', and *ke*, an element found in *keya* 'turtle'. It is possible that the turtle derives from an Iroquoian creation myth in which the culture heroine falls through the sky into a great sea and is rescued on the back of a turtle, upon which she creates the land. A relationship, then, is found between the Iroquoian heroine and Falling Star. (For other parallels to Iroquoian mythology, see Hertzberg, 1966).

But the Oglala Moon is clearly a woman, whom Buechel describes as the " 'man in the moon', thought of as a woman by the old Sioux, with a lot of clothes on" (Buechel, 1970:183). The woman stirs the kettle and ladles out food (*wanna woze yelo* 'now she ladles it out') and is also making the fire when she is known as *winyan ceic'iti* 'the woman makes her own fire' (from *winyan* 'woman'; *ceti* 'fire'; and ic'i, reflexive infix). A woman who is laden with clothes is called *hoke win s'e* 'in the manner of the woman in the moon', which refers to pregnancy, as I shall demonstrate.

Wi is found as a marker in some words indicating stages of life. For example:

hokšila:	boy	*wicincala:*	girl
koškalaka:	young man	*wikoškalaka:*	young woman
wicaša:	man	*winyan:*	woman
wicaȟcala:	old man	*winunȟcala:*	old woman

Hokšila is the conventional term for boy, but at an earlier period it simply meant undifferentiated child. The term for pregnant is *hokši ikpignaka*, which can mean to place a child in the abdomen or tie a blanket around the waist. The woman in the moon then is certainly pregnant when she is said to be laden with clothes. The term for being in labor with child is *hokši kiksuye*, literally "to remember *hokši*." *Ho* is a prefix related to a camp circle, and *kši* as a radical element means "to be bent or doubled up." Thus we find a deep structural relationship between the moon as mother and creator, the camp circle, and the child.

Koškalaka is derived from *koška* 'venereal disease' (transmitted by women) and *laka* 'to consider'; hence the term for young man reflects his new-found interests of a sexual nature. What is interesting is that males are not marked until they reach a marriageable state, *wicaša* 'man' and *wicaȟcala* 'old man'. *Wica* is regarded by most lexicographers as a male prefix (see particularly Buechel, 1970:576). But it also fulfills other functions: it is incorporated with verbs and other nouns to make them abstract, and is also used as the prefix indicating the third person plural in the objective case. However, it is never used alone; thus *wicaša* is a male *ša* 'red' but also, by extension, 'vagina'. *Wicaȟcala* 'old man' is also a synonym for father-in-law (although *tunkan* or *tunkaši* is proper) and is usually glossed as "veritable male, very male." As a suffix *ȟca* indeed means "very, really," but as a verb signifies "to blossom." This latter usage seems to me more appropriate for describing a male and female who have gone through the stages of life, metaphorically, from seed to fruition.

In the female series above, all stages of life are marked by *wi*. The final stage, *winunȟcala* 'old woman', is related to the name of the first-born female (cf. table 3), i.e., *winona* (from *winu* 'female captive'), which is to say, the first-born has become an old woman.

From the standpoint of myth, man is a special case of woman. It is a woman who is differentiated to generate the day and night, thus providing a rationale for the empirical observation that woman can produce both man and woman, but man can produce neither. The myths and metaphors in everyday usage underscore the fact that woman generates food, as she generates mankind. In M[4] Falling Star brings a variety of food to Wind and his sons. But it is sacred food that she gives to her potential husband, food that cannot be depleted. The insurance that food will be abundant is symbolic of the continuity of society itself because the source of food and the source of the people are one. The unhappiness of Double-Face over her exile and isolation from her people initiates the transformation which gives rise to the population of the earth; and finally, in M[11], it is the White Buffalo Calf Woman who brings the sacred rites to the people so that the people may live. The sacred woman, upon leaving the camp circle, changes into a buf-

falo, thus enunciating that the source of life and the source of food
are inseparably one.

Another clue to the primacy of women in the mythological past
is the state in which we find Face before she receives her punishment from Škan. She is pregnant with Yum, the whirlwind, who as
a result of his mother's transgressions becomes an anomaly. He
does not grow up; and later, when his brothers establish the four
directions, he is assigned no specific direction of his own. We
assume that Yum's father is Wind, and possibly the myth maker
also makes this assumption. But would the people in Oglala society
make this same assumption, knowing what they do about the
frivolity and promiscuousness of Yum's mother? Given what we
know about contemporary Oglala society and the manner in which
dubious paternity is regarded, I think not. Yumni has all the
characteristics of a bastard (*atkuku wanice* 'no father on hand') and
wablenica 'orphan' (*wa* 'one who'; *ble* 'lake'; but more at 'clear';
and *nica* 'wanting, without', i.e., 'unclarified'). Metaphorically, the
child whose paternity is dubious is moved from one relative to the
next. He has no fixed place because he does not belong.

The Lakota term for Double Face is *Anukite* 'face on both
sides', but she also appears to men in visions, and in the real world,
in the form of a deer, or two deer women, one black (*sintesapela*)
and the other white (*taȟcawin*). The two faces of Double-Face and
the two deer women represent proper and improper sexual conduct, and underscore the dictum to select a spouse from a place
other than, as the Oglalas say, "the corner of one's own house." The
product of an indiscriminate sexual union is *anukiya* 'cross-breed,
hybrid' (from *anuk* 'on both sides' and *kiya* 'to cause, make,
generate'). Men become disorderly or crazy when they gaze upon
the ugly face of Double-Face or have sexual relations with the deer
women because in reality indiscriminate sexual unions between
close kin create chaos in the kinship system. Present-day Oglalas
are still perplexed when they discover that they can call a relative
by more than one kinship term. The older people place emphasis
on teaching their grandchildren the proper kinship terminology so
that they will know who they are. The improper selection of a
spouse can lead only to disorder and, symbolically, death, as is
enunciated in M[11] when the White Buffalo Calf Woman appears to
the two hunters. She is clearly a relative of the people, yet one of

the hunters desires her. He is immediately enveloped in a mist, and when the mist rises he has been transformed into a pile of bones.

Man's overall need to reconcile his relationship between nature and culture is further complicated by his need to distinguish between male and female sexuality. The inversion of the North and West Winds reflects confusion in a system that at one time clearly indicated the male-female relationship. Man is a subset of woman, not only in the empiricality of childbirth but in linguistic terminology which identifies the stages of life. There is no need to identify the males who belong to the premarital stages, but after marriage, the relationship of man to woman changes in that future offspring must know where they belong. It is the male categories which are marked female, thus enunciating where the man still belongs: to his mother's people. This suggests that at one time the antecedents of the Oglalas lived in a matrilineal society and that the pressures of European contact and subsequent warfare with neighboring tribes caused a breakdown in the matrilineal system. I would still agree with Howard that the Oglalas emerged out of a patrilineal society, but at a later transitional stage. The larger transition would suggest that the antecedents of the Oglala were at an earlier period matrilineal-matrilocal, but after the migrations onto the prairie changed to a patrilineal-patrilocal, and finally, cognatic-patrilocal and neolocal system.

At a conscious level, the notion of matrilineality has been forgotton, but at an unconscious level aspects of matrilineality persist. If one views the birth order of the Four Winds as a model for ordering social relations, then the birth-order names which seem to defy translation at a conscious level begin to make sense. The first four names are suggestive of a mythical period before primacy was assigned to the West Wind. If we compare the attributes of the Four Winds with the birth order of children, we see the following relationships:

BIRTH ORDER

FOUR WINDS	HUMANS	
	Male	Female
North	Caske	Winuna
West	Hepan	Hapan
East	Hepi	Hepistinna
South	Watcato	Wanska

The second- and third-born of the Four Winds, that is, the West and East, are contrasted in a familiar way. The West Wind, which corresponds with the second-born male and female humans, is undifferentiated. But the East Wind and the corresponding third-born males and females are differentiated thus: the female name (of a dominantly male direction) is found in a diminutive form (Hepistinna). Stated another way, the difference between the West and East Winds and their corresponding human birth-order names is that the East (male) is a diminutive form of the West (female).

Kinship terminology also provides some insight in postulating matrilineality for an earlier period. The term *ina* 'mother' (and mother's sister[s]) is the common vocative form. But *hun* 'mother' is the possessive form (*mihun* 'my mother'; *hunku* 'his or her mother'). Curiously, *hun* is also found in *hunkake* 'ancestors', who are those deceased through whom one claims descent. The total number of deceased spirits is called *tunkašila* 'grandfather', but the deceased spirits to whom one is related are *hunkake*. *Ina* is a variant of *winu* 'female captive' and the two terms for mother suggest two kinds of reckoning: *ina*, mother by virtue of marriage; and *hun*, a mother by virtue of descent. The second term for mother and the term for ancestor also appears in the abstract form *wicahunku*, which I gloss as "motherhood" (but read "matriline") and *wicahunkake* 'ancestral line'. *Hunka* 'the making of relatives' also seems logically related.

Finally, if we are to find another clue for matrilineality other than the recurring theme that man is somehow a subset of woman, where might it lie? I suggest that the relationship between the woman in the moon who builds her own fire provides a partial answer. *Ceti* 'to build a fire', from which the term *oceti* 'fireplace' is derived and which forms Oceti Šakowin in earlier times probably signified lineage, i.e., people of a woman's fire. Although at the conscious level there is no memory of a period in which women occupied a primary role in the organization of Oglala society, at an unconscious level the metaphor of matrilineality persists.

Chapter 16

RELIGION AND IDENTITY

The Grandfathers

The need to reconcile the irreversibility of death is overcome in the reincarnative religious system of the Oglalas. The distinction between life and death in such a system is blurred. The ghosts of the dead appear at will and communicate with the living. The souls of the living disappear during rituals and communicate with the deceased. The two worlds are mirror images of each other and they are conjoined by a continuum, an ethereal road which passes across the sky in a southerly route and dips beneath the earth, only to reemerge again in the north, the land of pine, and breath, and life.

Somewhere between the earth and clouds, so the Oglalas say, the spirit helpers live, waiting to be coaxed from the sky by the utterance of the proper prayers and songs by the sacred persons. These spirit helpers are called *Tunkašila*, the Grandfathers. They along with animals, birds, insects, and the like are called upon by sacred persons so that the people, the Oglalas, may live. The Grandfathers are efficacious in curing illnesses, particularly the social maladies brought to the people by the white man. Their wisdom is passed down through the generations from the first period of time when the universe was only partially shaped.

These are the *wakan*, the sacred. They are *wakan* because they are capable of transforming a hopeless and futile world into one which is, at least temporarily, relieved of the constraints imposed upon the Oglalas by the white man. When the sacred rites are performed properly, the common universe, one acknowledged by the Oglalas to be controlled by the white man's technology, is transformed into a sacred universe, one controlled by the power of *Wakantanka*.

I initially began by asking how was it possible that the Oglalas maintained a distinct social and cultural identity despite the overwhelming odds in favor of assimilation. In the past it has been assumed a priori that a subordinate society is destined to change by mere contact with a dominant one. Studies of acculturation became the instrument for explaining the extent to which small societies were indeed affected by the imposition of a new culture. They focused on how individuals were able to adjust to a new social and cultural milieu over which they had no control. But the nature of acculturation studies dictated that they focus on the obvious, that is, the content of culture, its social relations, and at this level of research one could find change.

I opted for an approach to explaining society which is complementary, not antithetical, to acculturation studies. In order to understand the Oglalas, or other societies, it is necessary to examine the extent to which social and cultural values have persisted. But values do not lie at the level of social relations, only their artifacts do. The approach which I chose required that I examine society at a level which is not obvious, the underlying structure of social relations. In this final chapter, by way of summary and conclusion, I will focus on the significance of social structure as it relates to the persistence of Oglala social and cultural identity.

THE PROCESS OF IDENTITY

Wallace has demonstrated that when traditional values in society are shattered by foreign intrusion, people consciously attempt to construct a more satisfying culture (Wallace, 1956). One of the millenarian movements in anthropological literature is, of course, the ghost dance movement, which ended for the Sioux on the Pine Ridge Reservation with the Wounded Knee massacre. Interestingly, Wounded Knee has never been regarded as a religious symbol. The occupation of the massacre site by members of the American Indian Movement on February 27, 1973, one lasting seventy-one days, occurred for historical reasons centering on the injustices sustained by not only the Oglalas but by all Indians at the hands of the white man. The ghost dance itself was not critical in understanding Indian-white relationships. It died out as quickly as it began because in most respects, from a structural position, it was foreign to Oglala religious ideology. The contents of the ghost dance—the songs, prayers, trances, and dance itself, as they were learned from the prophet, Wovoka—were transformed in such a way that they conformed to ritual customs consonant with Oglala practice. But the doctrine of the ghost dance, one strongly influenced by the prophet's Christian training, was not in keeping with the sacred persons' knowledge of how the universe functions. The idea of cataclysm, for example, must certainly have been novel and interesting to the Oglalas, as were the notions of a massive influx of deceased human and animal spirits that would be transformed back into their corporeal states. The reincarnative system of the Oglalas could not accord this kind of transformation without denying the existence of the fundamental aspects of man, the *šicun, tun, ni,* and *nagi.*

Although the ghost dance was prematurely aborted with the massacre at Wounded Knee, it is unlikely that it would have survived much longer in its particular form. Old values would have been reinstituted so that the structure conformed to the original religious system. The most obvious, and most complex, idea to be dealt with in the ghost dance ideology was that Jesus was coming to earth. The Oglalas, in accordance with missionary training, could see the analogue between the white man's god and *Wakantanka,* the omnipotence, the all-pervasiveness, and the potency. But *Wakantanka* could never have a son, although certain of its aspects could. The attributes related to Jesus, particularly the miracles, suffering, and the nature of death, were attributes that the Oglalas associated with their culture hero, Inktomi, who was in fact part god.

What was important about the ghost dance movement, as far as the Oglalas are concerned, was not its religious overtones, but its political ones. It came at a time when the native sociopolitical system had become otiose. The *itancan,* the *tiyošpaye* leaders, were still alive, but powerless. Traditionally, they had led with the consent of their people, as long as they could maintain respect based on their acuity, wisdom, and bravery. If the leaders did not live up to the expectations of their followers, then they were shunned and new leaders were solicited. But with the establishment of the reservation and the strict control by the United States government, the people could only listen to the harangues of their once-wise chiefs about the injustices that had befallen the Oglalas, and the warrior's glory, which was remembered in the *wicooyake* and the honor songs. The Oglalas could listen, but there was no course of action.

In the ghost dance, it was the established religious leaders, the sacred persons, who came into prominence in a way reflective of the war leaders of another generation. They organized the ghost dancing and made decisions for the people that would have been made by the *tiyospaye* leaders several decades earlier. They began to attract a following of adepts, people who sought counsel, not over the location of the buffalo herds and enemy camps, but over day-to-day needs, the cultural dilemma of reservation living. The sacred persons gave their people a new form of hope and a new form of organization, and they led with the consent of their people as long as they could maintain their ritual authority. The ghost dance ended, but the transformation had been made: the role of the *tiyospaye* leader was now the role of the ritual specialist. The *tiyospayes* themselves were over time transformed into the fixed communities which are today found at Pine Ridge. The content of Oglala social relations changed; but the form, the structure, the relations between leader and follower persisted.

At the same time, various Christian sects began an intensive salvation program on the reservation. Churches were built, schools founded, the civilization process begun. The missionaries attempted to make Christianity as appealing and explicable to the Oglalas as they could. Bibles, psalms, and prayer books were translated into Lakota, and the masses and services were often conducted in the native languages by polyglot missionaries or bilingual native catechists. The Christian events, the holidays and conferences, were structured along Indian lines: meetings in circular shades reminiscent of the sun dance arbor, large campgrounds, feasts, and intervening events which recalled buffalo-hunting days. The Christians were convinced that their mission to convert the pagans was coming to fruition, particularly when among the congregation one could count the Oglala religious leaders themselves, participating in holy communion and taking their humble position before the face of God in the front pew of the church. This, coupled with the a priori assumption of faith that Christianity would ultimately conquer evil and ignorance, was regarded as a sacred sign by the ecclesiastics that God's will was being done. Yet at the same time, they were unaware that they had introduced an organizing principle that was more relevant to continuity in Oglala culture than it was to the acceptance of the faith. The organizing principle recalled the grandfathers' admonition to seek a spouse outside the corner of one's *tiyošpaye*. The Oglalas became members of Christian churches that were located in their own communities; entire communities joined the same denomination. But when it came time to choose a spouse, they tended to select one from another Christian denomination. I do not know that this choice was consciously made, but it was a logical one, given what we know about earlier organizing principles.

RELIGION AS ETHNIC BOUNDARY

The distinction between Oglala social and cultural identity and other possible identities should be regarded as a process rather than a category. The boundary which delineates Oglala society from non-Indians, or even non-Oglalas, is ideational. The Oglala is very much aware of the technological environment that surrounds his society. He participates in it. He wears a white man's clothing, lives in a white man's house, and works at a white man's job. But when he seeks to affirm his own identity as an Oglala, he moves along the continuum to the only institution available to him that is distinct from the white man. He seeks identity in a religious system whose structure has remained in many respects constant since European contact. Even the values he associates with the white man's technology are capable of being Oglala. The extent to which an Oglala uses this technology—money, cars, clothes, education, travel, employment and so on—is not in itself an indication of the extent to which he is acculturated. Acceptance of the white man's technology, particularly when the Oglala has no choice but to accept it if he is to survive, does not necessarily mean acceptance of the white man's values associated with that technology.

This is not to say that there are not Oglalas living on the Pine Ridge Reservation or in off-reservation communities who do not identify with the old way of life. And it is not to say that there are not Oglalas who are irreligious. The majority of Oglalas, like the majority of any people, tend to cluster in the midrange of a continuum. At one end of the continuum we find those sacred persons and spirits of the Grandfathers, the singers and other ritual specialists, and the old people whose total way of life is religious. It is near their homes that we find the sweat lodges, the vision pits, and the sacred tobacco offerings hanging in the trees. It is from these homes that men arise early in the morning and sing in a loud voice to the rising sun and pray to *Tunkašila Wakantanka* for a good day. It is here that the days slip into dusk to the accompaniment of prayers cast upward through smoke from a sacred pipe. Here the native language is spoken, and the grandchildren are reminded of their kinship obligations.

At the other end of the continuum is the white man's world. It is represented on the reservation by the omnipresence of the federal government, the Bureau of Indian Affairs, the Oglala Sioux Tribal Council, the welfare programs, the educational system, and other agencies. The Oglalas who must, move along this continuum and participate in the non-Oglala side. Some are in high offices in the government, and some are accused of having sold out to the white man: the "apples" and "Uncle Tomahawks" who only play at being what their kinsmen really are.

The majority of people living in the midrange move back and forth along the continuum situationally. At the white man's end of the scale they observe technology and change. But at the Oglala end, they see ideology and continuity. There they find a connection with the past expressed in the concept of *wakan*, that which is sacred, but also, that which is old. The continuity extends back into time long before the European arrived. Those who wish to be part of this continuous stream will move toward the Oglala end, consciously or unconsciously. Sometimes it is mere curiosity which brings an Oglala back to his traditions; sometimes it is illness of a sort, a symbolic illness for which no medical practitioner has a remedy at the white man's end of the continuum.

It is symbolic illness, or Indian sickness, that creates a need for the sacred persons, and which brings the common people in touch with the sacred. Symbolic illness provides the reason for transforming the white man's universe into an Oglala one, and guarantees that Oglala society will persist as a religious institution. The boundary which delineates Oglala religion, then, also delineates Oglala society. By passing back and forth along the continuum, the process of ethnic identity enables the traditional Oglala society and the white man's bureaucracy to coexist.

The significance of social structure to continuity in Oglala society is highlighted in the logical way in which replication occurs over time and space. The heptadic structure, which in turn is divided into tripartite components, enables the Oglalas to order their universe today as it did in times past. As I have shown in Chapter 13, the sacred numbers four and seven not only are employed to underscore relations in the mythical past, but serve as verbal categories for arranging the social organization of the Oglalas at the level of reality. There is continuity over time and space, and rarely is the ordering principle changed.

Again in Chapter 14, I demonstrated that the ritual use of space, particularly the symbolism of the circle and contrasts between accretions and depletions in a universe whose energy is finite, enables the Oglalas continually to transform the white man's world of technology into a sacred Oglala universe where old values are assigned to recent phenomena.

Finally, in Chapter 15 I emphasized that both myth and ritual serve to rationalize human behavior at the level of social relations. What is striking is that at a deep structural level, the manner in which the Oglalas order their social relations has remained relatively constant for the period from initial contact to the present.

Using my own field data and historical documents, I have reconstructed the religious system of the Oglalas for about 1700 and compared it with contemporary religion. I found it useful to invoke ideas originally advanced by Lévi-Strauss, particularly his notion of "bundles of relations" at the mythical level, and expand them to include political designations and ritual components. Moreover, Lévi-Strauss's notion of *bricolage* has been critical in understanding what in fact has been replicated over time and space. It cannot be denied that the modes of social and cultural expression, that is, the cultural content, have changed for the Oglalas. But it is striking just how much of the same seemingly finite cultural tools and materials seems to be reassembled to form new shapes of Oglala thought.

The number of *Yuwipi* and *Yuwipi*-like rituals has increased since the mid-sixties, and it is in these rituals that we see the dynamics of Oglala religion, even more so than in the sun dance. The *Yuwipi* rituals are held in the communities, and it is the specific relationship between the *Yuwipi* man and his adepts that replicates the relationship between the *tiyošpaye* leader of old and his followers. *Yuwipi* is dynamic because it meets the needs of the Oglalas in their own community. Its contents are new, but its form is old. It ensures its adepts, although not consciously, of continuity: old *Yuwipi* men are replaced by new ones, guaranteeing that Oglala society will not die. The heir to ritual authority is known far in advance of the older *Yuwipi* man's abdication. For a short time the two live together in the community, and the old and the new overlap so as not ever to separate fully the past from the present. The philosophy of *Yuwipi* is rather simple: to live with all my relations, *Mitak' oyas'in*. And it is the formal reiteration of this prayer at the end of the *Yuwipi* rituals that gives the Oglalas hope for the future through wisdom from the past.

PHONOLOGICAL KEY

The Oglalas speak Lakota, a Siouan dialect which they share with the Sicangus, Hunkpapas, Mnikojus, Sihasapas, Oohenunpas, and Itazipcos, collectively known as Tetons. The dialect is similar to and mutually intelligible with the Nakota (Yankton) and Dakota (Santee) dialects. The relationship between the discrete political units and their respective dialects is taken up in Chapter 1.

The orthography developed by Riggs (1852, 1872, 1890, and 1893), and modified by Buechel (1924, 1939, 1970) essentially serves as the model for the orthography employed throughout this book. Phonemes and their equivalent letters appear as follows:

Vowels. Lakota has eight vowels, five oral and three nasal:

a   Low, oral, approximately as in father. Written *a*.
ą   Low, nasal, approximately as in calm. Written *an*.
e   Mid, front, oral, approximately as in they. Written *e*.
i   High, front, oral, approximately as in machine. Written *i*.
į   High, front, nasal, approximately as in seen. Written *in*.
o   Mid, back, oral, approximately as in open. Written *o*.
u   High, back, oral, approximately as in boot. Written *u*.
ų   High, back, nasal, approximately as in boom. Written *un*.

In formal Lakota, sentences end in vowels with the exception of *ske*? 'it is said'; *nacece*? 'I suppose'; and *sece*? 'I think'. The glottal stop, however, is not written (*ske, nacece, sece*). One word ends in *w* (*haw* 'greetings', 'yes'), but it is traditionally written *hau* or occasionally *how*.

Consonants. Lakota has twenty-eight consonants, of which twenty-one represent seven consonantal triads (*p, t, k, c, z, ž,* and *x*), each of which is comprised of a voiced, aspirated, and glottalized

member. The remaining seven consonants are $w, y, l, m, n, h,$ and
ʔ.

p   Bilabial, voiced as in *boy.* Written *p* when word initial, *b* when
    first position in consonant cluster.
pᶜ Bilabial, aspirated as in *pin.* Written *p.*
pʼ Bilabial, glottalized. No English equivalent. Written *p'.*
t   Alveolar, voiced, as in *dim.* Written *t.*
tᶜ Alveolar, aspirated, as in *tin.* Written *t.*
tʼ Alveolar, glottalized. No English equivalent. Written *t'.*
k   Velar, voiced as in *got.* Written *k* when word initial, *g* when first
    position in consonant cluster.
kᶜ Velar, aspirated, as in *kick.* Written *k.*
kʼ Velar, glottalized. No English equivalent. Written *k'.*
c   Alveopalatal, voiced, as in *jaw.* Written *c.*
cᶜ Alveopalatal, aspirated, as in *church.* Written *c.*
cʼ Alveopalatal, glottalized. No English equivalent. Written *c'.*
z   Alveolar, voiced, grooved, as in *zip.* Written *z.*
s   Alveolar, aspirated, grooved, as in *sip.* Written *s.*
sʼ Alveolar, glottalized, grooved. No English equivalent. Written *s'.*
ž   Alveopalatal, voiced, grooved, as in *azure.* Written *j.*
š   Alveopalatal, aspirated, grooved, as in *shake.* Written *š.*
šʼ Alveopalatal, glottalized, grooved. No English equivalent.
    Written *š'.*
ɣ   Velar, voiced, as in Spanish *cigaro.* Written *g.*
x   Velar, aspirated, as in German *nach.* Written *h̃.*
xʼ Velar, glottalized. No English equivalent. Written *h̃'.*
w   Bilabial, voiced, as in *water.* Written *w.*
y   Alveopalatal, voiced, as in *yes.* Written *y.*
l   Alveolar, voiced, as in *link.* Written *l.*
m   Bilabial, voiced, as in *mink.* Written *m.*
n   Alveolar, voiced, as in *not.* Written *n.*
h   Glottal, voiceless, as in *hat.* Written *h.*
ʔ   Glottal, voiceless. Written as *'.*

A NOTE ON SOURCES

I believe a further word is in order with respect to the methods by which I reconstructed Oglala religion, particularly because the reconstruction period ranges over a relatively long period of time—from about 1700 to the present.

As I have stated, my chief sources have been Brown (1953), Densmore (1918), Dorsey (1894), Neihardt (1932), Walker (1917), and Wissler (1912). Of these authors, I have relied mainly on Walker and Wissler for earlier data. The two men spent time together on the Pine Ridge Reservation. Walker, a physician, collected texts between 1897 and 1914; Wissler investigated societies in 1903. Presumably, their informants were old men; Walker's informants died before his monograph was published. Inasmuch as "distance" anthropology was in vogue during those years (and this is borne out in the texts), the investigators not only recorded what they saw at the turn of the twentieth century, but also made inquiries into the nature of religious ceremonies in the times of their informants' fathers and grandfathers. Thus, their work, combined with my own, provides information that easily encompasses the period from the latter part of the eighteenth century to present times.

There are, of course, problems in reconstructing the period between 1700 and 1750. The Jesuit *Relations* gives us some clues about the emergence of the Oglalas as a discrete political entity during this period, but little of a specific nature is known about their religious ceremonies. This must have been a time in which the overall transition from a sedentary to a nomadic subsistence system had its effects on religious values, and the time when the sun dance was regarded as primary among the Oglalas and other

Tetons, while the mystery dance was the focus of religion among the Santees.

The other investigators all report similar religious ceremonies for the Oglalas and other Sioux for roughly the same period. Neihardt and Brown came later, and both dealt with the famous Oglala medicine man Black Elk. Black Elk's own narratives begin with buffalo-hunting days, and generally corroborate the notions of Oglala religion discussed by Walker and Wissler. Dorsey and Densmore provided good cross-references to Oglala religion even though their own work was done among other Lakota and Dakota peoples.

During my initial contact with the Oglalas, in 1948, there were still seven men living around Pine Ridge who had fought Custer. Survivors of the Wounded Knee massacre were even more numerous. These old people with whom I came in contact were always eager to talk about the old days. I had the great privilege to know many of the men whose fathers were the tribal leaders of another generation.

From 1948 on, I learned to speak Lakota, not for academic reasons (I was fourteen), but out of a love for Indian tradition. My interests focused on music, dance, and religion: I learned these things not to simply record them, but to do them. My emphasis on linguistic and structural analysis is partly influenced by my early days on the Pine Ridge Reservation. In my visits over a twenty-seven-year period I marveled at the sense of continuity I witnessed among the people and their reluctance to change their values despite the ever growing need to change their technology.

Over these long years I have had particularly intimate contact with the residents of Red Cloud Community, a small hamlet located one mile west of Pine Ridge Village. Most of the people there are descendants of the old chief Red Cloud and have not changed many of their attitudes about life. Except for new homes, new cars, televisions, and other conveniences, their values are still irrefutably Oglala: the native language is spoken as a first language, and the young people as well as the old attend the religious functions of the community.

As my interests became more directed, my research in 1966 and 1967 was supported by the Phillips Subcommittee of the American

Philosophical Society. In 1971, Wesleyan University supported my research for the purpose of making revisions in my masters thesis, "Yuwipi Music in Cultural Context," and permitted me to participate in the first Lakota Language Conference at Pine Ridge. In 1968–70, I made additional trips to Pine Ridge for the purpose of investigating the sun dance and other religious and secular functions. Additional interviews were conducted off the reservation between 1966 and 1970 in various locations. I returned again during the summers between 1971 and 1974 to do work relevant to my doctoral program at the University of Pennsylvania.

All the interviews were conducted in Lakota and English, and rarely were interpreters used except to verify ambiguous issues. Most of the interviews were tape recorded; others were simply noted and read back to informants for correction. I acquired approximately one hundred hours of tape recordings, not all of which are related to religion, but which encompass a wide range of ethnographic data.

A great deal of emphasis has been placed on etymologic considerations in this study. Being competent in Lakota, of course, greatly contributes to discovering relationships that otherwise might go unnoticed. In addition, throughout the writing, I was never without Eugene Buechel's *Lakota-English Dictionary* (Buechel, 1970), which gave me great inspiration—and frustration—throughout the four months of editorial work. Father Buechel, self-admittedly, was an old-fashioned grammarian and not a linguist. However, it should be noted that his research made my own much easier because he was a devoted naturalist, and cross-referenced lexical items with larger categories related to botany, ornithology, zoology, and what would now be called ethnopharmacology. The frustration came mainly from being chained to thirty thousand lexical items during the research, and being constantly afraid of missing something in the daily process of thumbing through Buechel's magnificent opus.

Finally, the most important resources to me were my friends, people for whom the term *informant* seems inappropriate. Some of them (possibly none of them) will agree with how I analyze Oglala belief, and I take full responsibility for the interpretation. Nevertheless, it would be wrong to end this book without mentioning the names of those who gave me so much of their time and their culture. An asterisk following the name or title signifies that they may be counted among the *Tunkašila* and *Hunkake:*

John Colhoff (White Man Stands in Sight)*; Mr. and Mrs. Edgar Red Cloud, Mr.* and Mrs. Henry White Calf, John Gray Blanket*, Gilbert White Whirlwind*, LeRoy White Whirlwind*, Mr. and Mrs. Willie Bear Tail*, Pete Stands Up*, Mr. and Mrs. Henry Make Shine, Mr. and Mrs. Francis Janis, Mr. and Mrs. Clarence Janis, Frank Afraid of Horses*, Zona Fills Pipe, Sam Loves War*, Silas Helper*, Mr. and Mrs. Jerome Wolf Ears*, Daniel White Eyes*, Mr. and Mrs. Charles Red Cloud, Mr. and Mrs. William Horn Cloud, Mr. and Mrs. Richard Elk Boy, Edgar Burns Prairie, Jim White Dress, Mr. and Mrs.* George Plenty Wolf, Mr.* and Mrs. Owen Brings, Mr. and Mrs. Melvin Red Cloud, Alice Red Cloud*, Burgess Red Cloud, Mr. and Mrs. Frank Fools Crow, Mr. and Mrs. Oliver Red Cloud, Lorenz Hunter, Mark Big Road, Levi Fast Horse*, Howard Blue Bird, Harry Jumping Bull, Joseph Eagle Hawk*, John High Eagle*, John Sitting Bull*. Joe Shake Spear*, Francis Brown, and Sidney Willow*, who are Arapahos, were also helpful.

Lila pilamayayapelo!

BIBLIOGRAPHY

Ardener, Edwin. 1970. "Witchcraft, Economics, and the Continuity of Belief." In Mary Douglas, ed., *Witchcraft, Confessions and Accusations*. London: Tavistock.

Barth, Fredrik, ed. 1969. *Ethnic Groups and Boundaries*. Boston: Little, Brown and Co.

Blom, Jan-Petter. 1969. "Ethnic and Cultural Differentation." In Fredrik Barth, ed., *Ethnic Groups and Boundaries*. Boston: Little, Brown and Co.

Boas, Franz. 1897. *The Social Organization and Secret Societies of the Kwakiutl Indians*. Report of the U.S. National Museum for 1895. Washington, D.C.

——. 1966. *Kwakiutl Ethnography*. Edited by Helen Codere. Chicago: University of Chicago Press.

Boas, Franz, and Ella C. Deloria. 1932. "Notes on the Dakota, Teton Dialect." *International Journal of American Linguistics* 7:3–4.

Boas, Franz, and John R. Swanton. 1911. "Siouan." In *Handbook of North American Indian Languages*. Bureau of American Ethnology Bulletin 40, pt. 1. Washington, D.C.

Bowers, Alfred W. 1950. *Mandan Social and Ceremonial Organization*. Chicago: University of Chicago Press.

Brown, Joseph Epes. 1953. *The Sacred Pipe*. Baltimore: Penguin Books, 1971.

Buechel, Eugene, S.J. 1924. *Bible History in Teton Sioux*. New York: Benziger Brothers.

——. 1939. *A Grammar of Lakota*. St. Louis: John S. Swift and Co.

——. 1970. *A Lakota–English Dictionary*. Pine Ridge, S.D.: Red Cloud Indian School.

Bushotter, George. 1887–88. Lakota texts, MS. National Anthropological Archives, Smithsonian Institution, Washington, D.C.

Chapple, E. D., and Carleton Coon. 1942. *Principles of Anthropology*. New York: Henry Holt and Co.

Clark, Ann. 1941. *The Pine Ridge Porcupine*. Lawrence, Kans.: Haskell Institute.

Colson, Elizabeth, 1949. "Assimilation of an American Indian Group." In Paul Bohannan and Fred Plog, eds., *Beyond the Frontier: Social Processes and Cultural Change*. Garden City: Natural History Press, 1967.

Cooper, John M. 1944. "The Shaking Tent Rite among the Plains and Forest Algonquians." *Primitive Man* 17:60–84.

Deloria, Ella C. 1929. "The Sun Dance of the Oglala Sioux." *Journal of American Folklore* 42:354–413.

———. 1932. *Dakota Texts*. Publications of the American Ethnological Society, vol. 14.

Deloria, Vine, Jr., 1969. *Custer Died for Your Sins*. New York: Macmillan.

———. 1974. *God Is Red*. New York: Grosset and Dunlap.

DeMallie, Raymond J., Jr. 1971. "Teton Dakota Kinship and Social Organization." Ph.D. dissertation, University of Chicago.

Densmore, Frances. 1910. *Chippewa Music*. Bulletin of the Bureau of American Ethnology, no. 45. Washington, D.C.

———. 1918. *Teton Sioux Music*. Bulletin of the Bureau of American Ethnology, no. 61. Washington, D.C.

———. 1932. *Menominee Music*. Bulletin of the Bureau of American Ethnology, no. 102. Washington, D.C.

Dorsey, J. Owen. 1894. *A Study of Siouan Cults*. Eleventh Annual Report of the Bureau of American Ethnology. Washington, D.C.

Douglas, Mary. 1970. *Natural Symbols*. New York: Pantheon Books.

Durkheim, Emile. 1912. *The Elementary Forms of the Religious Life*. Reprinted New York: Free Press, 1965.

Durkheim, Emile, and Marcel Mauss. 1903. *Primitive Classification*. Chicago: University of Chicago Press, 1963.

Eastman, Charles A. 1920. *Indian Heroes and Great Chieftains*. Boston: Little, Brown and Co.

Eggan, Fred. 1937. *Social Anthropology of North American Tribes*. Chicago: University of Chicago Press.

———. 1950. *Social Organization of the Western Pueblos*. Chicago: University of Chicago Press.

Feraca, Stephen E. 1961. "The Yuwipi Cult of the Oglala and Sicangu Teton Sioux." *Plains Anthropologist* 6:155–63.

———. 1962. "The Teton Sioux Eagle Medicine Cult." *American Indian Tradition* 8:195–96.

———. 1963. *Wakinyan: Contemporary Teton Dakota Religion*. Browning, Mont.: Museum of the Plains Indian.

———. 1966. "The Political Status of the Early Bands and Modern Communities of the Oglala Dakota." (W. H. Over) *Museum News* 27:1–2.

Feraca, Stephen E., and James H. Howard. 1963. "The Identity and Demography of the Dakota or Sioux Tribe." *Plains Anthropologist* 8:20.

Firth, Raymond. 1961. *Elements of Social Organization.* 3d ed. Boston: Beacon Press.

Fletcher, Alice C. 1882. *The Sun Dance of the Ogallala Sioux.* Proclamations of the American Association for the Advancement of Science.

———. 1884. *The Elk Mystery or Festival of the Ogallala.* Peabody Museum Reports, vol. 3–4. Cambridge, Mass.

———. 1904. *The Hako: A Pawnee Ceremony.* Twenty-second Annual Report of the Bureau of American Ethnology, pt. 2. Washington, D.C.

Fletcher, Alice C., and Francis LaFlesche. 1911. *The Omaha Tribe.* Twenty-seventh Annual Report of the Bureau of American Ethnology. Washington, D.C.

Fugle, Eugene. 1966. "The Nature and Function of the Lakota Night Cult." (W. H. Over) *Museum News* 27:3–4.

Gallatin, Albert S. 1836. *A Synopsis of the Indian Tribes within the United States East of the Rocky Mountains, and in the British and Russian Possessions in North America.* Transactions and Collections of the American Antiquarian Society, vol. 2.

Geertz, Clifford. 1966. "Religion As a Cultural System." In Michael Banton, ed., *Anthropological Approaches to the Study of Religion.* London: Tavistock.

Goll, Louis J., S.J. 1940. *Jesuit Missions among the Sioux.* Saint Francis, S.D.: St. Francis Mission.

Goodenough, Ward H. 1963. *Cooperation in Change.* New York: Russell Sage Foundation.

Hassrick, Royal B. 1944. "Teton Dakota Kinship System." *American Anthropologist.* 46:338–47.

———. 1964. *The Sioux: Life and Customs of a Warrior Society.* Norman: University of Oklahoma Press.

Hertzberg, Hazel W. 1966. *The Great Tree and the Longhouse.* New York: Macmillan.

Hickerson, Harold, 1970. *The Chippewa and Their Neighbors: A Study in Ethnohistory.* New York: Holt, Rinehart and Winston.

Hodge, Frederick W., ed. 1907–10. *Handbook of American Indians North of Mexico.* Bulletin of the Bureau of American Ethnology, no. 30. Washington, D.C.

Howard, James H. 1954. "The Dakota Heyoka Cult." *Scientific Monthly* 78:254–58.

——. 1960. *Dakota Winter Counts as a Source of Plains History*. Bulletin of the Bureau of American Ethnology, no. 173. Washington, D.C.

——. 1965. *The Ponca Tribe*. Bulletin of the Bureau of American Ethnology, no. 195. Washington, D.C.

——. 1966. "The Teton or Western Dakota." (W. H. Over) *Museum News* 27:9–10.

Hurt, Wesley R., and James H. Howard. 1952. "A Dakota Conjuring Ceremony." *Southwestern Journal of Anthropology* 8, no. 3:28–29.

——. 1960. "A Yuwipi Ceremony at Pine Ridge." *Plains Anthropologist* 5, no. 10:48–52.

——. 1961. "Correction on Yuwipi Color Symbolism." *Plains Anthropologist* 6:11.

Hyde, George E. 1937. *Red Cloud's Folk*. Norman: University of Oklahoma Press.

——. 1956. *A Sioux Chronicle*. Norman: University of Oklahoma Press.

——. 1961. *Spotted Tail's Folk*. Norman: University of Oklahoma Press.

——. 1962. *Indians of the Woodlands*. Norman: University of Oklahoma Press.

Keating, W. H. 1825. *Narrative of an Expedition to the Source of St. Peter's River, Lake Winepeek, Lake of the Woods, & Performed in the Year 1823 by Order of the Hon. J. C. Calhoun, Secretary of War, under the Command of S. H. Long, U.S.T.E.* 2 vols. London: Cox and Bayliss.

Kemnitzer, Luis. 1968. "Yuwipi: A Modern Day Healing Ritual." Ph.D. dissertation, University of Pennsylvania.

——. 1970. "The Cultural Provenience of Objects Used in Yuwipi: A Modern Teton Dakota Healing Ritual." *Ethnos* 1:4 (Stockholm).

Kennedy, Edward M. 1969. "Foreword." *Indian Education: A National Tragedy—A National Challenge*. 1969 Report of the Committee on Labor and Public Welfare, United States Senate. Washington, D.C.

LaFlesche, Francis. 1921. *The Osage Tribe*. Thirty-sixth Annual Report of the Bureau of American Ethnology. Washington, D.C.

Lame Deer [John Fire], and Richard Erdoes. 1972. *Lame Deer, Seeker of Visions*. New York: Simon and Shuster.

Leach, Edmund R. 1954. *Political Systems of Highland Burma*. Boston: Beacon Press.

——. 1961. *Rethinking Anthropology*. London: Athlone.

——. 1970. *Claude Lévi-Strauss*. New York: Viking Press.

Lesser, Alexander. 1928. "Some Aspects of Siouan Kinship." *XXIII International Congress of Americanists*. New York. Pp. 563–71.

——. 1958. *Siouan Kinship*. Ph.D. dissertation, Columbia University. Ann Arbor, Mich.: University Microfilms.

Lévi-Strauss, Claude. 1949. *The Elementary Structures of Kinship*. Boston: Beacon Press.

———. 1962a. "Social Structure." In Sol Tax, ed., *Anthropology Today*. Chicago: University of Chicago Press.

———. 1962b. *The Savage Mind*. Reprinted Chicago: University of Chicago Press, 1966.

———. 1963. *Structural Anthropology*. New York: Anchor Books.

———. 1966. *The Savage Mind*. Chicago: University of Chicago Press. Original, 1962.

Linton, Ralph. 1940. *Acculturation in Seven American Indian Tribes*. New York: Appleton-Century.

Lowie, Robert H. 1913. *Dance Associations of the Eastern Dakota*. Anthropological Papers of the American Museum of Natural History, vol. 11, pt. 2. New York.

———. 1935. *The Crow Indians*. New York: Holt, Rinehart, and Winston.

Macgregor, Gordon H. 1946. *Warriors without Weapons*. Chicago: University of Chicago Press.

McNickle, D'Arcy. 1973. *Native American Tribalism*. London and New York: Oxford University Press.

Maranda, Pierre. 1972. "Structuralism in Cultural Anthropology." *Annual Review of Anthropology* 1:329–48.

Maynard, Eileen. 1969. "Some Notes on Denominational Preferences among the Oglala." *Pine Ridge Research Bulletin* 10:1–6.

Maynard, Eileen, and Gayla Twiss. 1970. *That These People May Live*. Pine Ridge, S.D.: U.S. Public Health Service.

Meyer, Roy W. 1967. *History of the Santee Sioux*. Lincoln: University of Nebraska Press.

Middleton, John. 1970. "The Religious System." In Raoul Naroll and Ronald Cohen, eds., *A Handbook of Method in Cultural Anthropology*. New York: Natural History Press.

Mirsky, Jeannette. 1937. "The Dakota." In Margaret Mead, ed., *Cooperation and Competition among Primitive Peoples*. Boston: Beacon Press.

Mooney, James. 1896. *Ghost Dance Religion and the Sioux Outbreak*. Chicago: University of Chicago Press, 1965.

Morgan, Lewis Henry. 1851. *League of the Ho-de-no-sau-nee, or Iroquois*. Rochester: Sage and Broa. Reprinted Seacacus, N.J.: Citadel Press, 1962.

———. 1871. *Systems of Consanguinity and Affinity of the Human Family*. Smithsonian Contributions to Knowledge vol. 17. Washington, D.C.

Murdock, George P. 1949. *Social Structure*. New York: Free Press.

Neihardt, John G. 1932. *Black Elk Speaks*. Reprinted Lincoln: University of Nebraska Press, 1961.

Nurge, Ethel. 1966. "The Sioux Sun Dance in 1962." *Proclamations of the XXXVI Congress of Americanists* 3:102–14.

Parkman, Francis. 1846. *The Oregon Trail*. Reprinted New York: Mentor Books, 1950.

Powell, John W. 1891. *Indian Linguistic Families of America North of Mexico*. Seventh Annual Report of the Bureau of American Ethnology. Washington, D.C. Reprinted Lincoln: University of Nebraska Press, 1966.

Powers, William K. 1963. "A Winter Count of the Oglala." *American Indian Tradition* 52:27–37.

———. 1967. "Okan, Sun Dance of the Blackfoot" (film review). *American Anthropologist* 69:561–62.

———. 1970. "Contemporary Oglala Music and Dance: Pan-Indianism versus Pan-Tetonism." In Ethel Nurge, ed., *The Modern Sioux: Social Systems and Reservation Culture*. Lincoln: University of Nebraska Press.

———. 1971. "Yuwipi Music in Cultural Context." Master's thesis, Wesleyan University.

———. 1972. "The Language of the Sioux." *Language in American Indian Education* (a newsletter of the Office of Education Programs, Bureau of Indian Affairs). Spring, pp. 1–21.

Radin, Paul. 1923. *The Winnebago Tribe*. Thirty-seventh Annual Report of the Bureau of American Ethnology. Washington, D.C.

———. 1956. *The Trickster*. New York: Schocken Books.

Ray, Verne F. 1941. "Historic Backgrounds of the Conjuring Complex in the Plateau and the Plains." In Leslie Spier, ed., *Language, Culture and Personality: Essays in Honor of Edward Sapir*. Menasha, Wis.: American Anthropological Association.

Redfield, Robert, Ralph Linton, and Melville J. Herskovits. 1936. "Memorandum for the Study of Acculturation." *American Anthropologist* 38:149–52.

Reese, Montana Lisle, ed. 1941. *Legends of the Mighty Sioux*. Reprinted Sioux Falls, S.D.: Fantab, Inc., 1960.

Riggs, Stephen Return. 1852. *Grammar and Dictionary of the Dakota Language*. Smithsonian Contributions to Knowledge, vol. 4. Washington, D.C.

———. 1869. *Tah-koo Wah-kan; or, The Gospel among the Dakotas*. Boston: Congregational Sabbath-School and Publishing Society.

———. 1872. "The Dakota Language," *Collections of the Minnesota Historical Society*, vol. 1. Minneapolis.

———. 1890. "A Dakota-English Dictionary," *Contributions to the North American Ethnology*, vol. 7. Washington, D.C.

————.1893. "Dakota Grammar, Texts, and Ethnography," *Contributions to the North American Ethnology,* vol. 9. Washington, D.C.

Robinson, Doane. 1904. *A History of the Dakota or Sioux Indians.* Reprinted Minneapolis: Ross and Haines, 1967.

Ruby, Robert H. 1955. *The Oglala Sioux: Warriors in Transition.* New York: Vantage Press.

Sandoz, Mari. 1942. *Crazy Horse: The Strange Man of the Oglalas.* New York: Alfred A. Knopf.

Schwatka, Frederick. 1890. "The Sun-Dance of the Sioux." *Century Magazine* 34:753–59.

Schoolcraft, Henry R. 1851. *Historical and Statistical Information respecting the History, Condition, and Prospects of the United States.* Philadelphia: J. B. Lippincott, Grambo.

Smith, J. L. 1967. "A Short History of the Sacred Calf Pipe of the Teton Dakota." (W. H. Over) *Museum News* 28:7–8.

Spindler, George, and Louise Spindler. 1971. *Dreamers without Power: The Menomini Indians.* New York: Holt, Rinehart and Winston.

Spiro, Melford E. 1966. "Religion: Problems of Definition and Explanation." In Michael Banton, ed., *Anthropological Approaches to the Study of Religion.* London: Tavistock.

Standing Bear, Luther. 1933. *Land of the Spotted Eagle.* Boston: Houghton Mifflin Co.

Steinmetz, Paul, S.J. 1969. "Explanation of the Sacred Pipe as a Prayer Instrument." *Pine Ridge Research Bulletin* 10:20–25.

Swanton, John R. 1905. "The Social Organization of American Tribes." *American Anthropologist* 7:663–73.

Sword, George. N.d. "Story of the Woman from the Sky." MS. Ed. by Ella C. Deloria. American Philosophical Society, Philadelphia.

Terrell, John Upton. 1974. *Sioux Trail.* New York: McGraw-Hill.

Thwaites, Reuben Gold, ed. 1896–1901. *Jesuit Relations and Allied Documents: Travels and Explorations of the Jesuit Missionaries in New France, 1610–1791.* 73 vols. Cleveland: Arthur H. Clark.

Tylor, Edward B. 1871. *Primitive Culture.* London: J. Murray.

Underhill, Ruth. 1965. *Red Man's Religion.* Chicago: University of Chicago Press.

Van Gennep, Arnold. 1908. *The Rites of Passage.* Reprinted Chicago: University of Chicago Press, 1960.

Vestal, Stanley. 1923. *Sitting Bull: Champion of the Sioux.* Norman: University of Oklahoma Press, 1956.

Walker, J. R. 1914. "Oglala Kinship Terms." *American Anthropologist* 16:96–109.

———. 1917. *The Sun Dance and Other Ceremonies of the Oglala Division of the Teton-Dakota.* Anthropological Papers of the American Museum of Natural History, vol. 16, pt. 2. New York.

Wallace, Anthony F. C. 1956. "Revitalization Movements." *American Anthropologist* 58:264–81.

———. 1966. *Religion: An Anthropological View.* New York: Random House.

Wallis, W. D. 1947. *The Canadian Dakota.* New York: American Museum of Natural History.

Wax, Murray L., Rosalie H. Wax, and Robert V. Dumont. 1964. "Formal Education in an American Indian Community," Supplement to *Social Problems,* vol. 11, no. 4.

Wissler, Clark. 1902. "Decorative Art of the Sioux," *Bulletin* of the American Museum of Natural History, vol. 13, pt. 3.

———. 1907a. "Some Oglala Dakota Myths." *Journal of American Folklore* 20:195–206.

———. 1907b. *Some Protective Designs of the Dakotas.* Anthropological Papers of the American Museum of Natural History, vol. 1, pt. 2. New York.

———. 1912. *Societies and Ceremonial Associations in the Oglala Division of Teton Dakota.* Anthropological Papers of the American Museum of Natural History, vol. 11, pt. 1. New York.

———. 1945. *Indians of the United States.* New York: Doubleday, Doran and Co.

Wright, Muriel H. 1951. *A Guide to the Indian Tribes of Oklahoma.* Norman: University of Oklahoma Press.

Zimmerly, David. 1969. "On Being an Ascetic: Personal Document of a Sioux Medicine Man." *Pine Ridge Research Bulletin,* 10:46–69.

ACKNOWLEDGMENTS

A number of people have contributed to my understanding of Oglala religion, and the anthropological perspectives within which this book is framed.

My foremost debt is to the Oglalas, particularly the people of Red Cloud Community, who permitted me to grow up in their society and share in their culture when I had become dissatisfied with my own. They were my first teachers and I hope that they will accept my effort to explain Oglala religion in anthropological terms as an honest one. I have learned their religion, but they have lived it.

I regard my wife, Marla, as my coequal in the research. The Oglalas named her well, *Tacannunpa Wakan Win*, Her Holy Pipe, a name which illustrates the high esteem in which she was held by her Oglala kin and friends. Her acuity as a researcher is matched only by her sensitivity to Oglala community life. My sons, Jeff and Greg, were my constant companions at Pine Ridge and taught me much about growing up Oglala. Named, respectively, *Wicahpi Ska*, White Star, and *Wamniomni*, Whirlwind—suitable names at that—they demonstrated how easy it is to share with others more than the culture of one's birth.

Although full responsibility for any deficiencies in the book is mine, a number of people read the manuscript and offered useful suggestions during the initial stages of writing. I am particularly grateful to Professors Brian Spooner, Sandra Barnes, John Witthoft, and Anthony Wallace, of the University of Pennsylvania; and Dr. William C. Sturtevant of the Smithsonian Office of Anthropology.

During earlier graduate studies at Wesleyan University, Professor David P. McAllester made me aware of cultural relativism, a perspective which is etched indelibly throughout the preceding pages. Professor Willard Walker gave me my first insights into linguistics. A number of other persons contributed to my understanding of anthropology directly or indirectly: William Davenport, Ward Goodenough, Dell Hymes, A. V. Kidder II, Igor Kopytoff, Alan Mann, Ruben Reina, David Sapir, and Bernard Wailes.

Linda Kelley typed the manuscript and supervised editorial revisions masterfully.

INDEX